JUNK DRAWER

MATERIAL CULTURE PERSPECTIVES

The series publishes innovative studies on material culture in literary, visual, and historical studies. The series seeks titles that engage with physical objects—broadly defined and including their formal attributes, ascribed functions, contribution to larger processes and practices, or symbolic significance—to explore historical and critical questions regarding the formation, dissemination, consumption, and contestation of material cultures and their ideologies, and how these affect any number of human pursuits, from scientific investigations to everyday material life. Books may address a wide range of topics, including matters of race, sexuality, or class, and encompass local or global contexts. The series also invites treatments that offer provocative, reflective, and theoretically informed approaches to material culture studies in the twenty-first century.

JUNK DRAWER

WHAT WE LEAVE BEHIND

EDITED BY
SANDER L. GILMAN AND BARBARA VON ECKARDT

PHOTOGRAPHS BY BARBARA VON ECKARDT

UNIVERSITY OF DELAWARE
UNIVERSITY OF DELAWARE PRESS
NEWARK

ISBN 978-1-64453-423-6 (cloth)
ISBN 978-1-64453-422-9 (paper)
ISBN 978-1-64453-424-3 (epub)

Cataloging-in-publication data is available from the Library of Congress.
LCCN 2025042990

A British Cataloging-in-Publication record is available from the British Library.

♾ The paper used in this publication meets the requirements of the American National Standard for Information Sciences—Permanence of Paper for Printed Library Materials, ANSI Z39.48-1992.

Composed in Chronicle (Jonathan Hoefler) and Whitney (Tobias Frere-Jones)

Book design by Robert L.Wiser, Silver Spring, MD

udpress.udel.edu

Distributed worldwide by Rutgers University Press

Manufactured in the United States of America

TABLE OF CONTENTS

ACKNOWLEDGEMENTS

We are grateful to Jerry Samet for encouraging Barbara to turn her "junk drawer" project into a book. And many thanks to Julia Oestreich, the Director of the University of Delaware Press, for her unflagging enthusiasm for the project throughout its development and to Holli Flanagan and Josephine Chaet for their insightful editorial work. We also wish to thank Martin Brückner, Professor of English and Director of the Winterthur Program in American Material Culture, University of Delaware, and Sandy Isenstadt, Professor and Chair of the Department of Art History at the University of Delaware, for their invaluable suggestions in shaping the final manuscript.

LIST OF PLATES AND FIGURES

I. PLATES

PHOTOGRAPHS BY BARBARA VON ECKARDT

II. ESSAY FIGURES

INTRODUCTION

A ROAD MAP TO JUNK DRAWERS, PHOTOGRAPHS, AND MEANINGS

SANDER L. GILMAN

A "junk drawer," as we usually encounter it in daily life, is, quite literally, a drawer in which we throw miscellaneous odds and ends we don't know where to put or that we don't have the time or patience to put away properly. Although ordinary junk drawers vary from household to household, they typically include mostly practical items like scissors, bag clips, thumbtacks, toothpicks, spare keys, and loose change.

The photographs in this book document the contents of a quite different—though related—junk drawer, not an actual drawer in someone's home but a collection of seemingly miscellaneous stuff sold on the online marketplace eBay (usually by an eBay reseller), specifically labeled "junk drawer" and "from [X] estate." Presumably, the most valuable items of the estate from which they derived have been either claimed by a family member or relative, sold, or contributed to a charity as having some potential value or use. What remains are the scraps, the leftovers, and the fragments, seen by the estate agent or seller as having no significant intrinsic, market, or utilitarian value except as part of a "junk drawer" collection. Like their common namesake, these collections consist of small- to medium-sized objects but, interestingly, and in contrast to more typical junk drawers, along with the usual utilitarian items, they often also include highly personal objects such as family pictures, baby shoes, vacation postcards, and jewelry, as well as things that speak to the cultural context in which they were produced and used.

Thus, in the end, these are just boxes of things that no one claimed from an estate, stuff that could not otherwise be sold or even given away. Perhaps not "junk" but leftovers, jumble, curios, bric-a-brac, stuff, bits and pieces that had had greater personal significances to the living (photos on the mantel, baby shoes in a baby box). The reason they ended up in a junk drawer collection on eBay was because the person who tossed them into a box no longer shared that affective connection and thus saw these items essentially as junk: things that, maybe even *because* of their personal significances, at that instant could not be imagined as having market value as defined at an estate sale. In Barbara Von Eckardt's lens, they are recuperated, or perhaps even rescued, as images, transmuting their value into art.

Remember what Alice said when she got "very tired of sitting by her sister on the bank, and of having nothing to do: once or twice she had peeped into the book her sister was reading, but it had no pictures or conversations in it, 'and what is the use of a book,' thought Alice 'without pictures or conversations?'"[1] This is very much a volume of conversations about and through Von Eckardt's *Junk Drawer* pictures, both of and in the material world. It is not so much a road map in its conventional sense, a two-dimensional abstracted representation of the material world, but rather a GPS system that explores readings of Von Eckardt's images through the critical voices of our contributors, as well as her own. This is an experiment: can we provide enough differing perspectives for the viewer of the photographs, and through them the objects represented, to understand not only the complexity and layered meanings of our material world but also of our constant and contradictory rereadings of it in both aesthetic presentation ("art") and criticism ("interpretation")?

In asking the diverse and truly eclectic group of authors represented in this volume to respond to Von Eckardt's photographic project, she and I set very few guidelines. We did not specify that they use a certain method, tone, or voice, or adhere to a certain length or scope. We provided a sort of Rorschach test to gauge the contributors' perceptions of the project, and the objects photographed in it. The authors had online access to the photographs, as well as an early version of the artist's statement about how the objects were selected and how the photographs were produced. In other words, what they were viewing was already thrice removed from the objects in their putative original home, which became objects in an estate upon the death of their owner, and somehow ended up with an eBay reseller, who sold them to Von Eckardt, who then organized and scanned them and posted the scans on her website.

The result is a potpourri of responses employing various voices and representing various positions, some adversarial, and some reinforcing the artist's *Junk Drawer* project. As editors, Von Eckardt and I have now ordered the responses just as the artist ordered her objects in the photographs of the junk drawers. While the opening three essays address the question of "junk," and the latter four refer in one way or another to Barbara's photographs, our trajectory generally moves from essays that directly interrogate the images to those that ruminate more broadly on the problems inherent in image-making, from those that deal with the intimate, the micro, to those that address societal issues, the macro. We lumped the former under the "Reading the Junk Drawer Photographs" section of the volume and the latter under a section titled "Thinking about Junk."

Mary Bergstein, the psychoanalytically informed art critic whose book *Mirrors of Memory: Freud, Photography, and the History of Art* (2010) has already framed the question of how photographs and the idea of photography create a simulacrum of memory, approaches "junk" from the standpoint of objects and memory in her essay "What We Leave Behind." But the simulacrum is infused with scattered bits of secondhand trauma, no less appalling because they are represented in photography rather than experienced directly. Visual memory is littered with images of images, which we convert into the shape of our own memory. She suggests that the seeming immediacy of that already compromised record is engaged by the images in *Junk Drawer*, as Margaret Olin, as well as Laura Levitt and Ruth Ost, reiterate in their essays in the second part of the volume.

Daniel Cavicchi, a noted American Studies scholar of pop music, and author of a book on Bruce Springsteen and his audience, *Tramps Like Us: Music and Meaning Among Springsteen Fans* (1998), explores the reception of the photographed objects as problematic social speculation in his essay "Estate Curiosities." Can we understand the world in which such objects had functioned, he asks, or must we reconstruct it object by object, seeing each in juxtaposition with not only the other objects in each eBay box, but also our own understanding of the nuances of the cultures from which they came?

John P. Jacob, the McEvoy Family Curator for Photography at the Smithsonian American Art Museum, and a master scholar of American vernacular photographs as objects of critical investigation, evokes the idea of loss in our material world, the idea of "Ghost Stories." Vernacular photographs from the formal portrait to the Brownie snapshot can suddenly become the subjects of scholarly analysis. Indeed, "found" objects are loved by scholars, who believe them to be somehow less mediated, less constructed than art photographs or even than the conventions of the photographic portrait themselves. Where the objects are found seems as important as the objects themselves, guaranteeing their veracity. If only?

We need, however, to open up this specific project to the broader questions that it inherently entails. How do we "make" art out of the quotidian, or the imagined quotidian, objects of our world? And who can do these tasks? What is disposable? What is reproducible? These are certainly not new questions, but ones that demand our attention. Photographer and cultural critic Margaret Olin writes passionately about how photography created "art" out of "junk" from its very origins in her essay "From 'Junk' to 'Junked.'" Are the *Junk Drawer* objects, rather than being "junk," props in an elaborate game to define who (not what) really has value in our fluid and transnational society? And at what point does art, if indeed here the snapshots in the images serve as a surrogate for art, become junk? Does it depend on the immediate context, such as with fabulously expensive porcelain objects imported from China in the eighteenth century versus delftware copies of them, cheap and quickly mass produced? In today's antique market, they would be nearly equally expensive. Or what of the value of the most ubiquitous porcelain object of our age found in every home, the toilet, when transmuted into Marcel Duchamp's *Fountain* of 1917.

My contribution to this volume, an essay titled "How 'Junk' Becomes 'Junque,'" similarly looks at how the valueless achieves value, and how marginal or transient objects, at least in modernity, have presented real difficulties for both the interpreter and the collector, both in the sense of the junque collector and the junk man. As we have known at least since the time of Adam Smith, value exists and it is related to the desirability or necessity of the object. But that valueless objects can acquire value and valuable objects can lose it has always been understood, from the ancient Greeks, at least since Epictetus. But we seem to live in a world where the shift from one to the other—and back again—occurs with blinding speed but without any perceptible plan. TikTok determines "fashion" and clicks define value. Our greatest treasures may well turn out to be, as I suggest, objects that evoke emotional ties to the past, real or imagined, and infiltrate the present, for good or for ill.

Laura Levitt, a teacher of religious studies whose book *The Objects that Remain* (2020) argues for a rethinking of the material world after the Holocaust, and her colleague Ruth Ost, a historian and curator, engage in a dialogue addressing "Ordinary and Extraordinary Objects and their Afterlives" as seen through concepts of loss, trauma, and fragmentation. They attend to such questions as what the phrase "left behind" really means. They evoke borderlands (the West Bank/Palestine, the United States Southern border area), where abandonment seems to mean something very different in terms of time and space than it does in the quotidian world of eBay. Their dialogue format raises interesting questions, such as whether abandonment is a material state or a psychological one, but also interrogates itself: Are dialogues a sign of a truer search for meaning than that which is achieved in the monotones of academic essays? Is not the attempt to capture dialogue in the fixity of print as fraught as our attempt to capture the fluidity of the material world in a photograph? Can reflecting on "left behind" objects in a dialogue ameliorate the ultimate abandonment of community in our solitary last act, our death?[2]

Finally, South African-born art critic and historian Rhoda Rosen and her collaborator Amanda Leigh Davis engage in a debate about whether there can be traces of ownership in abandoned objects in "Artifacts and Access." Again, the contributors present a dialogue, but of a quite different tone than that of Levitt and Ost. Their joint focus is on the implied idea of an "archive," a space to mine interpretations, and an archive, pace Jacques Derrida, so constructed to not only catalogue but also generate meaning. But, with respect to Von Eckardt's images, at their core, it is not their sources but the view that they flee from any and all interpretation, including the social implications of any type of constructed past, that is problematic.

While there are a series of intertextual touchstones in this volume (Walter Benjamin and Roland Barthes, to no one's surprise, being two of them), the references create their own webs of meaning, not alone because of the disciplinary biases of the authors. But one other variable needs to be mentioned: each of the writers—including the artist and her coeditor—at some moment stops and draws not upon the canon but upon their own lived experience, the quotidian moments in their own lives, something that is shared only in the broadest sense and that makes each reading truly unique. They intercede at various levels of "reality," for even a virtual image is "real" in someone's universe. No two of these readers "see" the same objects, and that is the point of our volume. What you as the reader of these essays and the viewer of these images will take away is truly up to you. You will note the various voices in these essays, some very scholarly, some reflective, some critical, all responding in their own way to the *Junk Drawer* images and the claims about the objects in them, left behind, boxed, and then sold, without any describable meaning or origin.

You have purchased, Dear Reader, an object, a book with reproductions of images, now two stages away from the box sent by eBay to Barbara Von Eckardt. Whatever their original source, someone placed the objects into that box, separating them from all other objects. The box was sent, opened, and sorted again. The objects were then reproduced as scans, made virtual, no longer material objects, and then translated into printed images, now reproduced as pages in a book. If entropy has a truth in our material world, at some time, our book too will wind up in the Oxfam equivalent of a junk box. Not created as junk, objects are transformed and reformed and reused and rethought—always real in the eye of the beholder, always teetering, as Mary Douglas warns us, on the edge of becoming a "blur, smudge [that] contradict or otherwise confuse accepted classifications."[3]

That junk may have been created as such is also a mantra in our age of the disposable, of the ephemeral, of the cheap. But it does not define our ever-shifting understanding of objects and the value we attribute to them. In a recent illustrated essay titled "Things I Find on the Ground," K.C. Councilor illustrates our dilemma. The frames begin: "There is so much interesting stuff on the ground. I'm talking about trash. Garbage." Not a litterer, indeed, also not a "save the earth type either," Councilor "love[s] trash in its natural environment. Disturbing it feels wrong like touching the wings of a butterfly." Some things are "a piece of someone's life left behind."[4] The reading by the artist gives the object its meaning.

1. Lewis Carroll, *Alice's Adventures in Wonderland* (Dover Publications, 1993), 1.
2. See in this context Sander L. Gilman, "Representing Dead and Dying Bodies," in David Hillman and Ulrika Maude, eds., *The Cambridge Companion to the Body in Literature* (Cambridge University Press, 2015), 149–62.
3. Mary Douglas, *Purity and Danger* (Routledge, 1966), 50.
4. K.C. Councilor, "Things I Find on the Ground," *Literature and Medicine* 40, 1 (2022): 25–28 (25).

ARTIST'S STATEMENT

BARBARA VON ECKARDT

I. THE PHOTOGRAPHIC PROJECT

The personal dimension of some of the eBay junk drawer objects initially drew my attention. Especially thrilling was discovering junk drawers with objects that were highly personal, in the sense of being private—someone's erotic playing cards, for example, or notes someone took on a napkin while on a religious pilgrimage. Such objects afforded me a glimpse of things that had not only been especially meaningful to their previous owners but were also not intended for the eyes of others. As literary scholar Marilyn Alquizola notes, when she did archival work for the first time, "This new experience for me was somewhat akin to intellectual voyeurism, as I felt a small thrill in invading someone's private papers."[1] In my case, of course, the thrill came in seeing and being in the presence of someone's private stuff.

The eBay junk drawers were fascinating in another way. Not only did they contain a lot of interesting personal objects and afford the odd voyeuristic thrill, but they also seemed, at least in part, testamentary—that is, the objects in the junk drawers seemed to "speak" about their owners. Or, to put it in a more epistemic way, they seemed "readable." I later found texts in fields such as personality psychology, history of philosophy, and material culture studies that helped me make sense of these notions, but initially, my understanding was purely impressionistic. All I understood at the time was that there seemed to be something about each object in my junk drawer boxes, and something about me (cognitively), that made it possible to form a reasonable hypothesis about the person who had owned that particular object. And that was a fascinating discovery.

Thus far, I have focused on the positive aspects afforded by discovering the junk drawers I eventually purchased and photographed. But finding these collections triggered another, more negative, reaction: dismay. There seemed something very wrong with the once personally meaningful stuff of a deceased person being sold on eBay. But why did I feel that this was wrong? And what about the junk drawer items caused this reaction? Again, the answer only emerged after months of reading the relevant literature.

It was the above two responses to the eBay junk drawer objects—their apparent readability coupled with my dismay—that prompted the *Junk Drawer* photographic project to purchase drawers and then photograph the objects within them as a way of both honoring the owners whom I glimpsed in the objects and contravening the depersonalization inherent in the objects' commodification.

I purchased eleven junk drawer boxes between 2014 and 2018 and photographed their objects from 2018 to 2019. The boxes came from all over the United States, including Spokane, Washington; Marseilles, Illinois; Jobstown, New Jersey; Columbus and Dayton, Ohio; Salt Lake City, Utah; Harrisburg, Pennsylvania; Green Bay, Wisconsin; and Boley, Oklahoma. (I no longer have location information for the other two.) The most I paid for any junk drawer box was thirty dollars. Since the various lots of stuff were sold by eBay resellers, I have no documentation regarding who the original owners were, but based on the contents of the boxes, especially the photographs included in them, it is reasonable to conclude that the owners were all white and middle class.

My original intention was to purchase only boxes for which all the objects came from a single estate and, hence, from a single owner, as this would enable a richer, more multi-faceted reading of the objects in any given box. And I initially believed that the descriptor "from estate" ensured such single ownership. I subsequently discovered that this was not the case. When several essay writers raised questions about whether all the items in any given box came from the same estate, I decided to survey some eBay sellers currently peddling "from estate" junk drawers as to what the description meant to them. The response was mixed. For some, it meant that all the items came from the same estate, but for others, sadly, it meant that each item came from an estate but that their estates of origin could be different. While the likelihood of multiple ownership of the items in some of my boxes obviously belies my original belief in one box-one estate, I maintain that this in no way undercuts the apparent testamentary nature of individual items. What it does do, however, is force us to look for internal evidence—specifically, the coherence of items in a box—to determine whether the contents of any given box come from a single estate.

Because I was primarily interested in the narrative potential of the objects in the boxes, I felt free to choose the junk drawer collections to purchase, as well as which purchased boxes to eventually photograph. In addition, although I initially intended to photograph every item in each of the boxes as part of this project, this proved not artistically viable. In other words, the process of going from the junk drawer collections available on eBay at the time I was looking to the photographs selected for this project involved many choices and some serious winnowing. Be that as it may, by the end of this process, I had 128 photographs of 323 objects (I counted some subcollections, such as a group of keys, as one item) from the eleven purchased boxes. Fifty of those photographs appear in this book.

I "photographed" the objects by placing them on an Epson V600 photo scanner and subsequently processed the resulting images in Adobe Photoshop with the Nik Silver Effex filter. I chose to desaturate the color of the original scans and give the images a slight sepia tone, not only for aesthetic reasons but also for a metaphorical one: sepia was originally used to extend the life of black-and-white prints, just as I am now attempting to extend the meaningful life of the junk drawer objects. Margaret Olin, in her essay in this volume, appreciates this point when she observes: “When junk is photographed as though it were precious, the meeting between the concept of junk and the homage paid to it by a photographer can impart the feeling of the uncanny, as do Von Eckardt’s photographs. This is a beautiful, redemptive light in which to regard photography” (see page 136).

II. THE PHILOSOPHICAL PROJECT

I noted above that my photographic project was inspired by two immediate reactions to the junk drawer items sold on eBay: first, the intuition that many of the objects could tell me something about the owner of the estates from which they came (that they were testimonial); and, second, a feeling of dismay that these objects were being commodified. Once I completed the photographic project, I took it upon myself to see if I could figure out what the psychological and philosophical basis of those two reactions could be.

OBJECT-TO-OWNER-ATTRIBUTE INFERENCES

The idea of “reading” an object is not new. Roland Barthes famously claimed the following:

> A garment, an automobile, a dish of cooked food, a gesture, a film, a piece of music, an advertising image, a piece of furniture, a newspaper headline—these indeed appear to be heterogeneous objects. What might they have in common? This at least: all are signs. When I walk through the streets—or through life—and encounter these objects, I apply to all of them, if need be without realizing it, one and the same activity, which is that of a certain reading: . . . this car tells me the social status of its owner, this garment tells me quite precisely the degree of its wearer’s conformism or eccentricity, this aperitif (whiskey, Pernod, or white wine an cassis) reveals my host’s life style.[2]

Note that a “reading,” for Barthes, is both an activity (an inferential process) and the result of such an activity (a judgment or conclusion). I call such readings “object-to-owner-attribute inferences,” a label that is ambiguous in the same way in that an “inference” can refer both to a process but also to a conclusion. Barthes grounds such readings in the semiotic properties of objects, drawing on Ferdinand de Saussure’s semiotics.[3] I prefer a psychological understanding grounded in cognitive psychology’s tradition of unconscious inference.[4]

The understanding I propose is built on two key ideas. The first, clearly articulated by Sam Gosling, is that ordinary (types of) objects are typically associated with characteristic roles vis-à-vis a user’s actions or mental state.[5] These roles come about in various ways: consumer objects are typically designed by a manufacturer to serve specific purposes; handmade and artistic objects’ roles are often designated by their creator; and some roles evolve spontaneously within subgroups in society. According to Gosling, there are three major kinds of roles: "behavioral residue," "person state regulator," and "material identity claim."[6]

- Behavioral residue: the intended or unintended material result or byproduct of an action. Examples of objects with this kind of role include a homemade birdhouse, a photograph, an empty pill bottle, or a dirty frying pan.
- Person state regulator: something that facilitates, enhances, or regulates actions, cognition, and emotion, bodily states, interpersonal attitudes, values, or motivational structures. Examples of objects with this kind of role include a hammer, music app, keys, contact lenses, political ads, medicine, books, movies and TV shows, or wall paint colors.
- Material identity claim: something that symbolizes, communicates, and/or maintains the owner's self-concept or a third-person identity attribution. Examples of objects with this kind of role include political buttons or sports awards.

The importance of these roles for my purposes is that they can mediate object-to-owner attribute inferences. They do so in two steps: first, by licensing an inference to the existence of a relevant action or mental state, and then by attributing that action or mental state to the owner of the object in question.

My junk drawer boxes contain examples of objects with all three roles. The theater program (PLATE 0.22), meal ticket (PLATE 0.08), and embroidery (PLATE 0.40) are all behavioral residues. The ownership of a theater program typically results from attending the theater performance described in the program; the possession of a used meal ticket typically results from buying food from a cafeteria, store, or restaurant that takes such tickets, with the number of holes punched indicating the number of meals bought; and the creation of a piece of handmade embroidery typically results from an act of embroidering. Actions presuppose actors. Thus, the causal action—attending, buying, or making—presupposes, and therefore points to, a specific attribute of the object's owner, in these cases that the owner attended *Blossom Time*; that the owner was entitled to (and bought) a certain number of meals from a ticket-taking venue; and that the owner embroidered a napkin. There are also many person state regulators—the smoking paraphernalia (PLATE 0.01), non-vintage photographs of persons and events (PLATES 0.07, 0.10, 0.12, 0.16, 0.24, 0.28, 0.30-0.37), and non-photographic travel memorabilia (PLATES 0.23, 0.26, 0.37-0.39). The smoking paraphernalia facilitates smoking; old photographs of persons and events facilitate remembering the persons and/or events photographed; and other kinds of memorabilia facilitate remembering the specific persons or events associated with them. From these facilitated actions, both behavioral and mental, we can infer the existence of an owner who performed the facilitated action—an owner who smoked or an owner who remembered. Finally, many items make a material identity claim. They declare, in effect, that the owner, whomever that was, self-identified with belonging to the military (PLATES 0.07, 0.09), or with belonging to a family (PLATES 0.28, 0.30, 0.34), had a religious affiliation (PLATE 0.33), made a political choice (PLATE 0.15), or partook in certain hobbies and interests (PLATES 0.05, 0.42, 0.47, 0.49). Given that each object belonged to a particular owner, we can infer that the identity claim suggested by the object was likely embraced by that owner.

But, you might protest, what if the object in question landed in a junk drawer box in a non-standard way—not by intentional acquisition but, say, by being inherited, or left by a neighbor, or found on the street? There are always counter-examples to canonical object-to-owner attribute inferences, which is simply to say that such inferences are not deductive. But that fact alone does not mean that such non-deductive inferences are all equally problematic.

The non-deductive inference form relevant here is what analytic philosophers now call "inference to the best explanation."[7] Given a set of facts, one determines the best possible explanation for those facts from a set of possible explanations that meet certain criteria, and then infers that the best possible, available explanation is, in fact, true (or, at least, probably true). Inferences to the best explanation occur frequently in both everyday life and science. Scientific examples include Charles Darwin's account of the origin of species, Ignaz Semmelweis's account of childbed fever, and John Snow's account of the causes of cholera.[8]

Armed now with our two key ideas—that objects have characteristic roles and that object-to-owner inferences are inferences to the best explanation—we can unpack the mystery of how (and by virtue of what) many junk drawer objects serve as testaments about their owners. They do so, I argue, as upon consciously perceiving and categorizing a junk drawer object, a person unconsciously infers, by means of an inference to the best explanation: first, that the object played a specific characteristic role in the past (that is, functioned as a behavioral residue of an action, as a person state regulator vis-à-vis actions, mental states, bodily states, etc., or as a material identity claim vis-à-vis the owner); and, second, that the owner of the object performed a characteristic action, or experienced a particular mental state, etc., brought about by the object. The conclusion of this two-part inference sometimes rises to the level of consciousness or, more minimally, results in an intuition or feeling that objects, like those in the junk drawers discussed here, can be testamentary.

There are ways of going beyond the basic object-to-owner inferences thus far considered. When the objects in a junk drawer box exhibit enough coherence to consider them as coming from a single estate (assuming that there is no direct evidence of that fact), one can consider those objects in relation to one another. When suitable background knowledge is available, one can go deeper by bringing that background knowledge to bear on the relevant objects.

For instance, one of the most coherent boxes in my junk drawer collection is Box 6, as most of its objects are photographs, the contents of which overlap significantly. As a result, the items in Box 6, taken together, lend themselves to telling a single story. Here is the story I am inclined to tell based on inferences. My guess is that the owner of the Box 6 objects was the woman depicted in PLATE 0.28, whom I infer to be the wife of the gentleman standing next to her. The man reappears in PLATE 0.30 standing next to two young adults whom I infer were the couple's children, and in PLATE 0.31 sitting in his car. The man and woman most likely lived in the house depicted in PLATE 0.31. There is a calling card for an insurance business in Salt Lake City, Utah. The man could have been Charles James Cayias, the president of that business. The son served in the military, as shown in PLATE 0.32. There are young children in PLATES 0.33 and 0.34, most likely grandchildren of the older couple. The fur coat in PLATE 0.28 and the jewelry and fancy lighter in PLATE 0.29 suggest that the wife enjoyed her wealth. Religion (likely the Eastern Orthodox Church) seems to have played an important part in her family's life (PLATE 0.33, 0.34). PLATES 0.37 through 0.39 suggest that the husband and wife traveled to Jerusalem on the ship *Coronado* and stayed at the Gloria Hotel in the Old City. PLATE 0.39 depicts notes taken on hotel stationery, mentioning Christ, Judah, the Tomb of the Virgin Mary, the Garden of Gethsemane, the Mount of Olives, and St. Helen. These seem to be notes taken by someone on the Passion of Jesus, the short final period before the death of Jesus, as described in the four canonical gospels. The notes strike me as written from the point of view of a devout Christian, which fits the family pictures of a priest (PLATE 0.33).

Box 3 also exhibits significant coherence but, in addition, provides multiple opportunities for utilizing background information to extend the object-to-owner inferences. Prima facie, the objects in Box 3 seem to tell the story of Fred Juergensen (PLATE 0.08), who played with toy soldiers as a child (PLATE 0.12), spent time in the military as an adult (PLATE 0.07), wore military insignias (PLATES 0.09, 0.11), had military buddies (PLATES 0.10, 0.12), used an oil can (PLATES 0.12), ate at a cafeteria at Fort Monroe in 1945 (PLATES 0.18), shaved with Gillette razors (PLATES 0.11), received mail in Mailbox 65 (PLATE 0.14), and likely voted for Roosevelt, Truman, Nixon, and Carter (PLATE 0.15).

These inferences can be extended by doing detective work. For example, from my own travels to the Southwest United States, I know that the tree depicted in PLATE 0.10 is a Joshua tree. A Google search reveals that Joshua trees (*Yucca brevifolia*) grow only in the U.S. Southwest, including the Mojave Desert.[9] Wikipedia further tells me that there was a World War II training camp in the Mojave Desert in 1942, the Desert Training Center, whose mission was "to train United States Army and Air Force units and personnel to live and fight in the desert, to test and develop suitable equipment, and to develop tactical doctrines, techniques and training methods."[10] Since the United States entered World War II in 1941 and the draft was mandatory, we can infer that Fred was serving in the military in 1942, and from the picture we can infer that he was posted at the Desert Training Center at that time.

My second reaction to discovering the junk drawer objects being sold on eBay for small sums of money was dismay. Why did I feel that? Three ideas are at the core of a possible answer. The first is the moral principle, associated with eighteenth-century philosopher Immanuel Kant, that people should be treated as ends in themselves rather than as means to an end. Kant said that we should "act in such a way as to treat humanity, whether in your own person or in that of anyone else, always as an end and never merely as a means."[11] Kant's use of the term "humanity" here does not mean human beings collectively. Rather, it means that collection of features that makes us distinctively human, which for Kant includes the capacity to adopt and pursue our own ends (e.g., aims, intentions), as well as other related rational capacities.[12] Kant's concern with our humanity is primarily a concern with our capacity to adopt moral ends, but there are other broader ways to understand what makes us distinctively human, and thus what makes people ends in themselves. One is to include in that understanding all those capacities and actions related to choosing our ends (goals, projects, plans), not just those connected to morality; another is to include all those capacities and actions related to choosing what makes our life meaningful.

The second idea that helped to provide insight into my dismay is that the respect for persons called for by Kant's principle, originally articulated as applying to the humanity of living persons, can be extended to two other dimensions—from persons to entities or attributes that are person-related, including their possessions, and from living persons to the deceased. From respect for possessions of the living and for the deceased, we can then triangulate to respect for possessions of the dead and seeing such possessions as ends in themselves.

Finally, the third idea is that there are different realms of value, and these can be in opposition to each other in the sense that moving something from one realm to another negates or interferes with its value in the original realm. My junk drawer objects, as originally owned, had value as objects of choice and personal meaning. If we accept the extensions of Kant's principle suggested above, then not only the persons who owned these objects but also the objects themselves should be treated with respect. But selling such objects on eBay is to treat them as commodities, in other words as objects of exchange, which is the exact opposite of treating them as ends in themselves. As a result, selling them on eBay violates the respect they are due. Hence, my dismay.

III. THE SCHOLARLY PROJECT

As the collecting and photographing phase of the *Junk Drawer* project got underway, I began to share my results with academic colleagues. Much to my surprise, I discovered that many found the project interesting not only in itself but also because it resonated with their areas of scholarship—history of photography, art history, memory studies, and American studies, for example. After conversations with Sander Gilman, a new appreciation of how this project might be expanded began to emerge, including not only photographic documentation of my junk drawer collection but also a set of essays by colleagues interested in material culture that would explore the collection and photographs of "junk" through the lens of their own discipline. Interestingly, this broader reconception led to a revision of my purpose in creating and photographing the junk drawer collection: from restoring the meaningfulness of the junk drawer objects from their devaluation via commoditization by photographing them, to also giving them new meaning by creating the opportunity for related scholarly exploration. This, then, became another scholarly project associated with the first photographic one, resulting in a fascinating and varied assortment of essays—a "junk drawer" itself of contemporary scholarship on objects that were left behind and the photographs of those objects, included in the pages that follow.

1. Marilyn Alquizola, et al., "The Bulosan Files: Another Layer in an Ongoing Dialogue," in *Writer in Exile/Writer in Revolt: Critical Perspectives on Carlos Bulosan*, ed. J.A. Cabusao (University Press of America, 2016), 261.
2. Roland Barthes, *The Semiotic Challenge*, rev. ed. (University of California Press, 1994), 157.
3. Ferdinand de Saussure, *Course in General Linguistics*, trans. R. Harris (Duckworth, 1983).
4. The concept of unconscious inference has a rich history in cognitive psychology, beginning with the work of Hermann von Helmholtz in the nineteenth century. Helmholtz proposed that perception involves unconscious inferences, suggesting that the brain uses past experiences to interpret sensory data, thus facilitating accurate perception of the environment (Hermann von Helmholtz, *Treatise on Physiological Optics*, vol. 3, trans. J.P.C. Southell [1867: Dover, 1962]). Over the last century, Helmholtz's idea has been reinterpreted. Recent versions of the unconscious inference hypothesis include J.A. Bargh and T.L. Chartrand, "The Unbearable Automaticity of Being," *American Psychologist* 54, no. 7 (1999): 462–79, and Gerd Gigerenzer, *Gut Feelings: The Intelligence of the Unconscious* (Viking, 2007).
5. Samuel D. Gosling, et al., "A Room with a Cue: Personality Judgments Based on Offices and Bedrooms," *Journal of Personality and Social Psychology* 82, no. 3 (2002): 379–98. Mihaly Csikszentmihalyi and Eugene Rochberg-Halton, *The Meaning of Things: Domestic Symbols and the Self* (Cambridge University Press, 1981), and Susan Fournier, "Meaning-Based Framework for the Study of Consumer-Object Relations," *Advances in Consumer Research* 18, no. 1 (1991): 736, have proposed similar schemes.
6. Gosling, et al., "Room with a Cue."
7. Inference to the best explanation is sometimes referred to as "abduction." Despite the widespread occurrence of abduction in both science and everyday life, there remain many philosophical questions about its explication. These include what counts as a possible explanation, what counts as the best explanation, why is it reasonable to infer from being a best explanation to being true or probably true. See Igor Douven, "Abduction," *The Stanford Encyclopedia of Philosophy*, last modified May 18, 2021, https://plato.stanford.edu/archives/sum2021/entries/abduction/, for recent discussions.

8. Charles Darwin, *The Origin of Species* (John Murray, 1872), 421; on Ignaz Semmelweis, see P. Lipton, *Inference to the Best Explanation*, 2nd ed. (Routledge, 2004), 74–90; on John Snow, see D. Tulodziecki, "A Case Study in Explanatory Power: John Snow's Conclusions about the Pathology and Transmission of Cholera," *Studies in History and Philosophy of Biological and Biomedical Sciences* 42 (2011): 306–16 (315).
9. Wikipedia, "Joshua Tree," last modified 2024, https://en.wikipedia.org/wiki/Yucca_brevifolia.
10. Wikipedia, "Desert Training Center," last modified 2024, https://en.wikipedia.org/wiki/Desert_Training_Center.
11. Immanuel Kant, *Groundwork of the Metaphysics of Morals*, ed. and trans. Mary Gregor and Jens Timmermann (1785; Cambridge University Press, 1997), 38.
12. On Kant's conception of "humanity" as the rational capacity to set and pursue ends, rather than simply human beings collectively, see Allen Wood, *Kant's Ethical Thought* (Cambridge University Press, 1999), especially Chapter 2; Christine M. Korsgaard, *Creating the Kingdom of Ends* (Cambridge University Press, 1996), especially Chapters 3–4; and Jens Timmermann, *Kant's Groundwork of the Metaphysics of Morals: A Commentary* (Cambridge University Press, 2007), esp. commentary on 4:429.

JUNK DRAWER: THE PHOTOGRAPHS

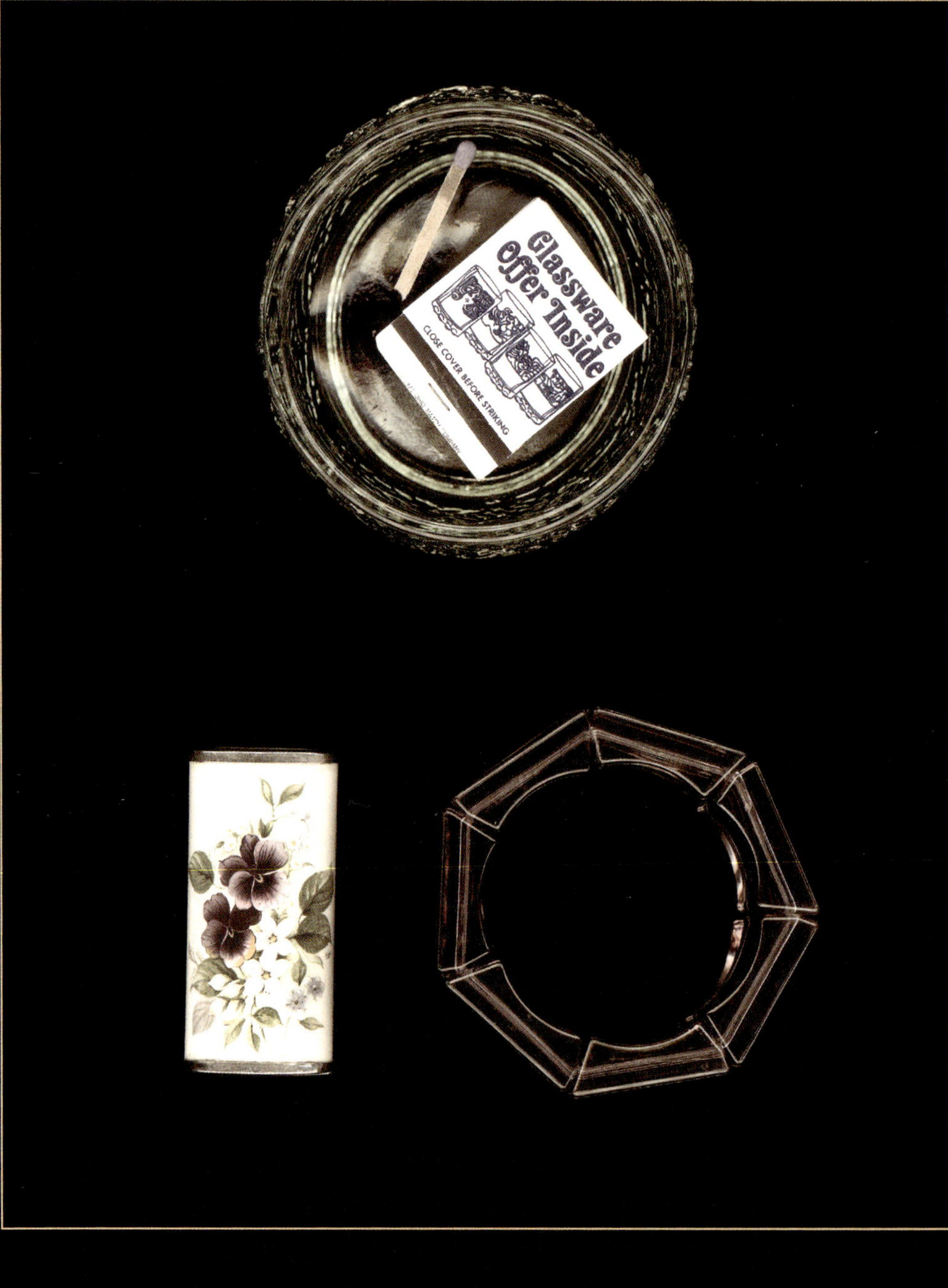

PLATE 0.01. *Ashtray, Matches, Lighter, and Bracelet* (Box 1).

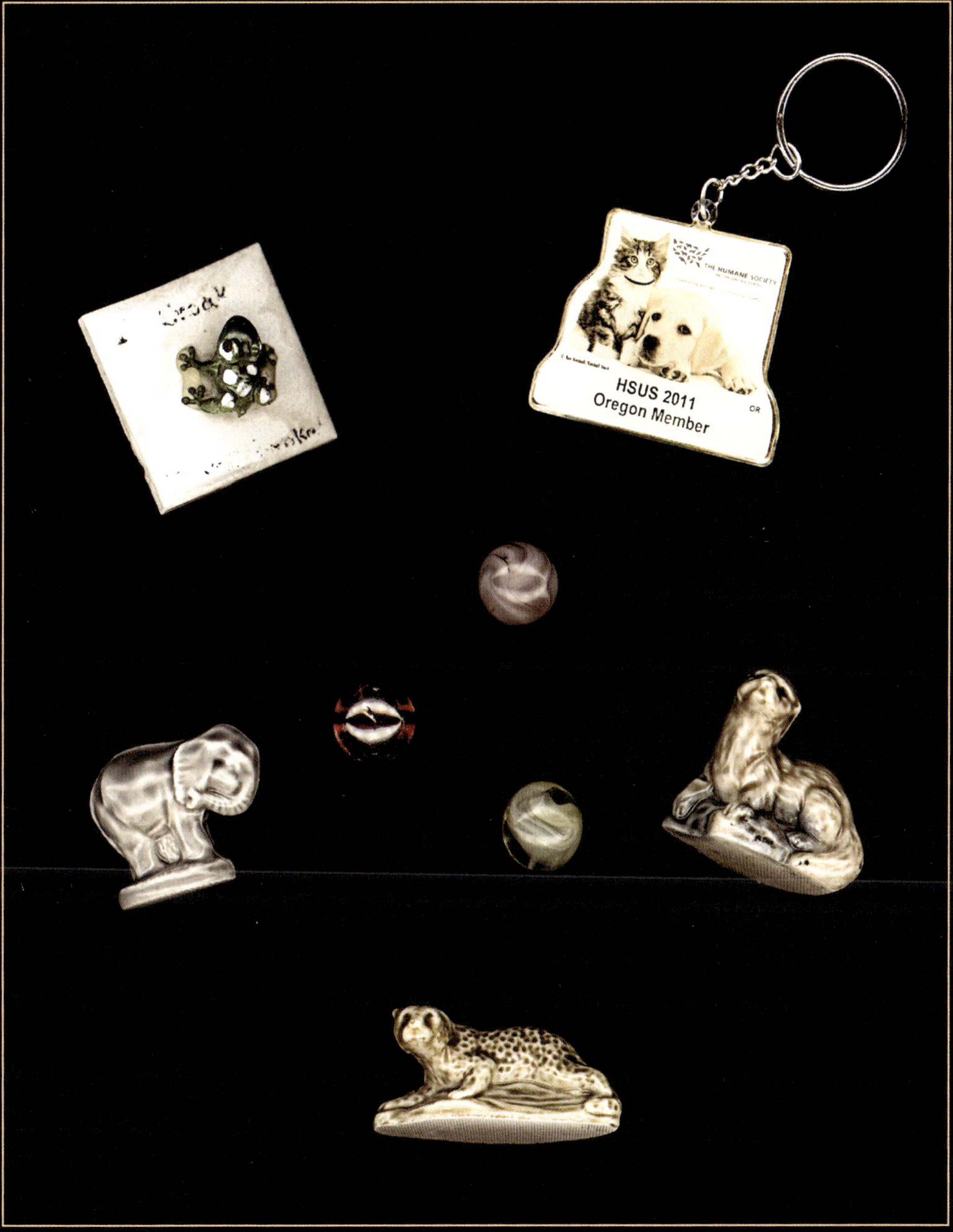

PLATE 0.02. *HSUS 2011 Key Chain, Marbles, and Small Animal Figurines* (Box 1).

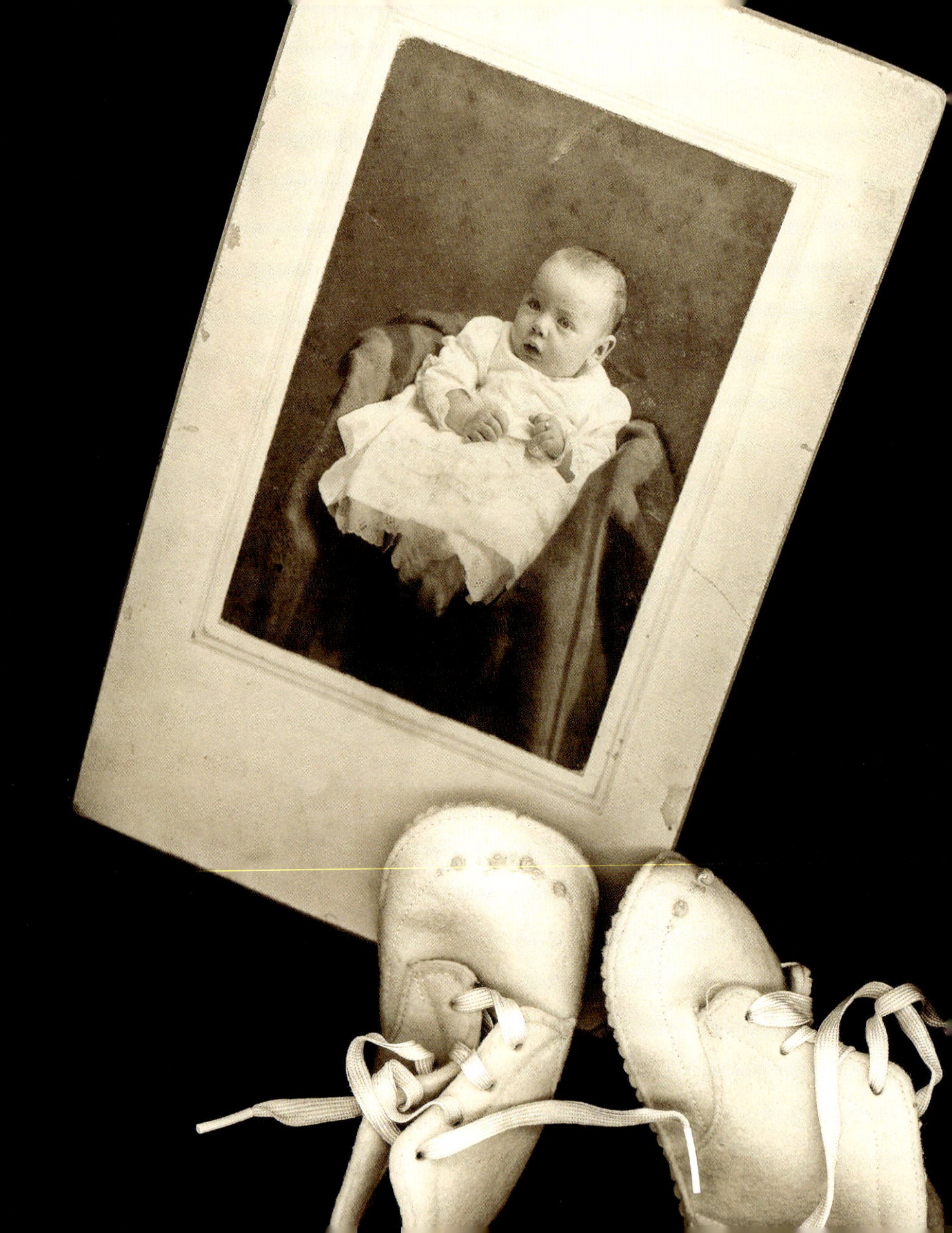

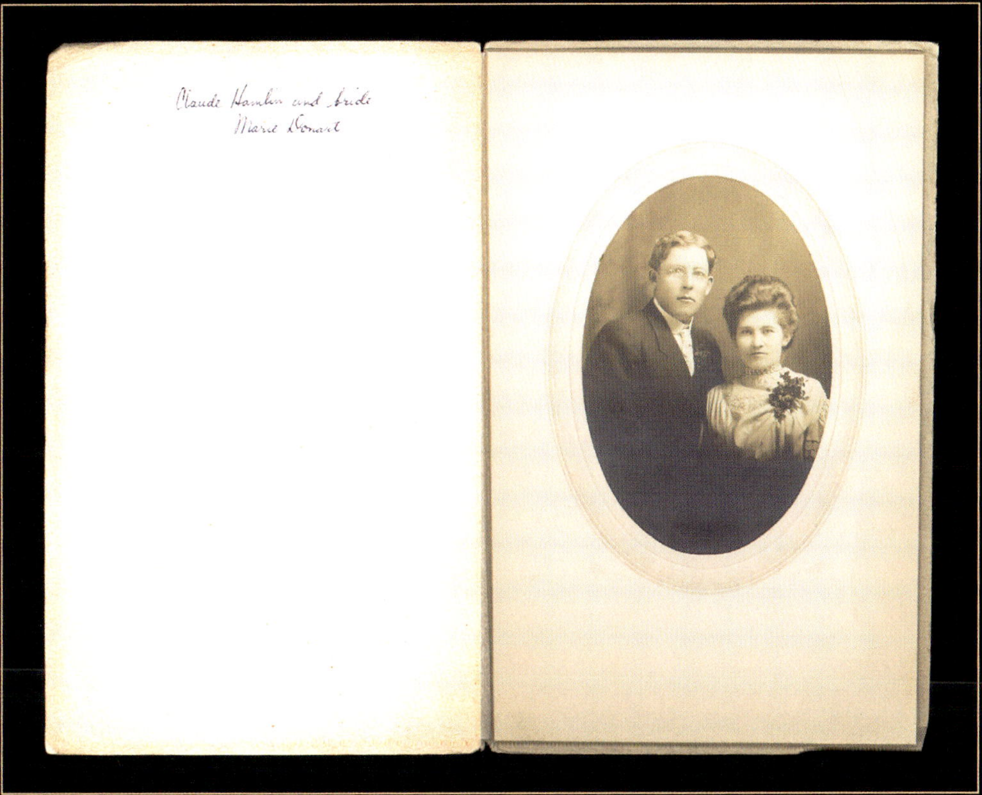

PLATE 0.04. *Formal Portrait of Claude Hamlin and Bride* (Box 1).

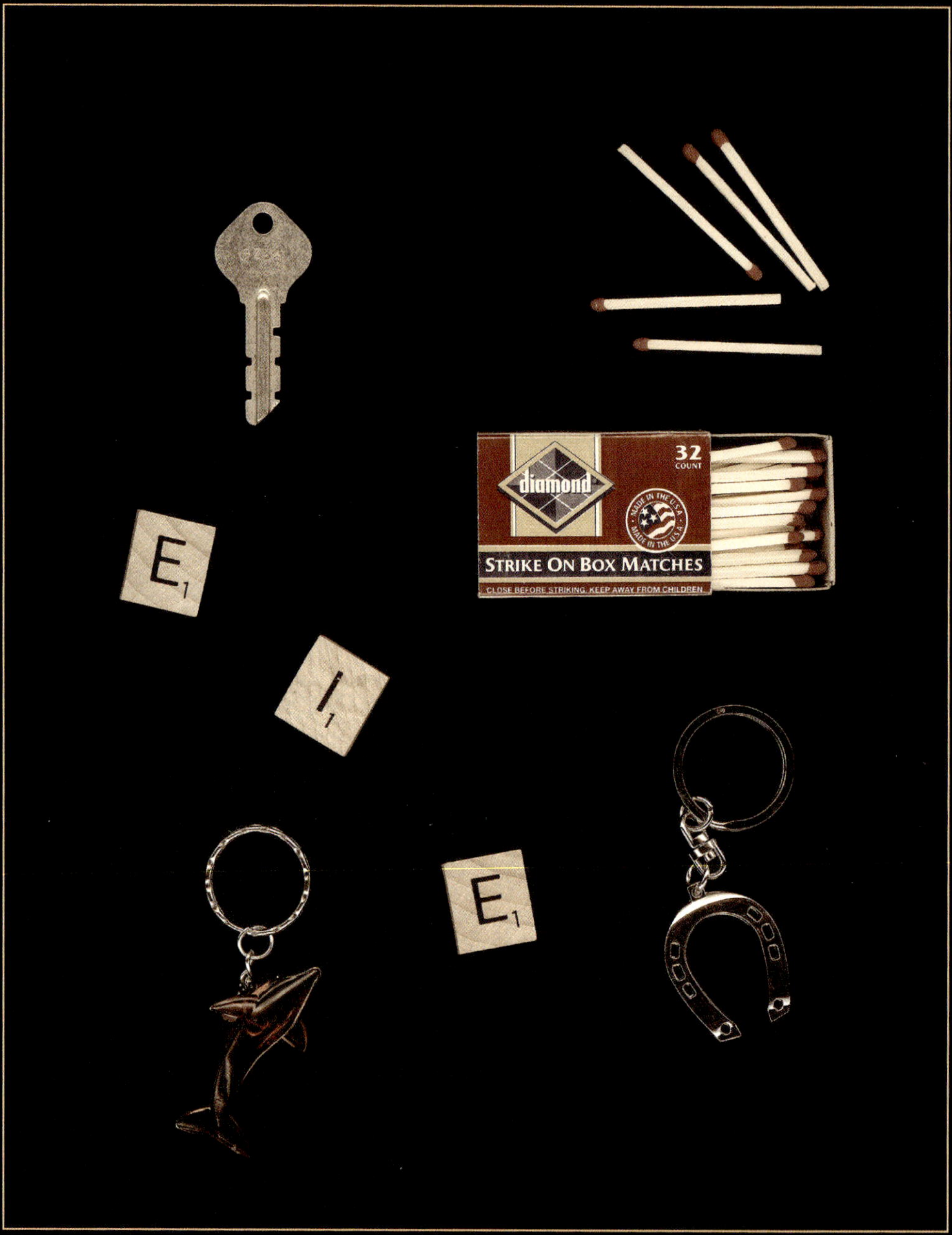

PLATE 0.05. *Diamond Matches and Other Odds and Ends* (Box 2).

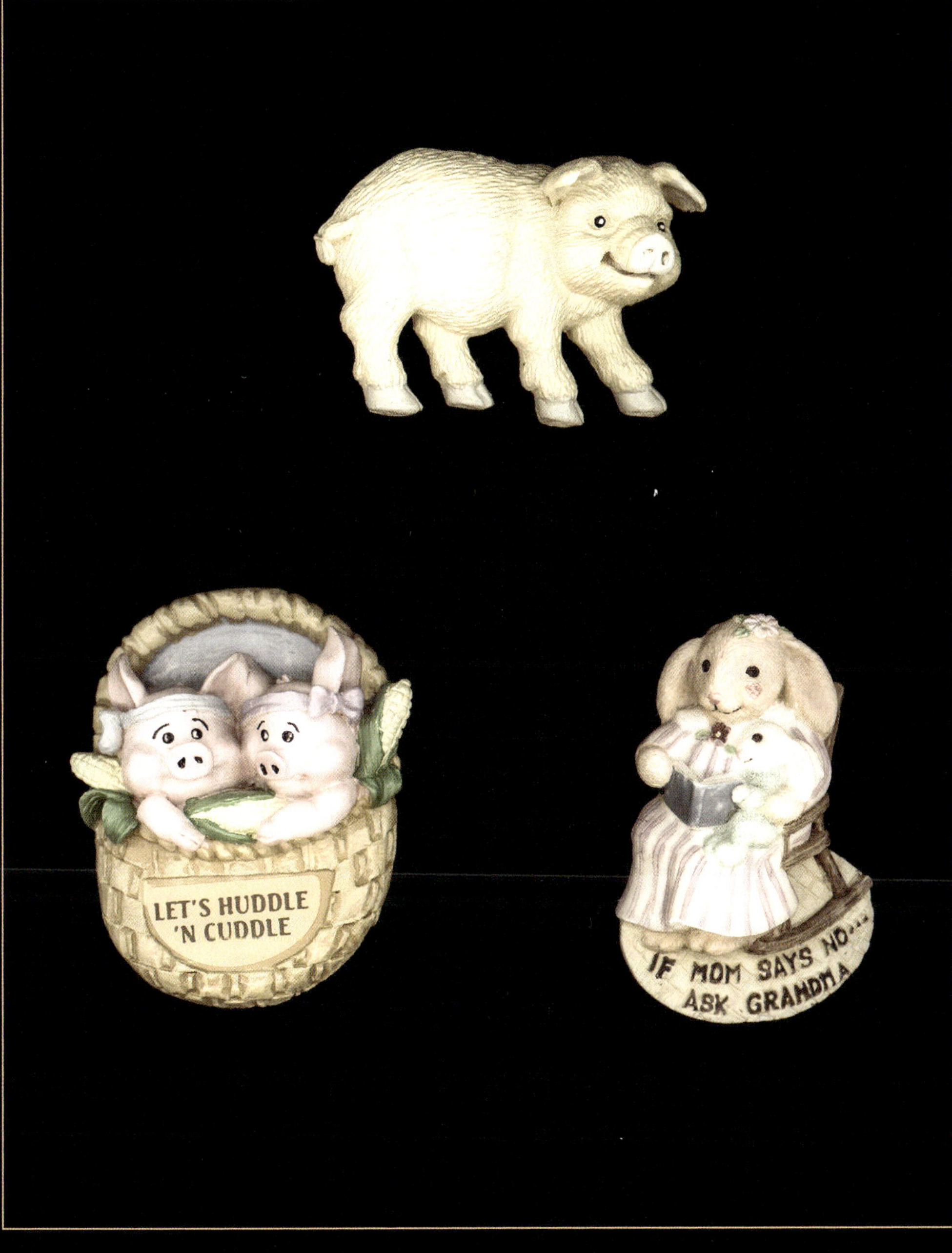

PLATE 0.06. *Grandma's Animal Trinkets* (Box 2).

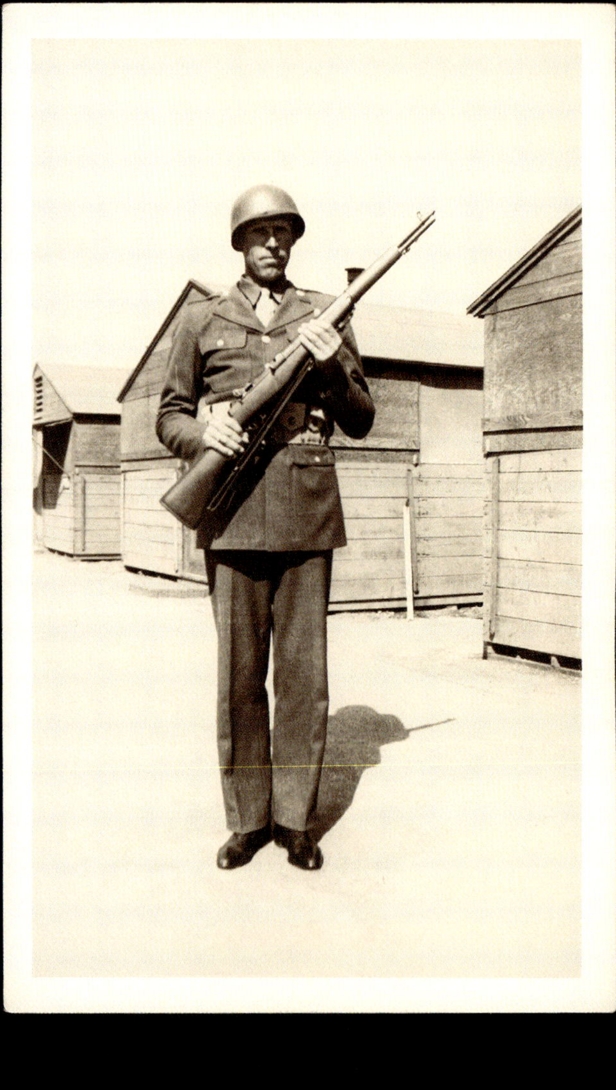

PLATE 0.07. Photo of Soldier Standing with Rifle (Box 3).

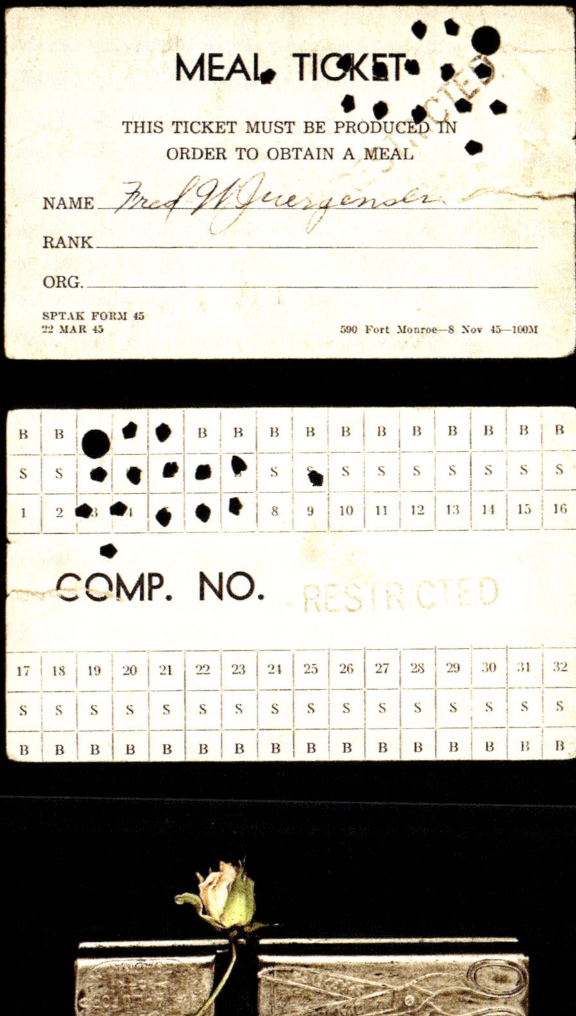
MEAL TICKET
THIS TICKET MUST BE PRODUCED IN
ORDER TO OBTAIN A MEAL
NAME Fred W Juergensen
RANK
ORG.
SPTAK FORM 45
22 MAR 45
590 Fort Monroe—8 Nov 45—100M
RESTRICTED
B B B B B B B B B B B B B
S S S S S S S S S S S
1 2 8 9 10 11 12 13 14 15 16
COMP. NO.
RESTRICTED
17 18 19 20 21 22 23 24 25 26 27 28 29 30 31 32
S S S S S S S S S S S S S S S S
B B B B B B B B B B B B B B B B

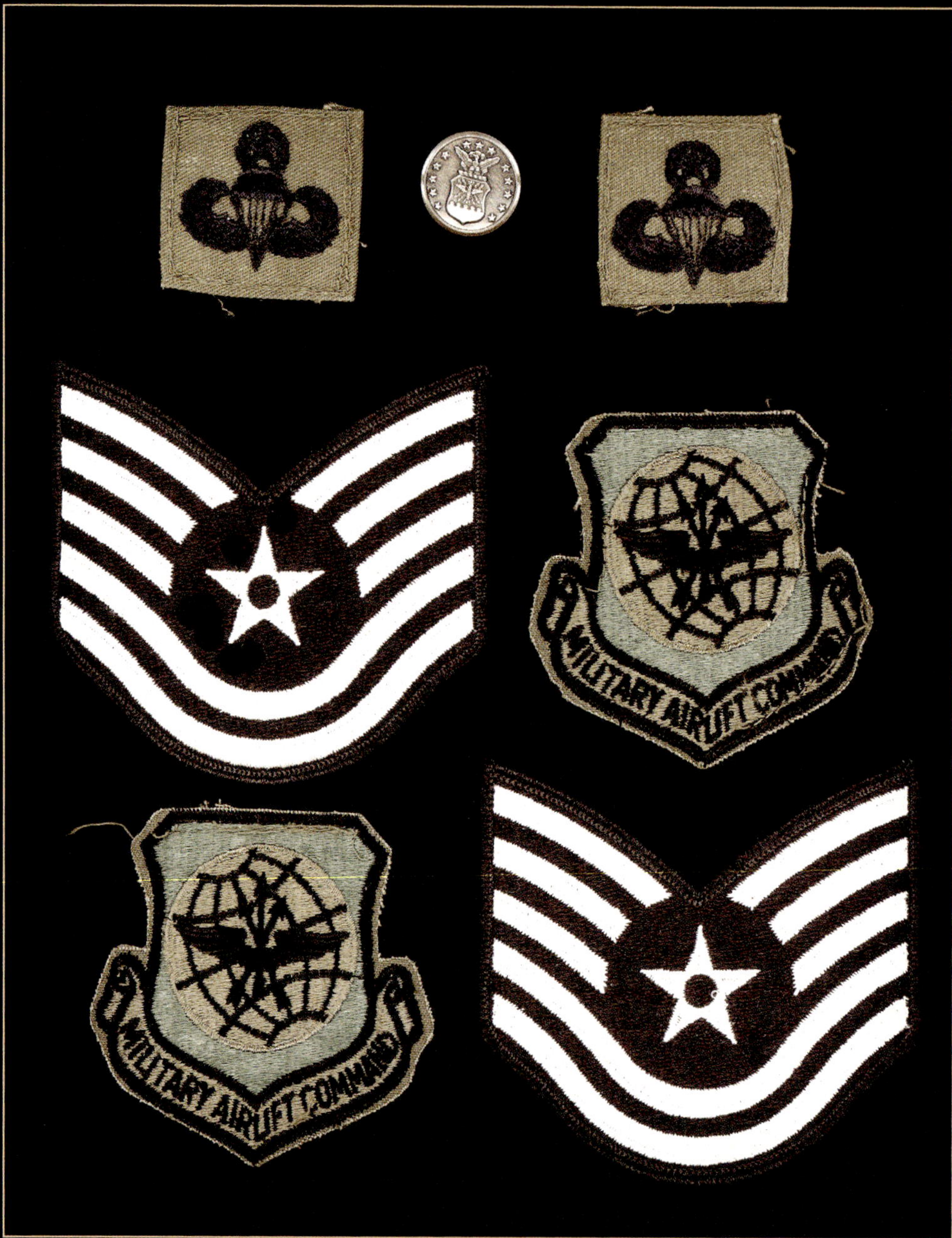

PLATE 0.09. *Insignias: Military Airlift Command* (Box 3).

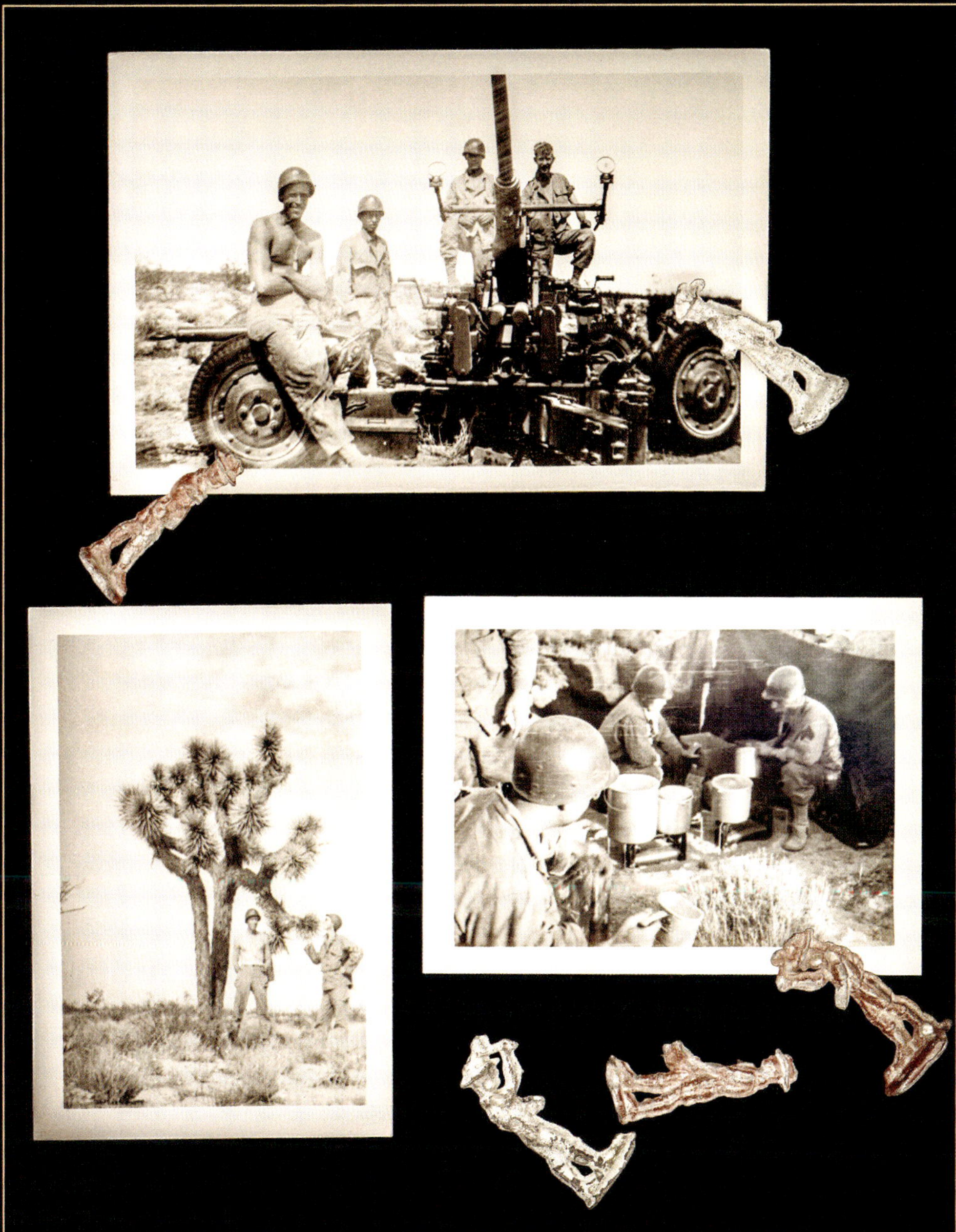

PLATE 0.10. *Snapshots of Soldiers at WWII Training Camp in Mojave Desert* (Box 3).

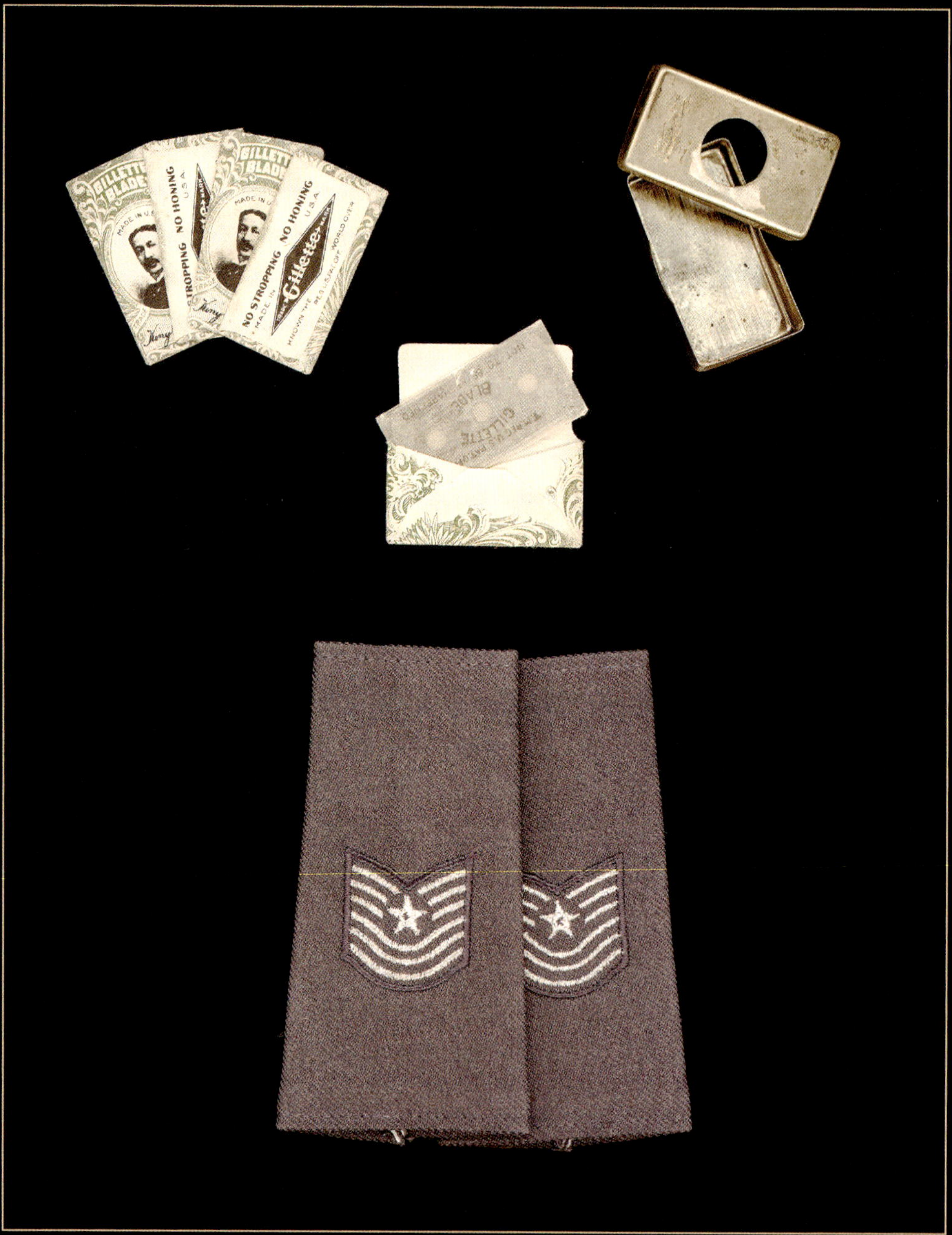

PLATE 0.11. *Gillette Razor Blades and Air Force E-6 Insignia* (Box 3).

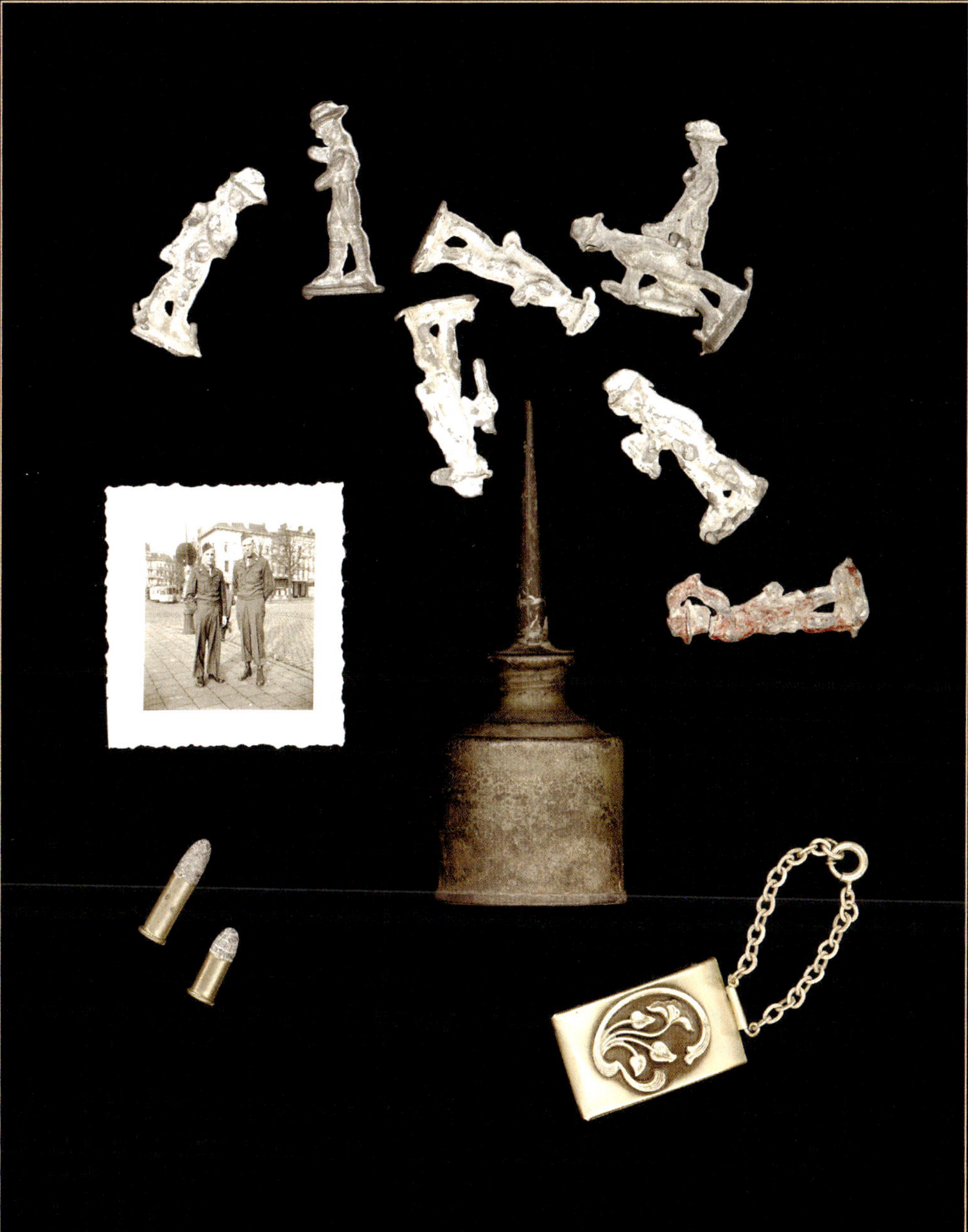

PLATE 0.12. *Metallic Toy Soldiers, Oil Can, Bullets, Photo of Two Soldiers* (Box 3).

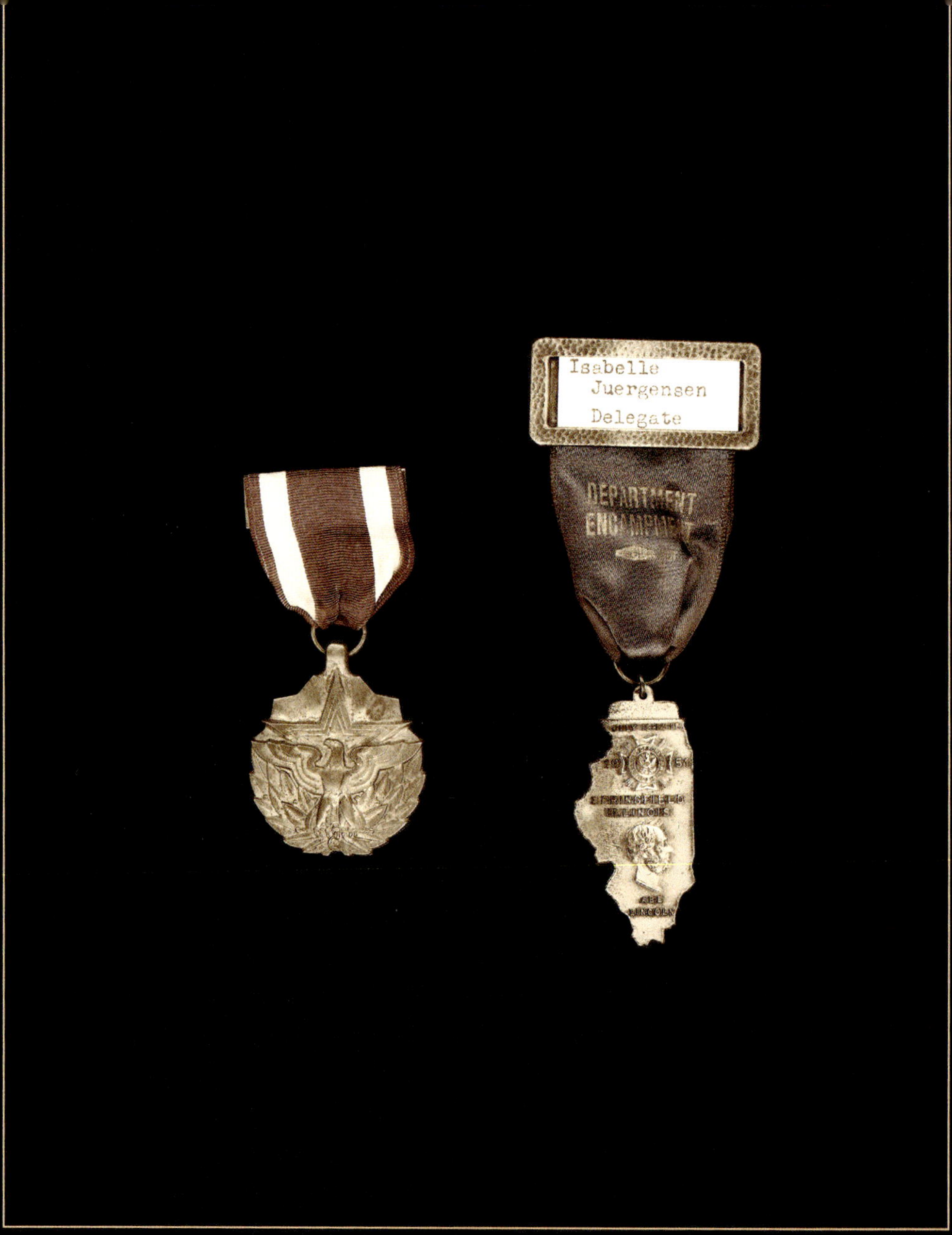

PLATE 0.13. *Isabelle Juergensen VFW Encampment Delegate 1951 Pin* (Box 3).

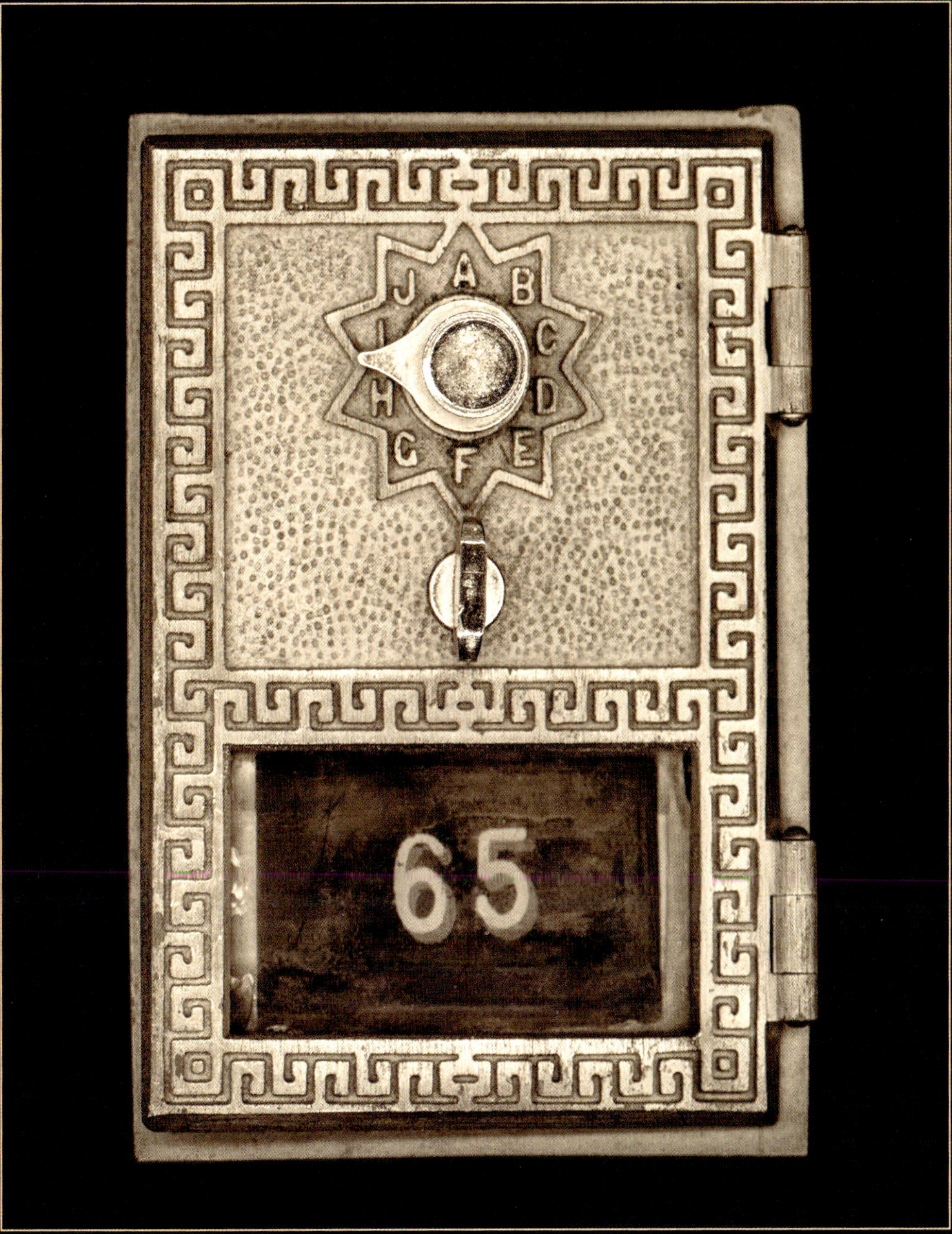
A B C D E F G H I J
65

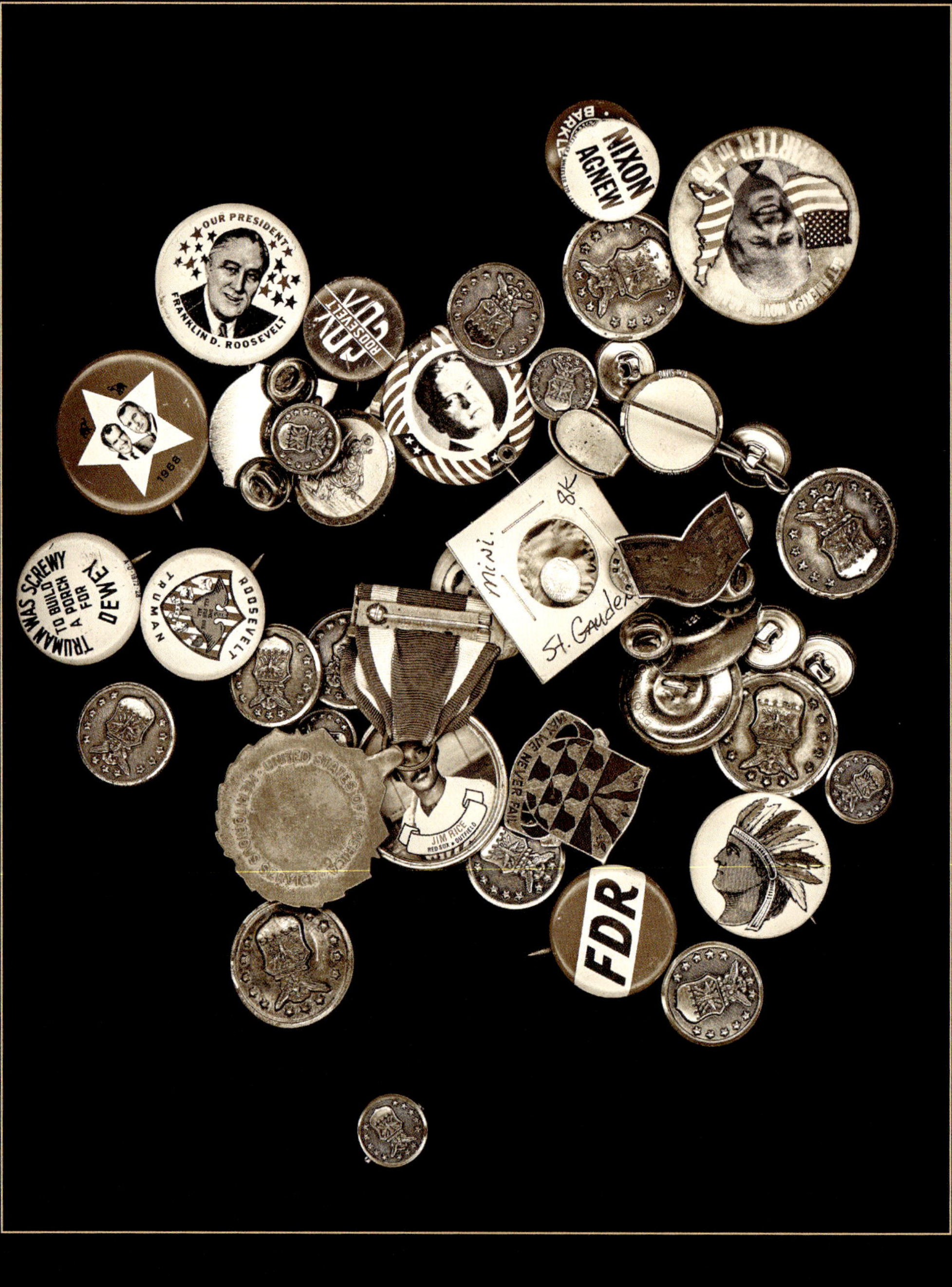

PLATE 0.15. *Political Buttons and Other Round Objects* (Box 3).

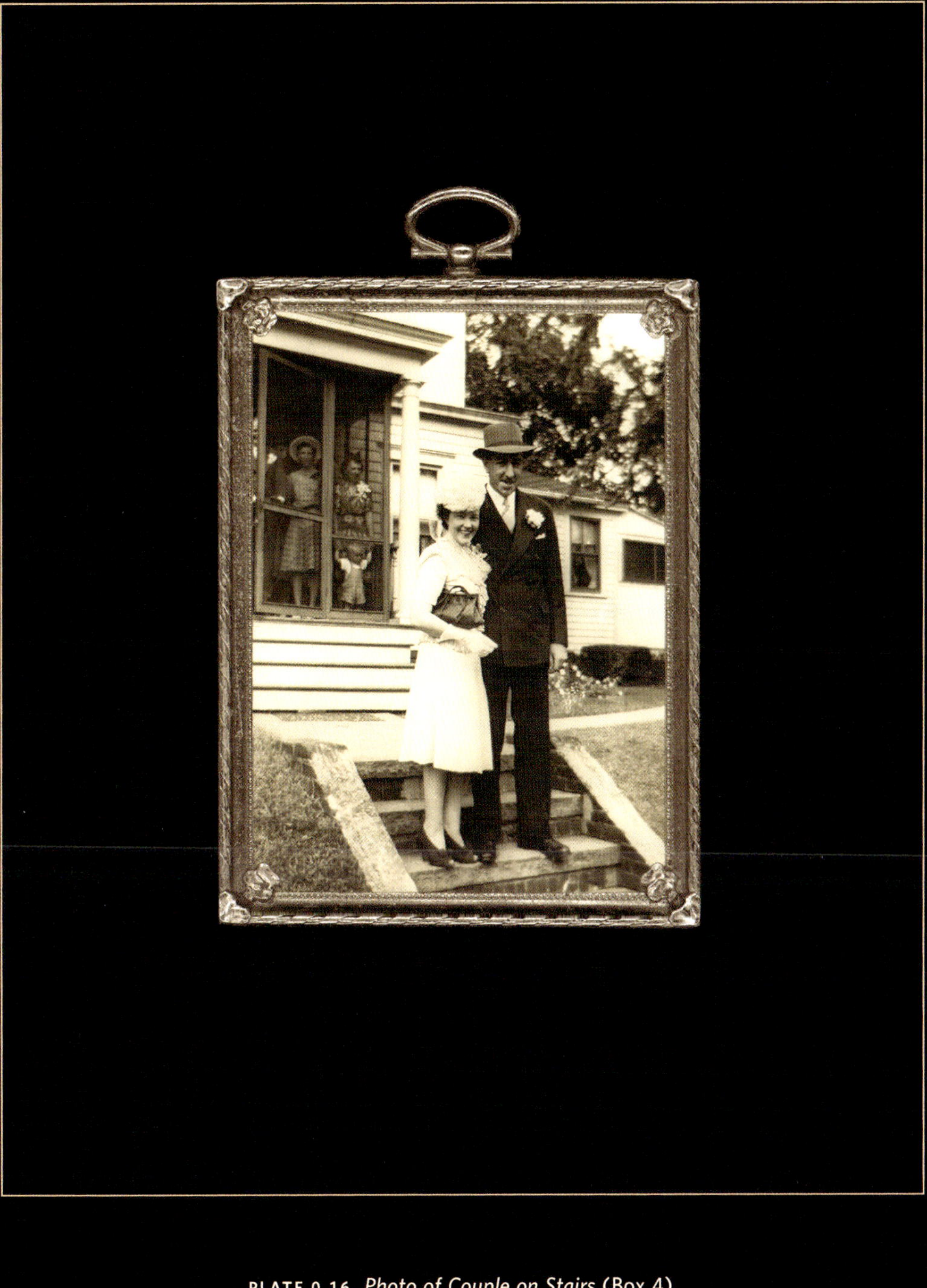

PLATE 0.16. *Photo of Couple on Stairs* (Box 4).

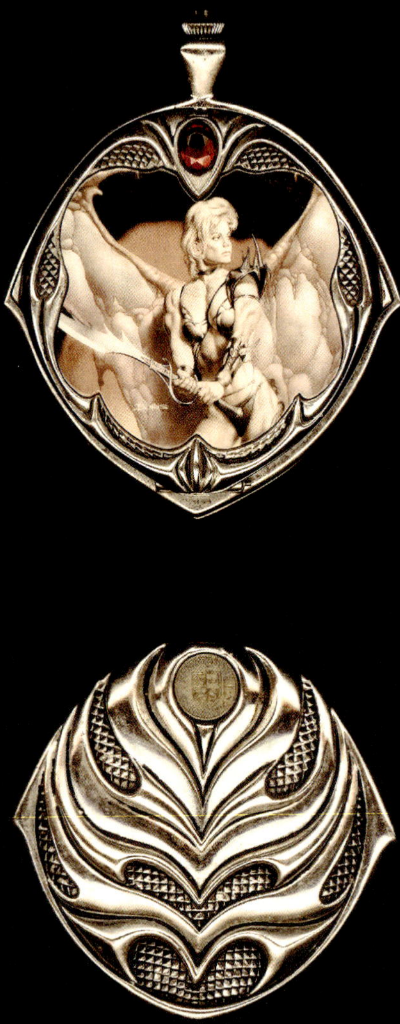

PLATE 0.17. *Muscular Angel Pocket Watch* (Box 4).

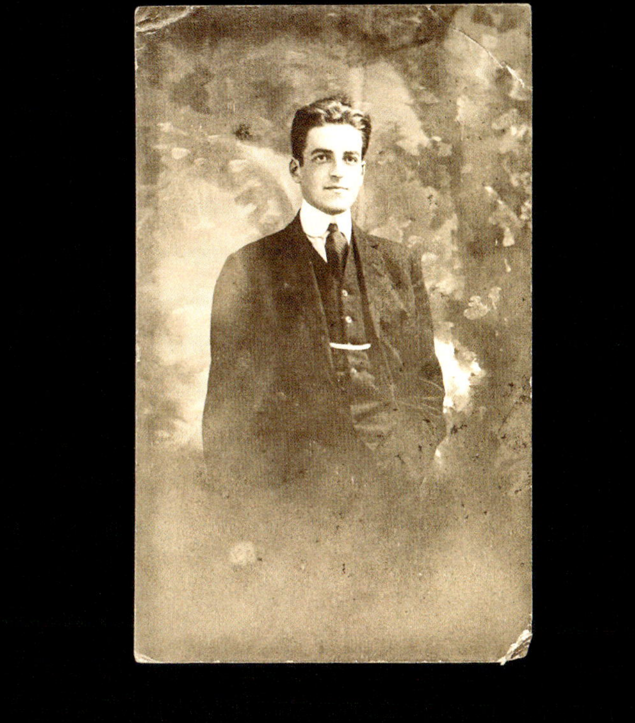

PLATE 0.18. *"For the Whole Bunch of Yez" Postcard, 1913* (Box 5).

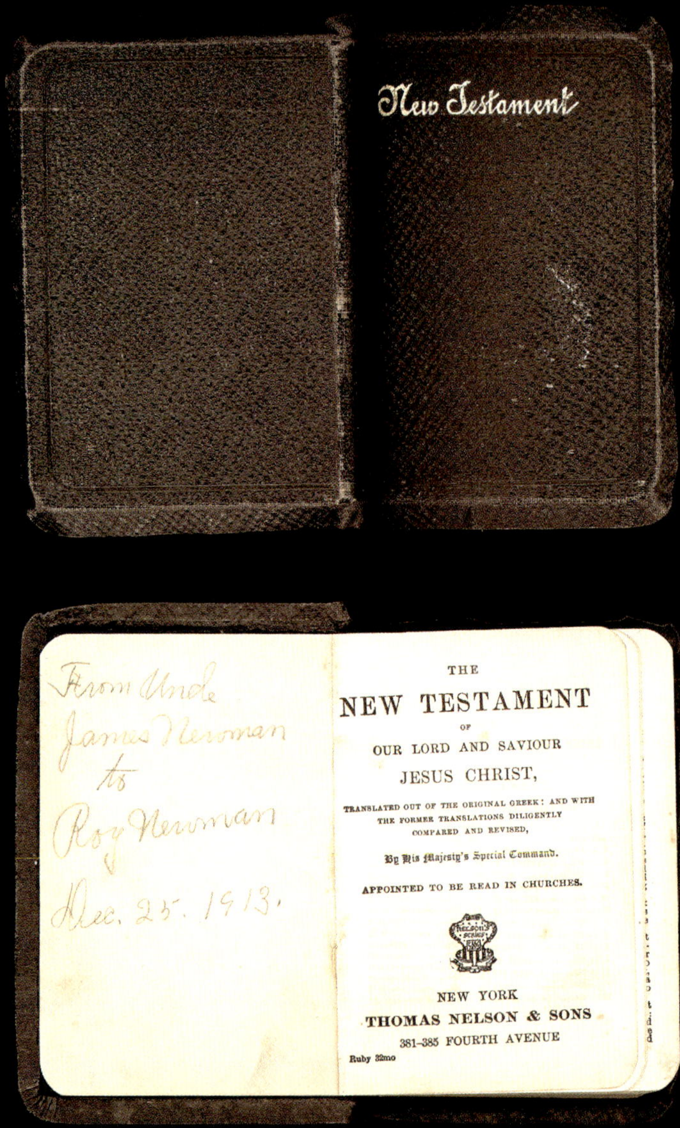

PLATE 0.19. *"From Uncle James Newman to Roy Newman Dec. 3, 1913" Bible* (Box 5).

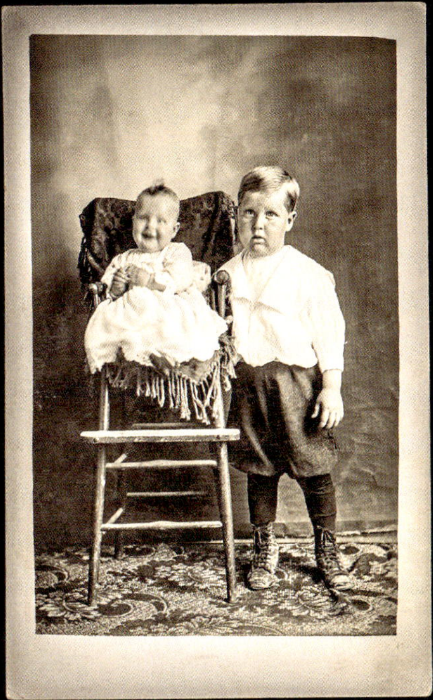

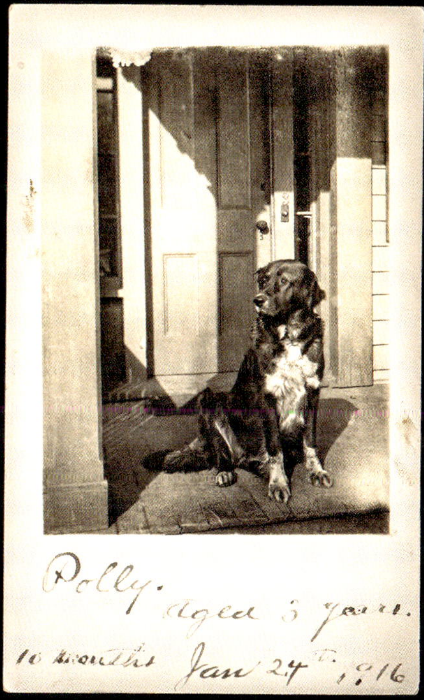
Polly.
aged 3 years.
10 months Jan 24th 1916

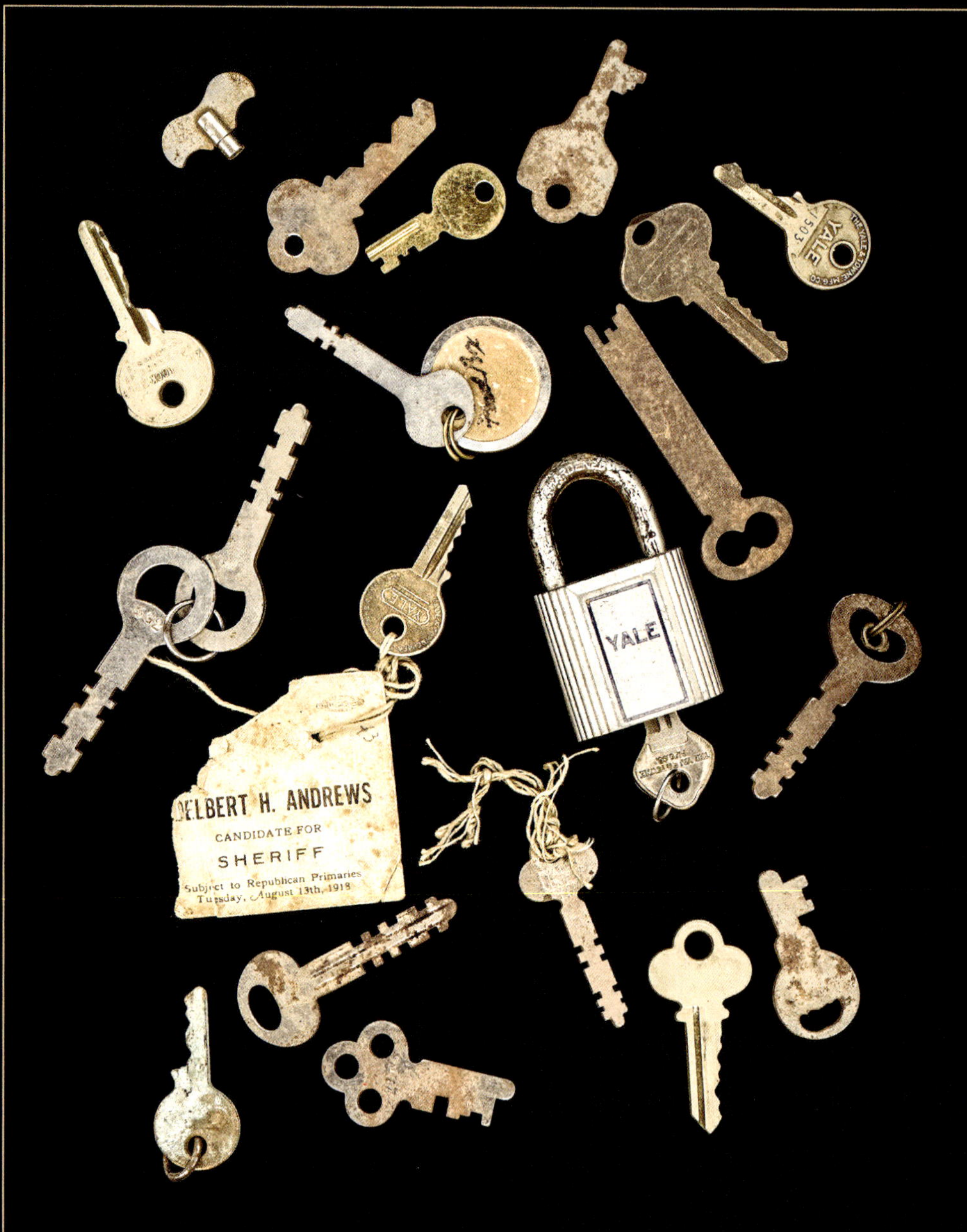

PLATE 0.21. *Assorted Keys, 1918* (Box 5).

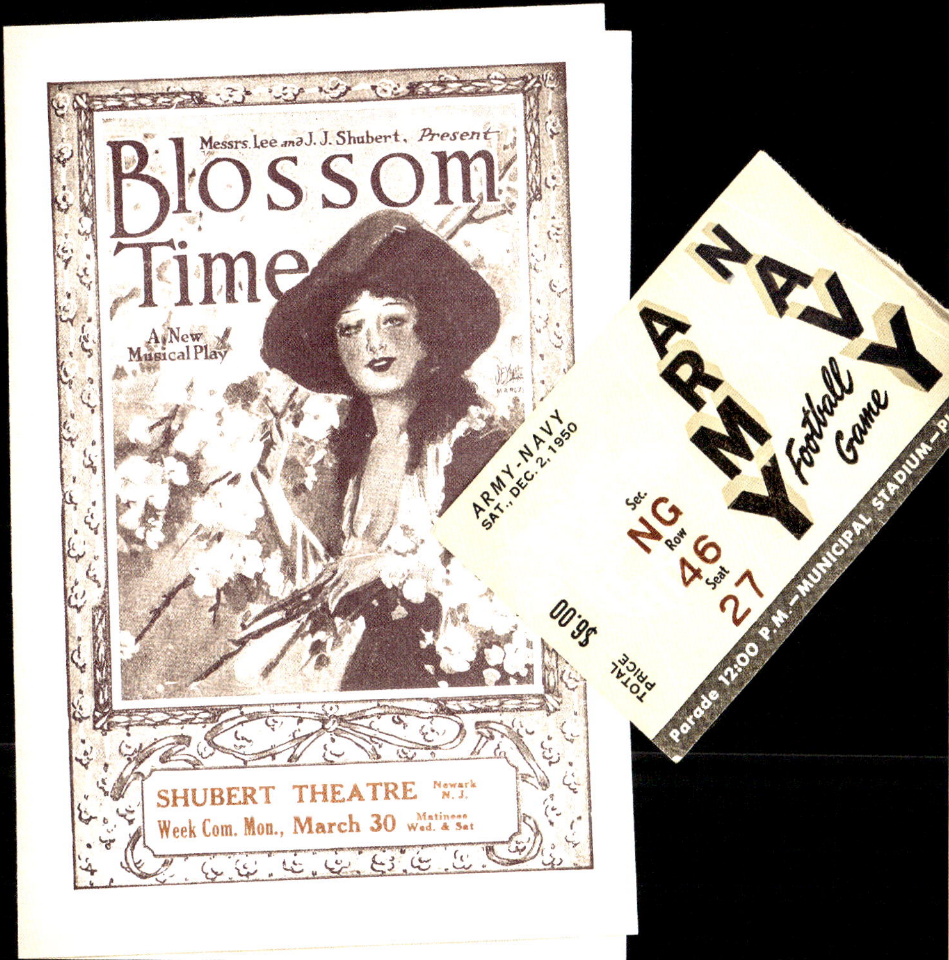

PLATE 0.22. Blossom Time *Program Shubert Theatre, 1922, and Army-Navy Game, 1950* (Box 5).

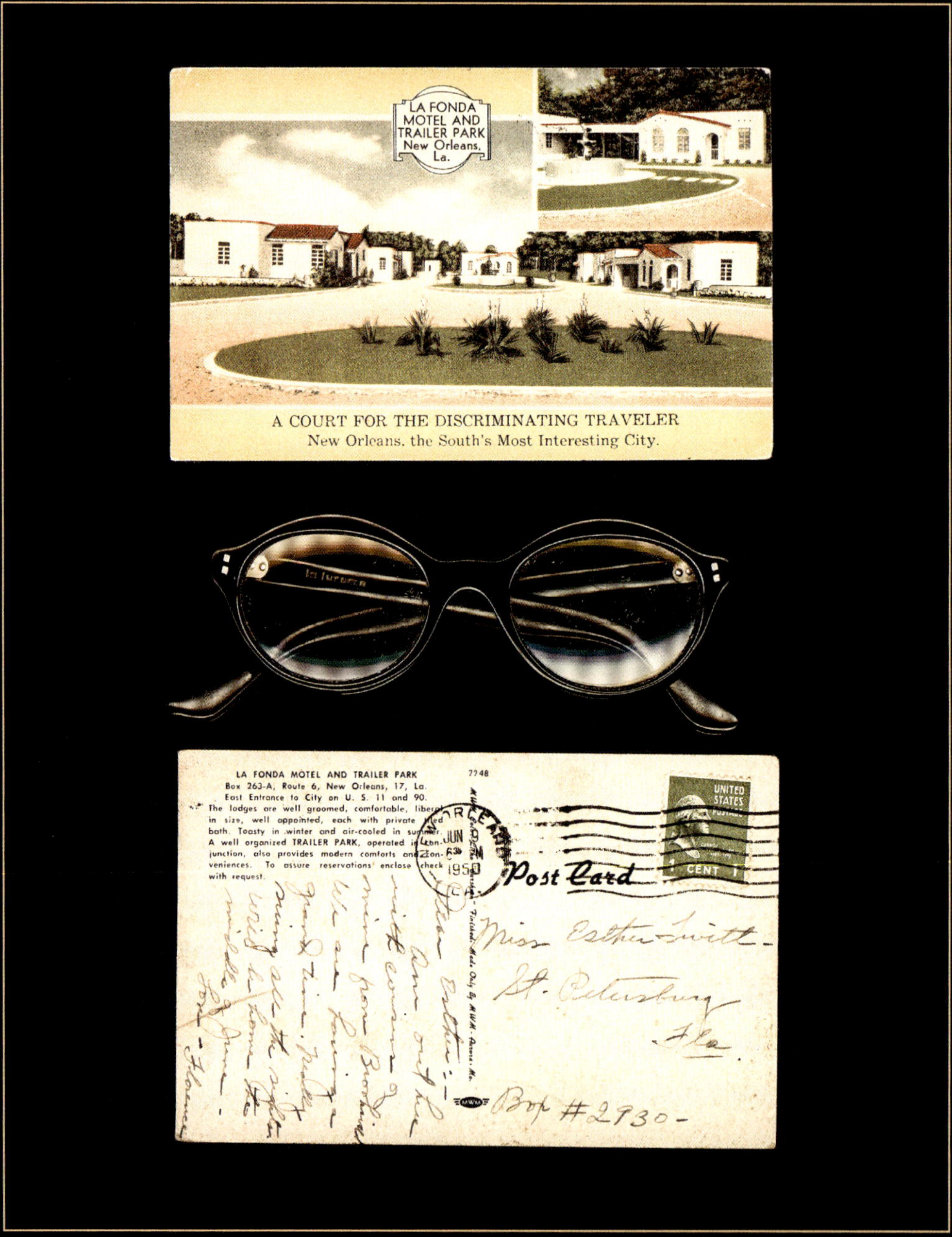

PLATE 0.23. *Postcard for La Fonda Motel, New Orleans, and Glasses* (Box 5).

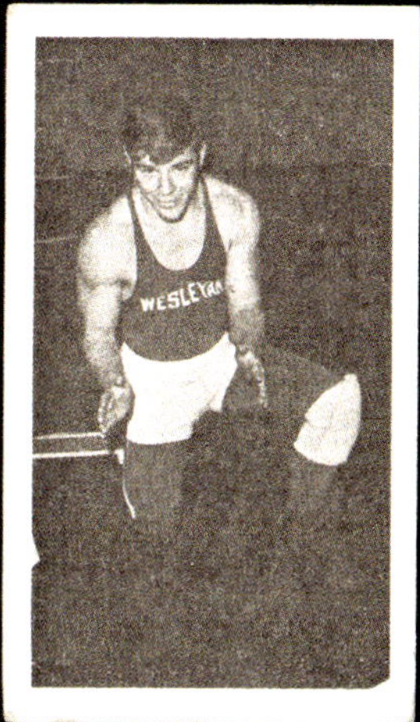

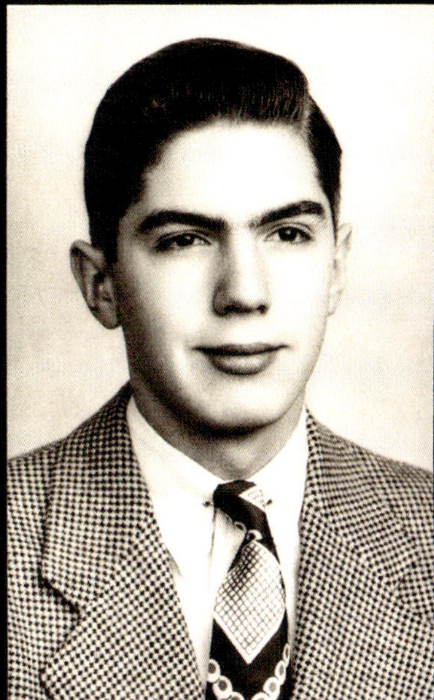

WRESTLING 1967-68

IOWA WESLEYAN COLLEGE
MOUNT PLEASANT, IOWA

Dec.	2	Wartburg Invitational	Away	9:30 A. M.
	9	Dubuque	Away	1:30 P. M.
	12	Kirksville	Away	7:30 P. M.
	15	Loras	Home	7:00 P. M.
Jan.	13	Southeast Missouri	Home	2:00 P. M.
	18	Simpson	Home	7:00 P. M.
	20	Knox - Double Dual	Away	1:00 P. M.
Feb.	10	Wartburg - Triple Dual	Away	1:00 P. M.
	14	Parsons	Away	7:30 P. M.
	17	Simpson	Away	1:00 P. M.
	21	Coe	Away	7:00 P. M.
	24	Missouri Valley	Home	1:00 P. M.
	28	Muscatine Jr. College	Away	7:00 P. M.

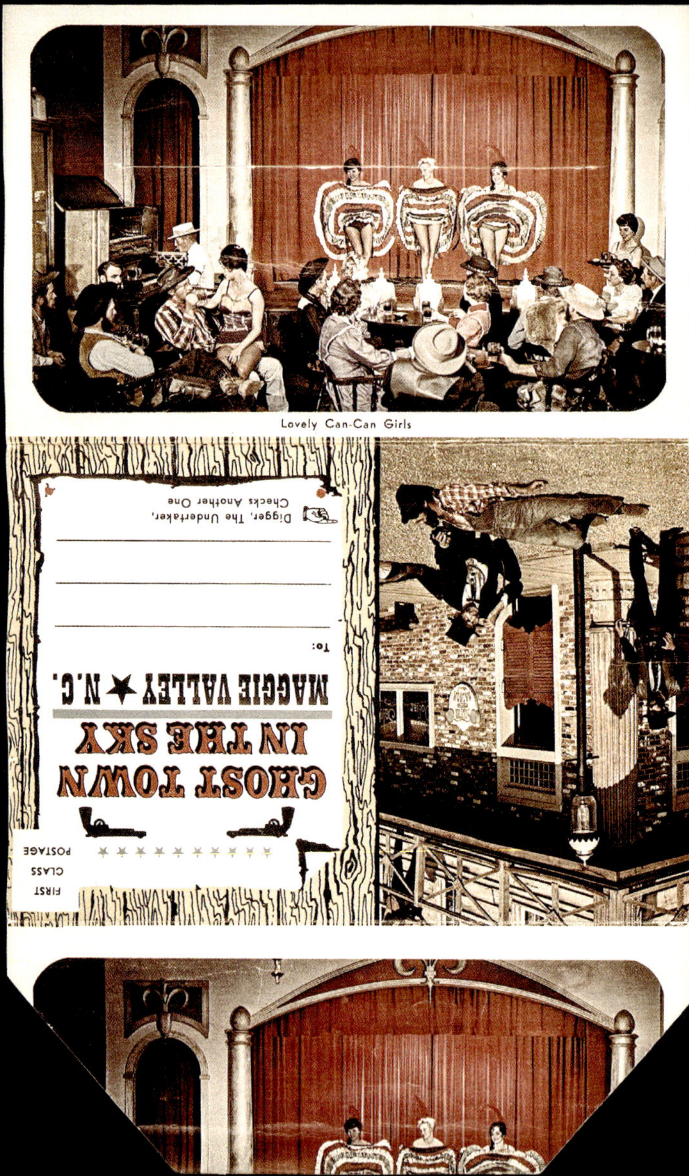

PLATE 0.25. *Ghost Town, N.C., Postcards 1961–2002* (Box 5).

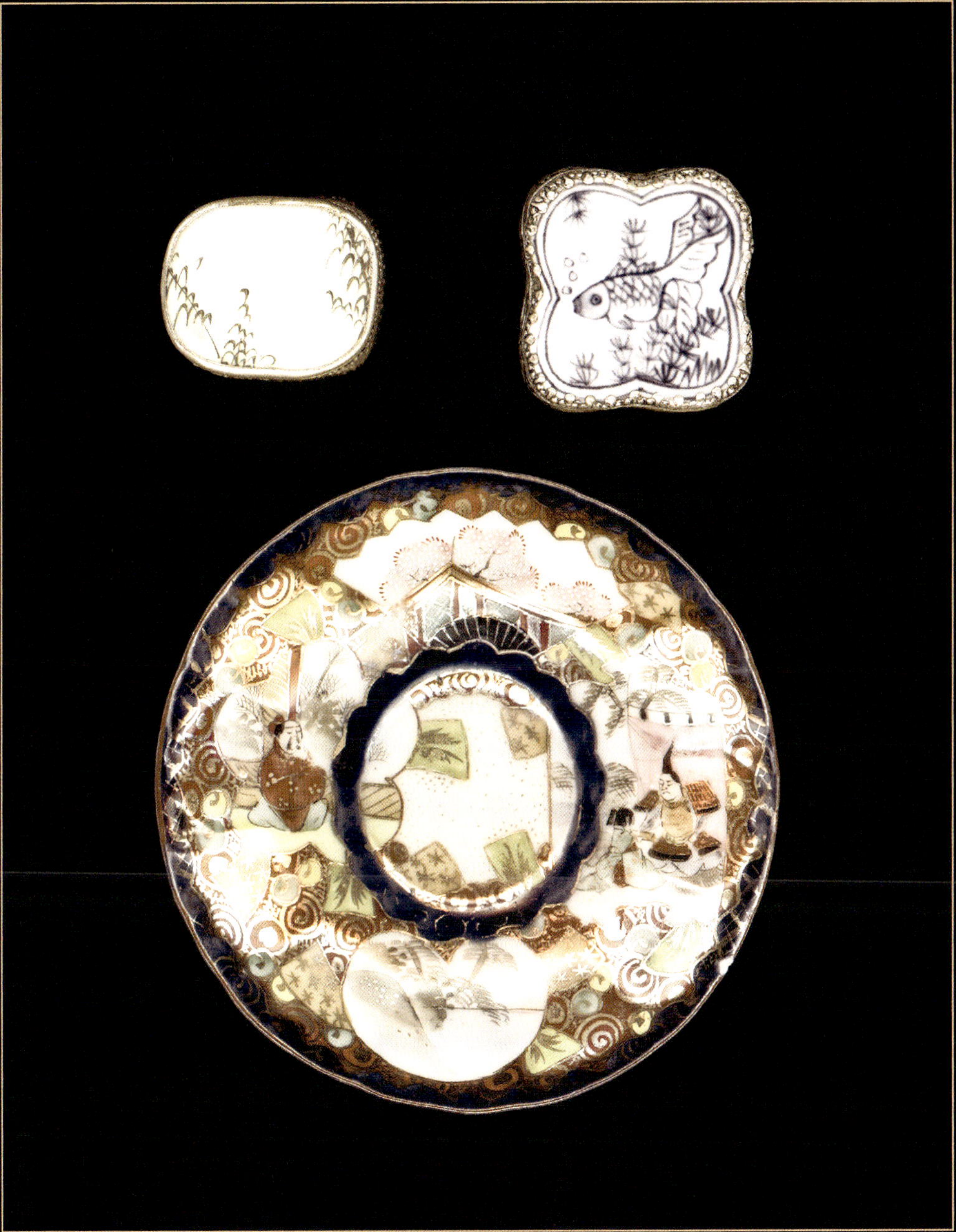

PLATE 0.26. *Asian-Themed Ceramic Ware* (Box 5).

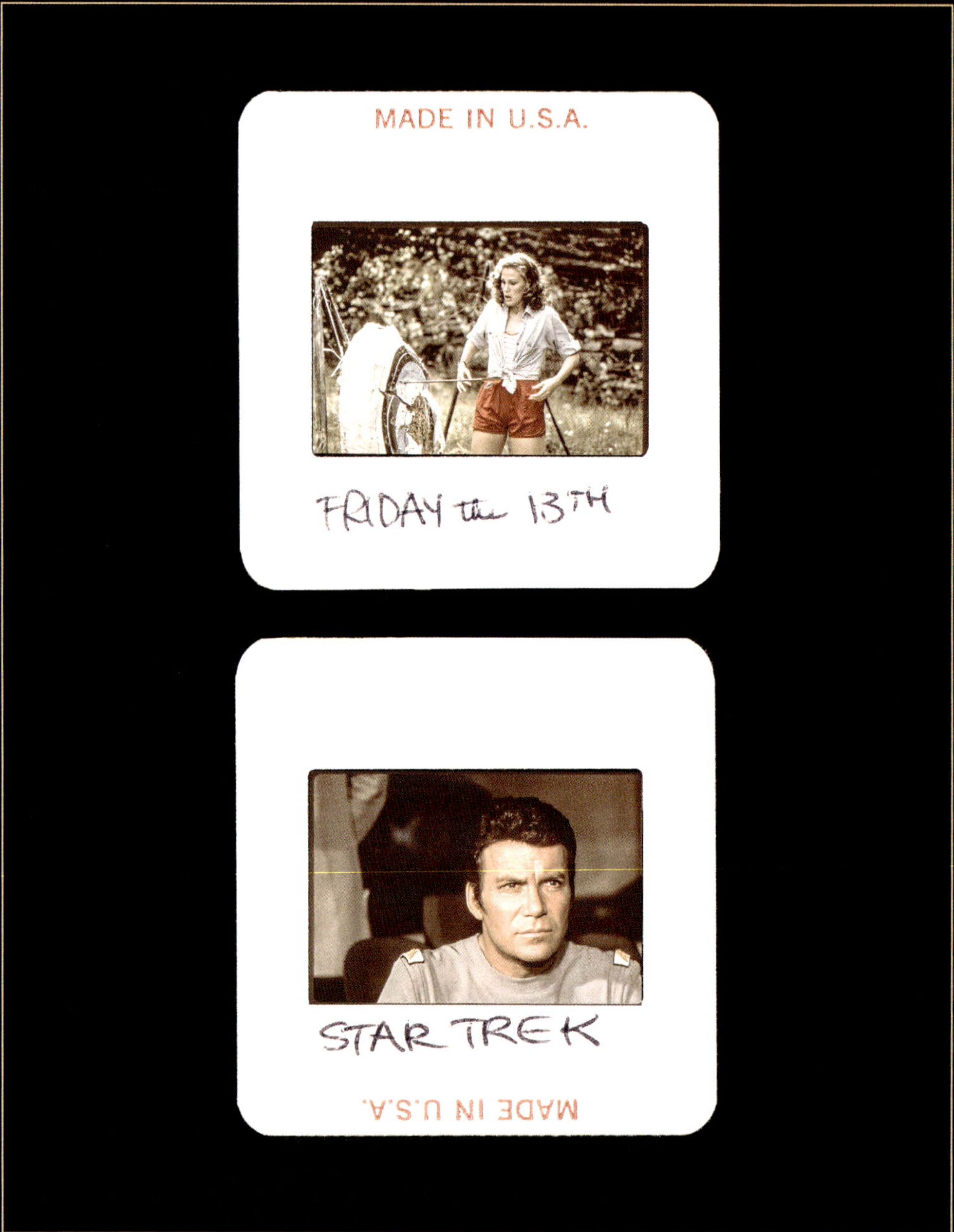

PLATE 0.27. *Slides of* Friday the 13th *(1980) and* Star Trek *(1979)* (Box 5).

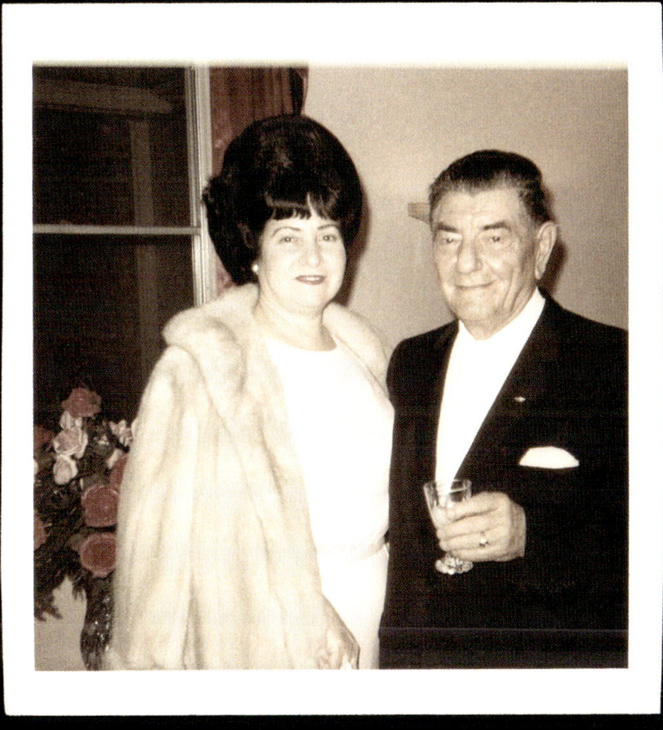

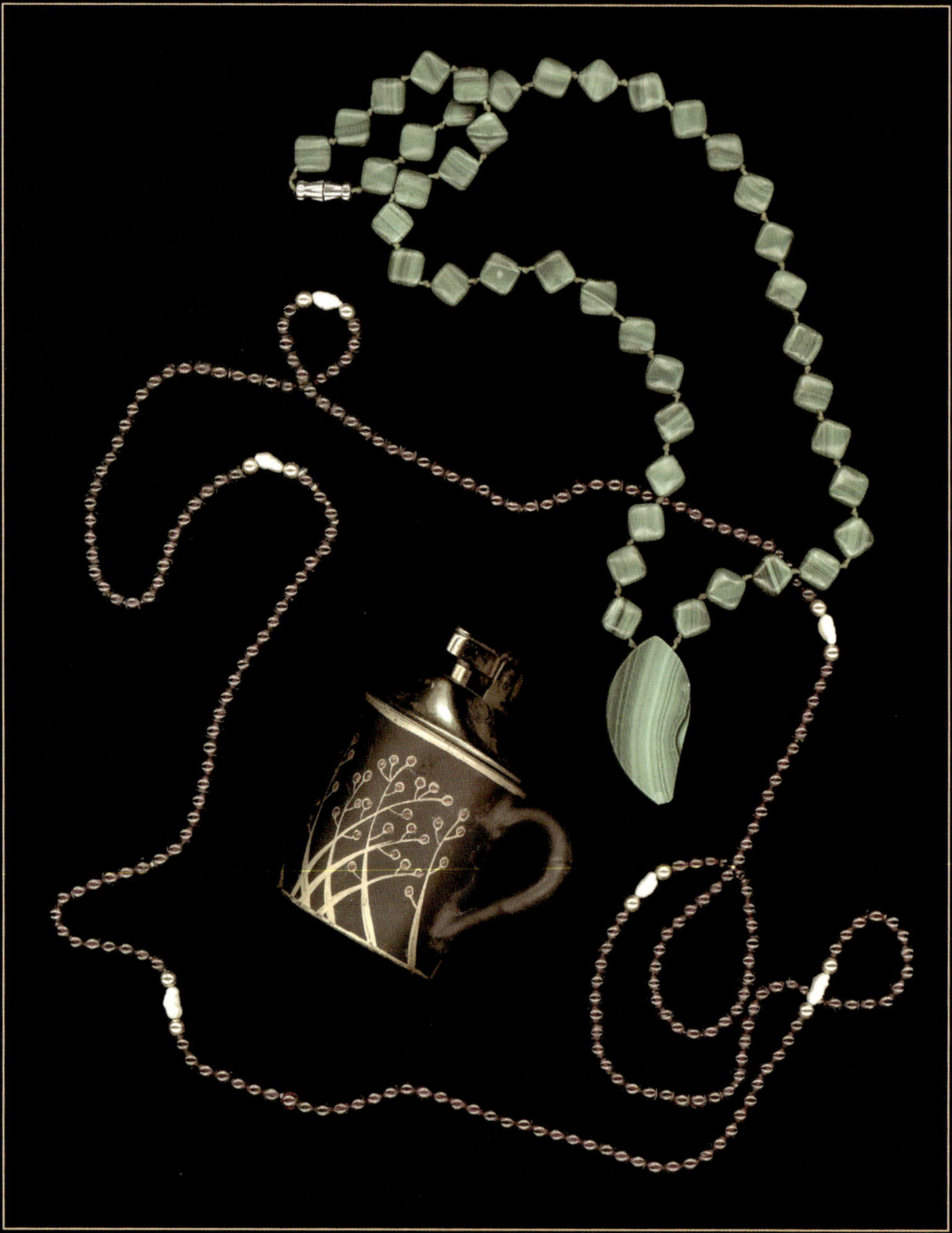

PLATE 0.29. *Green Necklace, Chain, and Cigarette Lighter* (Box 6).

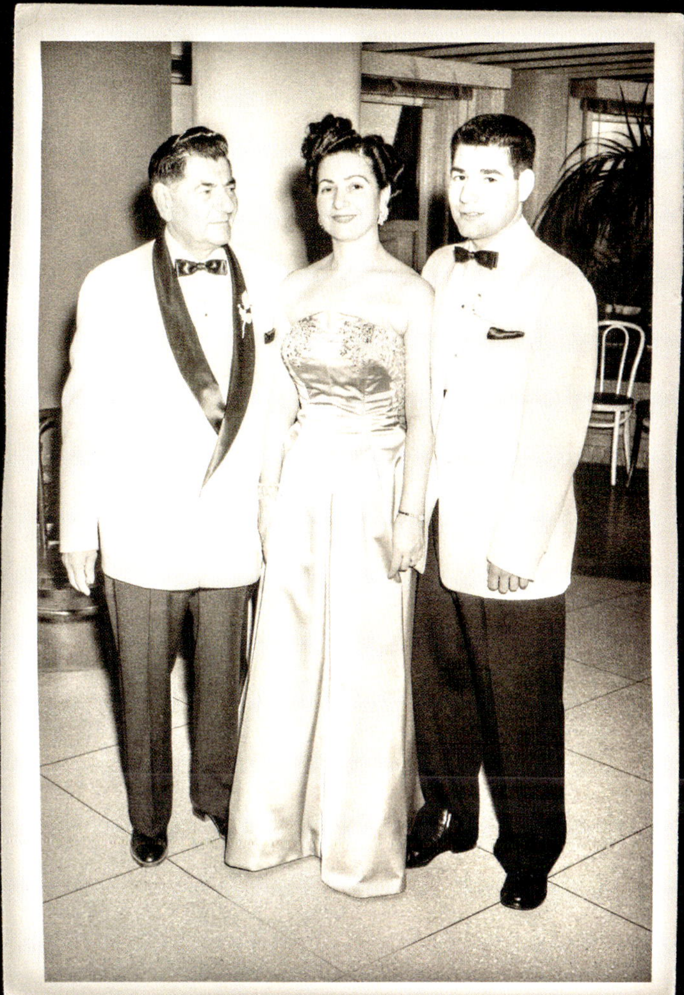

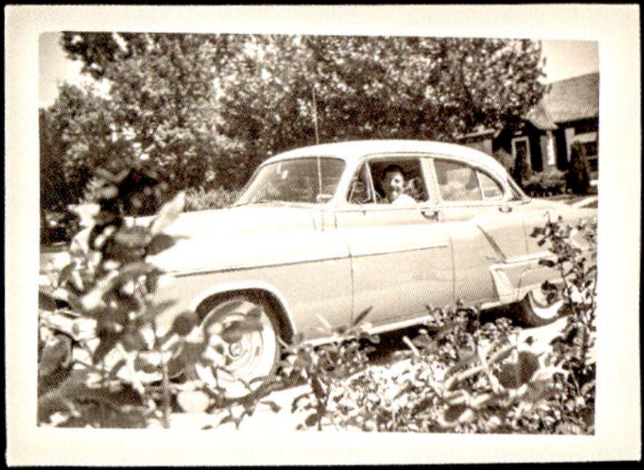

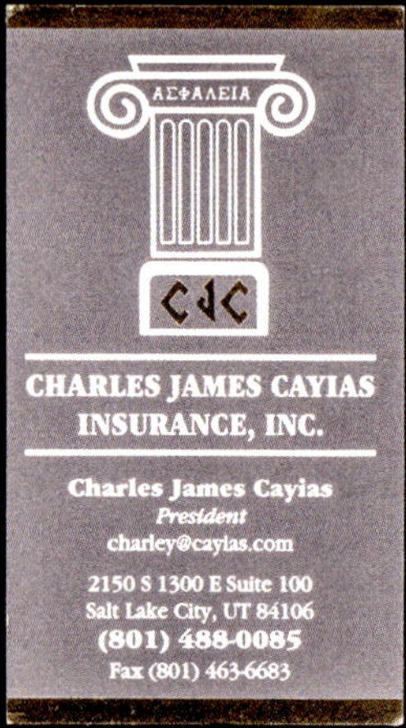

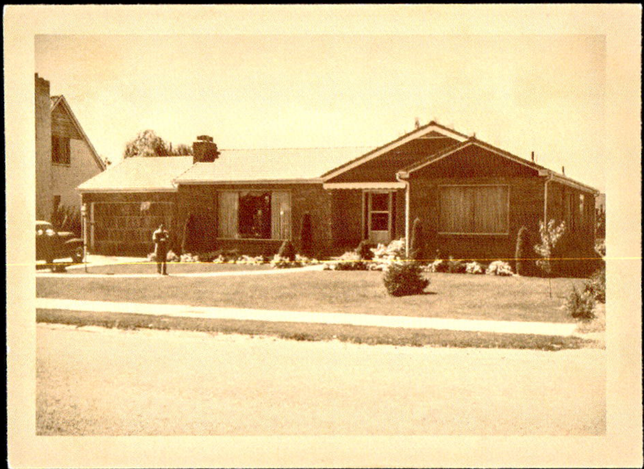

PLATE 0.31. *Photos of Car and House Plus Insurance Business Card* (Box 6).

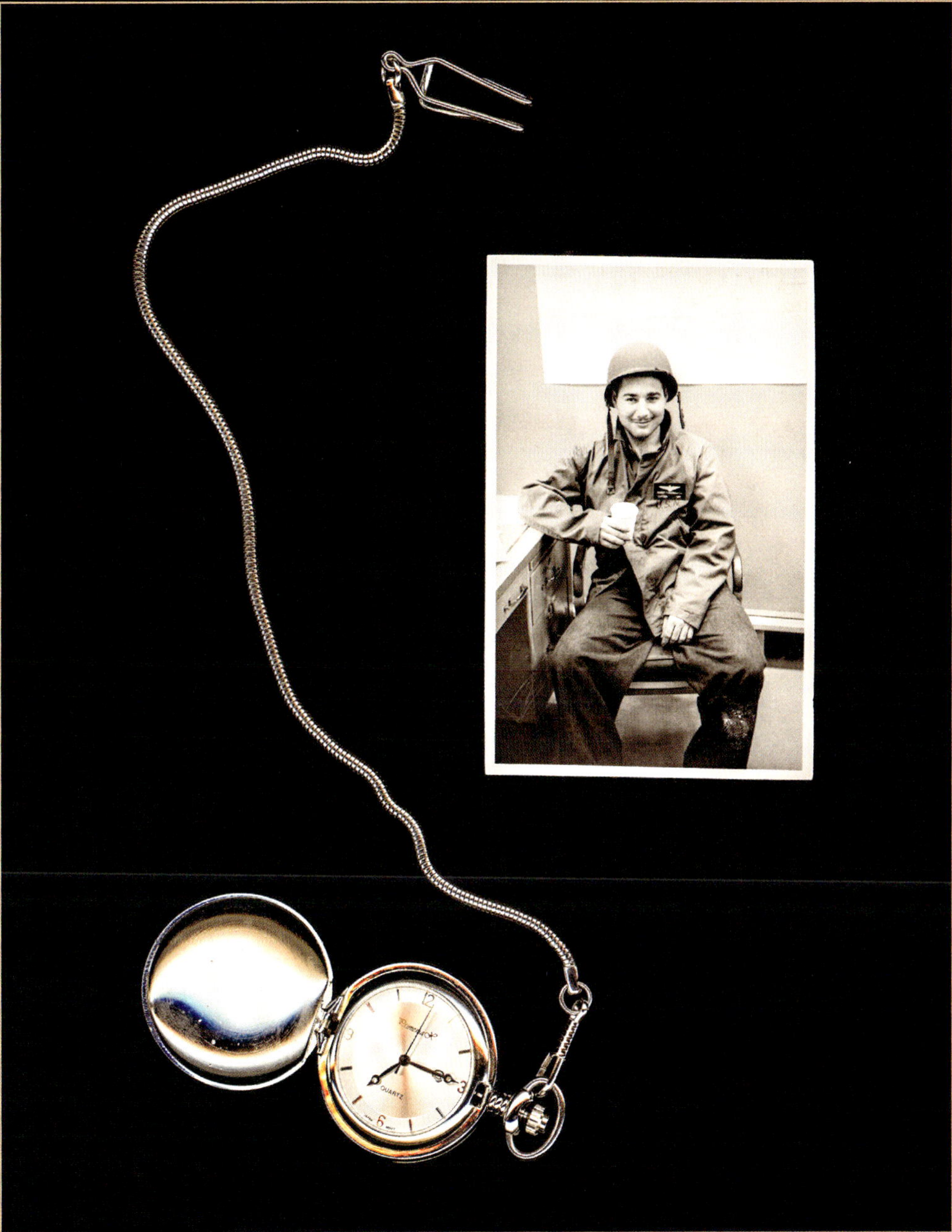

PLATE 0.32. *Photo of Soldier and Pocket Watch* (Box 6).

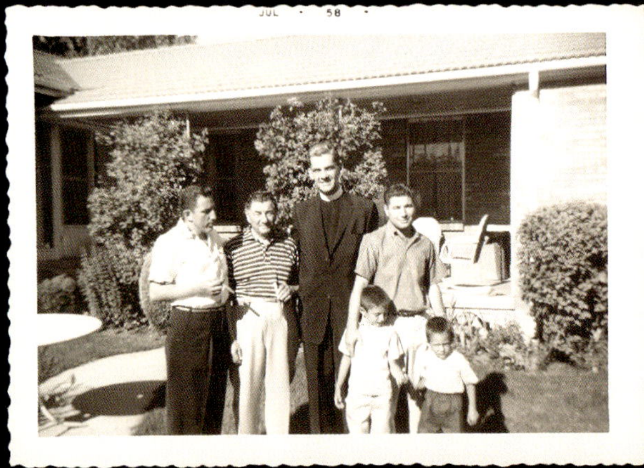

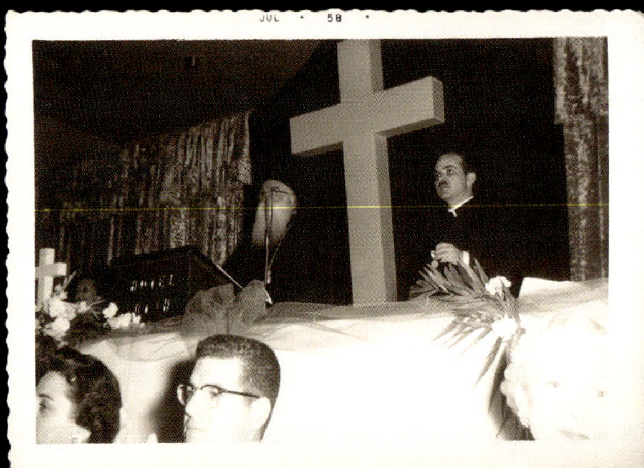

PLATE 0.33. *Photos of Family and Priest, 1958* (Box 6).

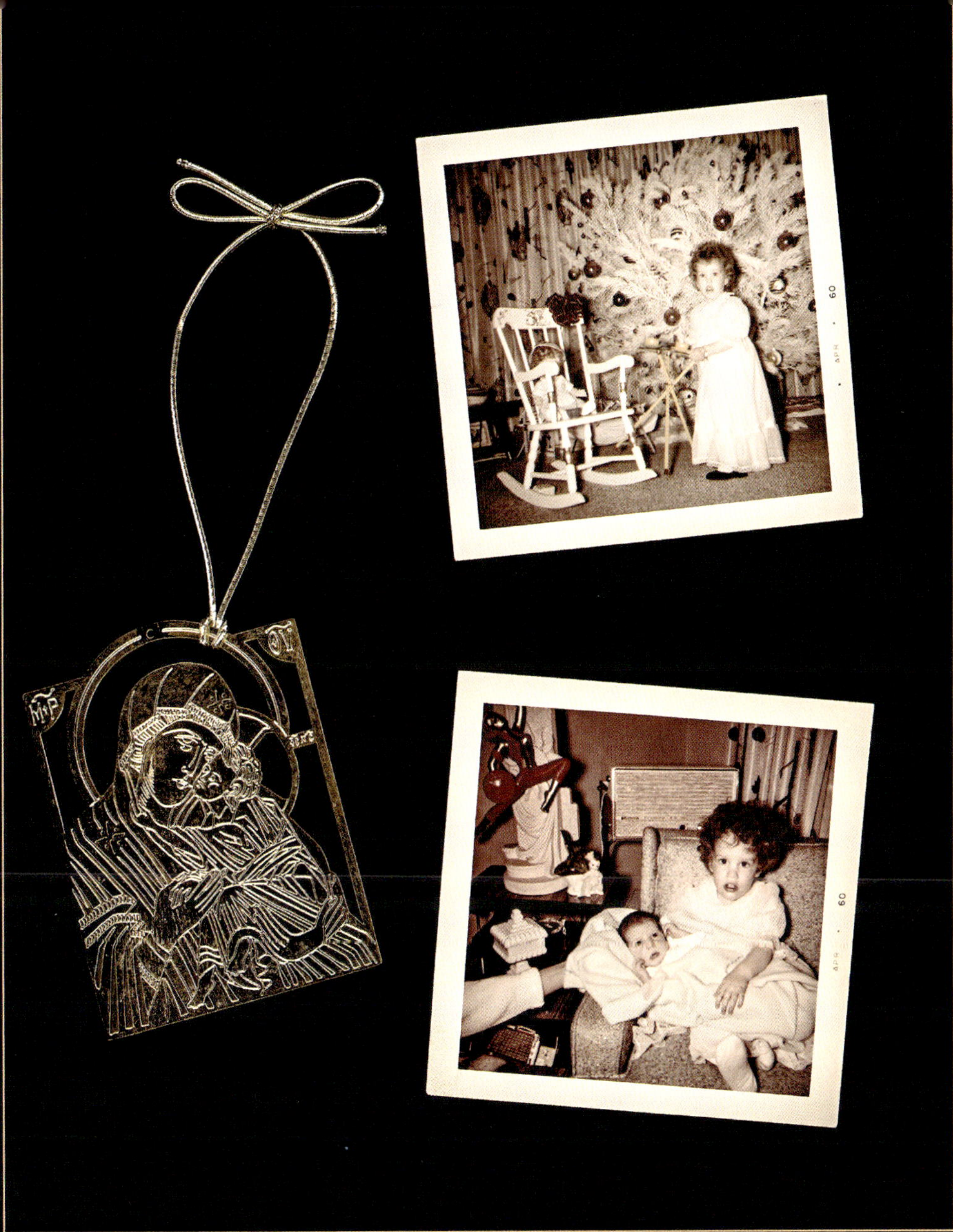

PLATE 0.34. *Two Small Snapshots of Children, 1960, and Religious Ornament* (Box 6).

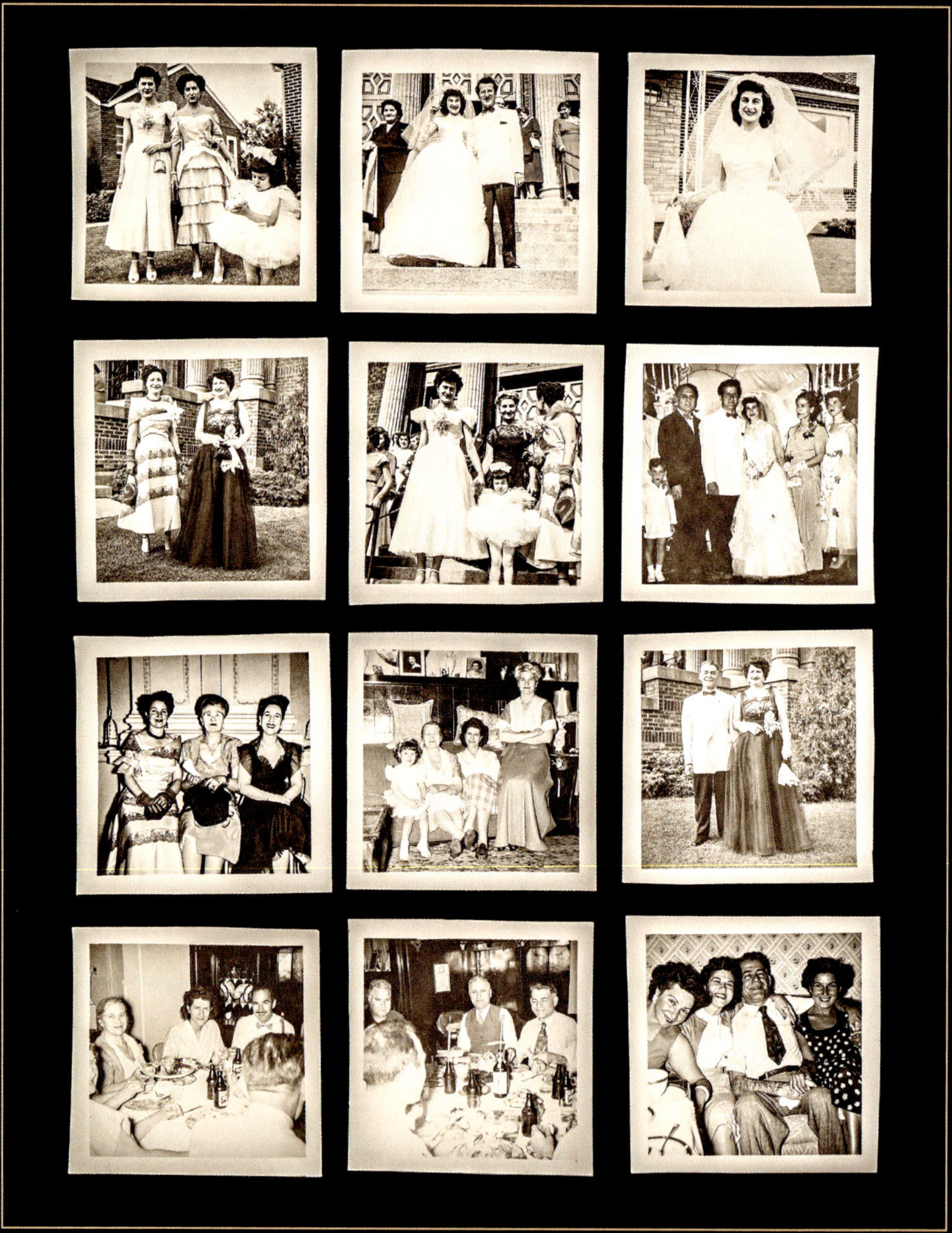

PLATE 0.35. *Twelve Small Wedding Photos* (Box 6).

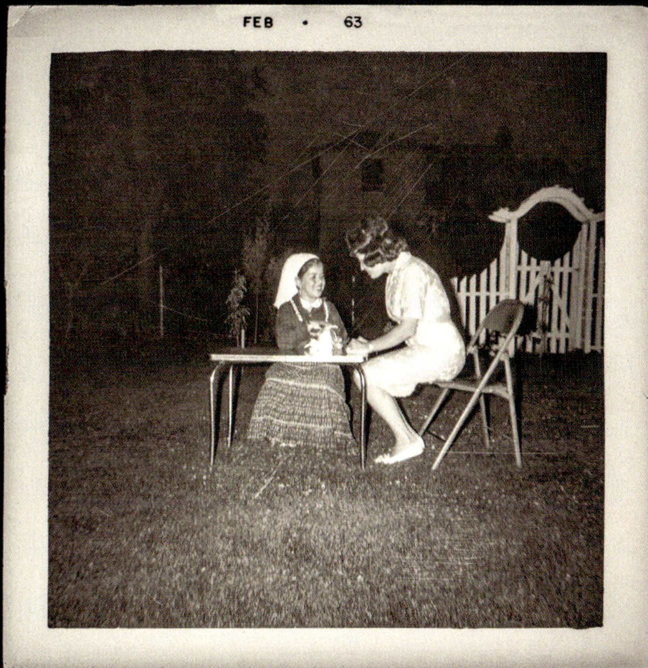
FEB • 63

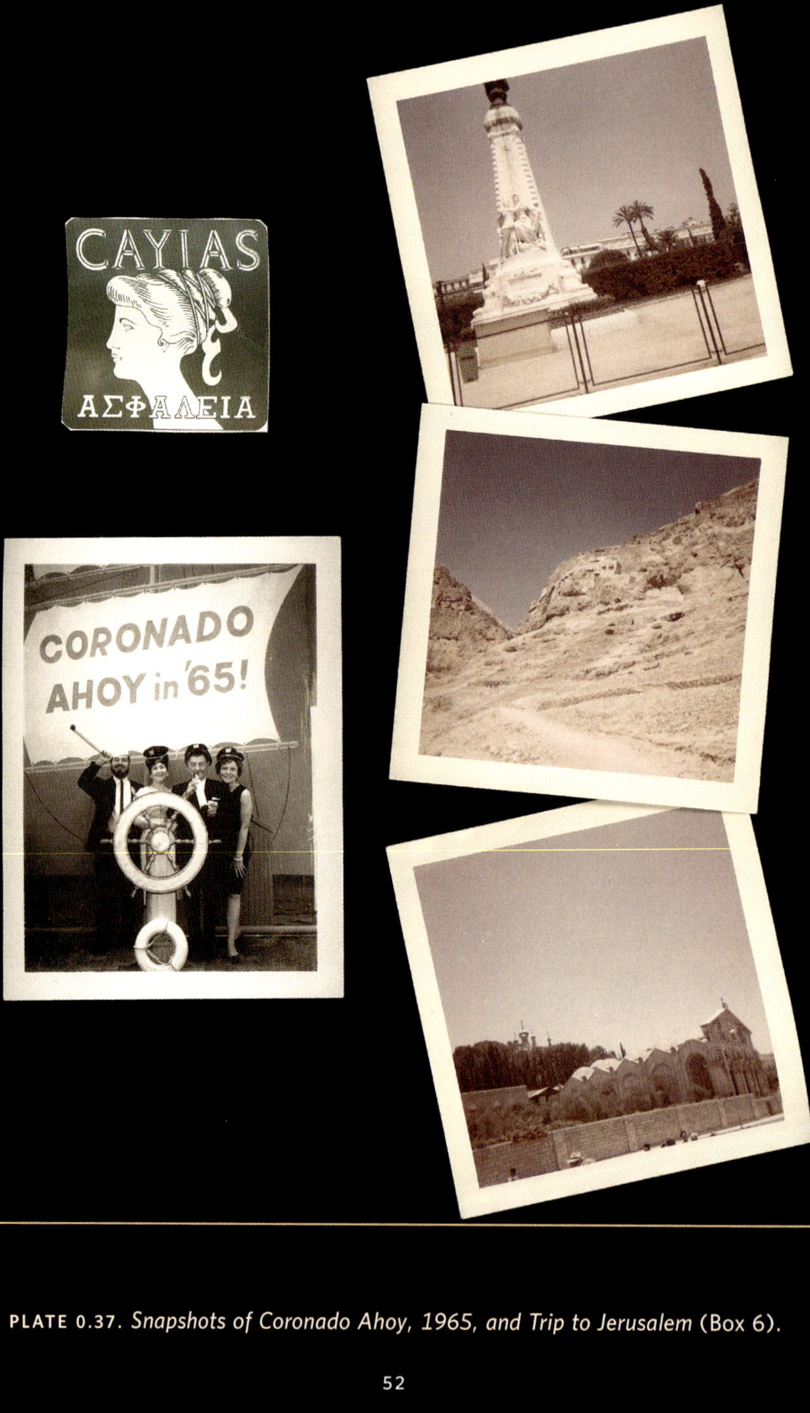

PLATE 0.37. *Snapshots of Coronado Ahoy, 1965, and Trip to Jerusalem* (Box 6).

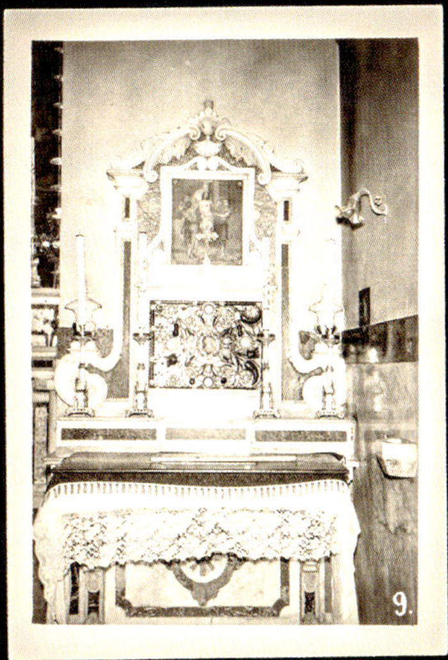

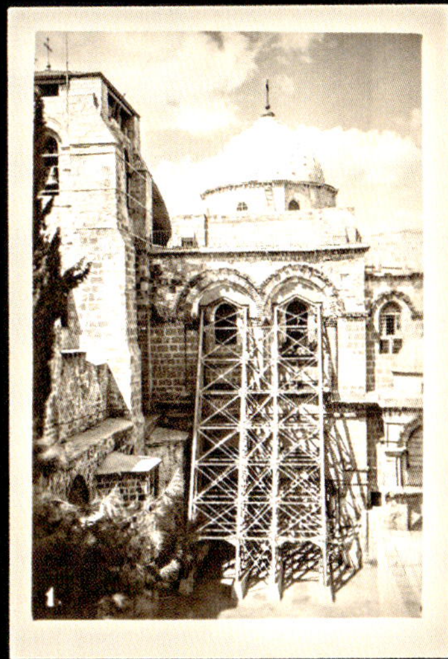

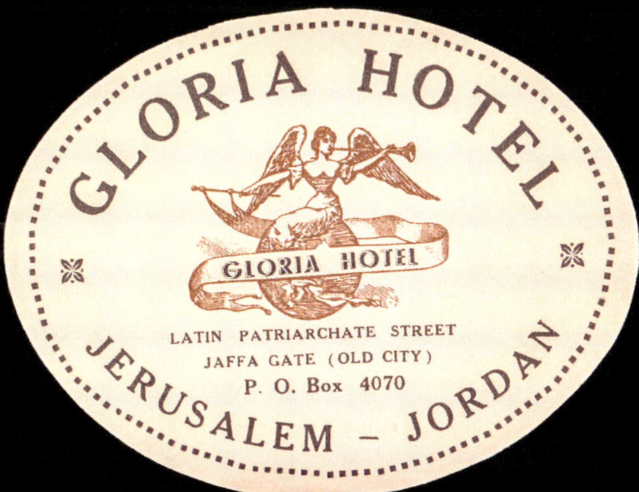

PLATE 0.38. *Gloria Hotel Address and Two Church Snapshots* (Box 6).

Gloria Hotel

Jaffa Gate (Old City)
P. O. Box 4070
JERUSALEM – JORDAN

Virgin Mary – lifted to heavens – didn't find her – disciples – sent belt down
Visited place of Ascension into Heaven after 40 days
St Helen built 327 – years beautiful church destroyed by Persians.
Saw Christ right foot print in Church of Ascension where Lord ascended into heaven

St Helen built church 327 – 333
Cause Jews bring new born up to 2 yrs be killed Christ taken to Egypt
Saw Father Artemios pent he built
Greeks pray by star only – right to hold service Greek Liturgy (Basilica main body of Church – represents cross) ✝
Monastery of Prophet Elias
Christ came & saw man planting rocks – dug up & found garbanzos.
Gethsemane lies between 2 hills
Moriah & Kidron Josaphat lies between
Gethsemane loved this spot to pray last time with scholars & the place Judas

took him to Caiphas –
~~horsed pass by~~
betrayed by Judas
Lord came with disciples
saw spot where betrayal took place
Judah came & kissed Lord & took him in
(Church where tomb of Virgin Mary
it has style of its own. Water running from each side buried by loose ground
from running water
Church built St Helen!

Christ realized – felt real bad & asked Lord not to drink glass of poison
Place where he prays
Judas came & got him
Garden of Gethsemane
Big rock Lord prayed last moments & sensed regretted crucifixation – prayed to father to avoid trouble punishment – then strength came & said follow as you wish.
Olive tree 2000 yrs old
Saw stone where he prayed
Convent of nuns – orthodox
Czar of Russia built)
Road of Mount Olives)
old road – Christ passed on donkey
Palm Sunday

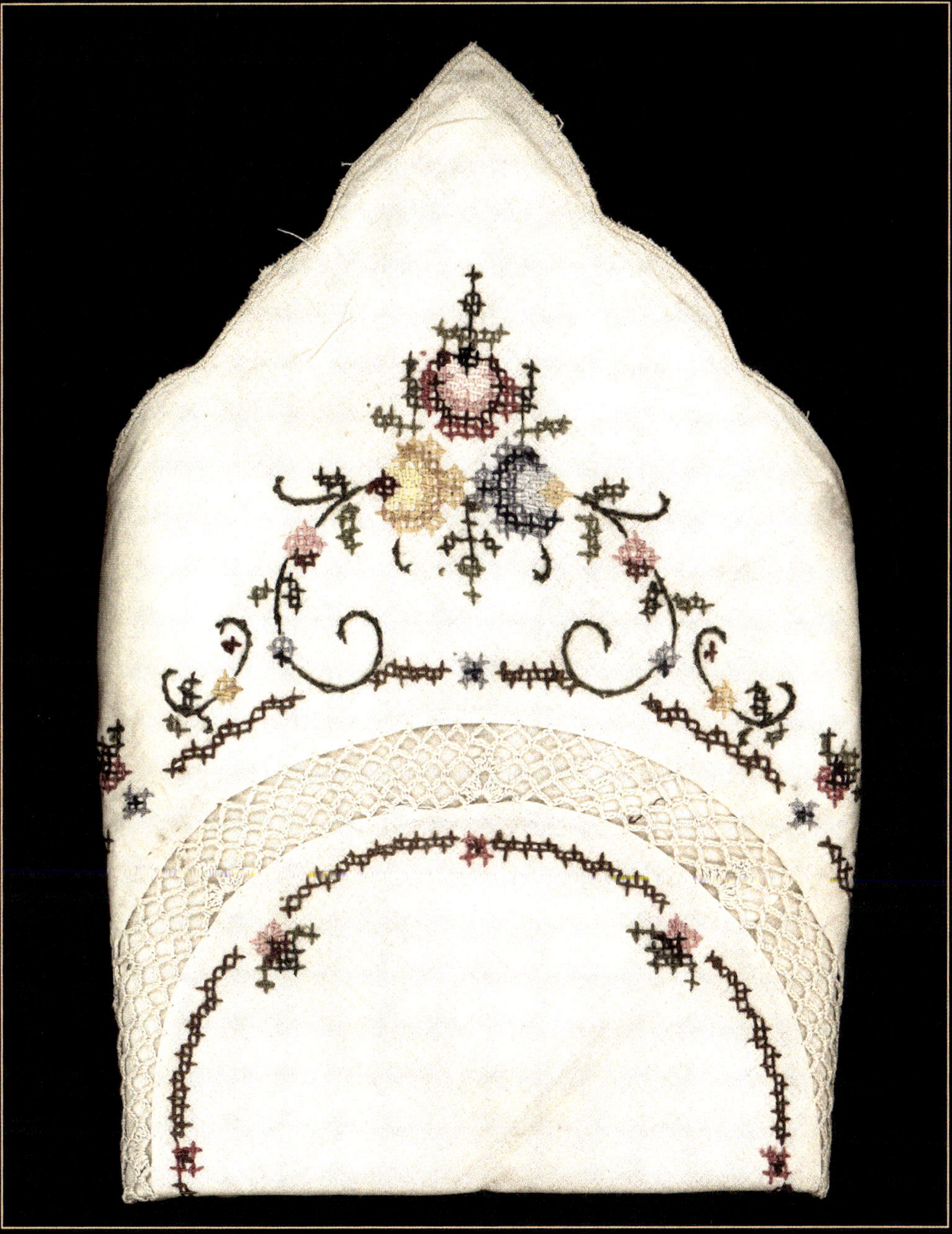

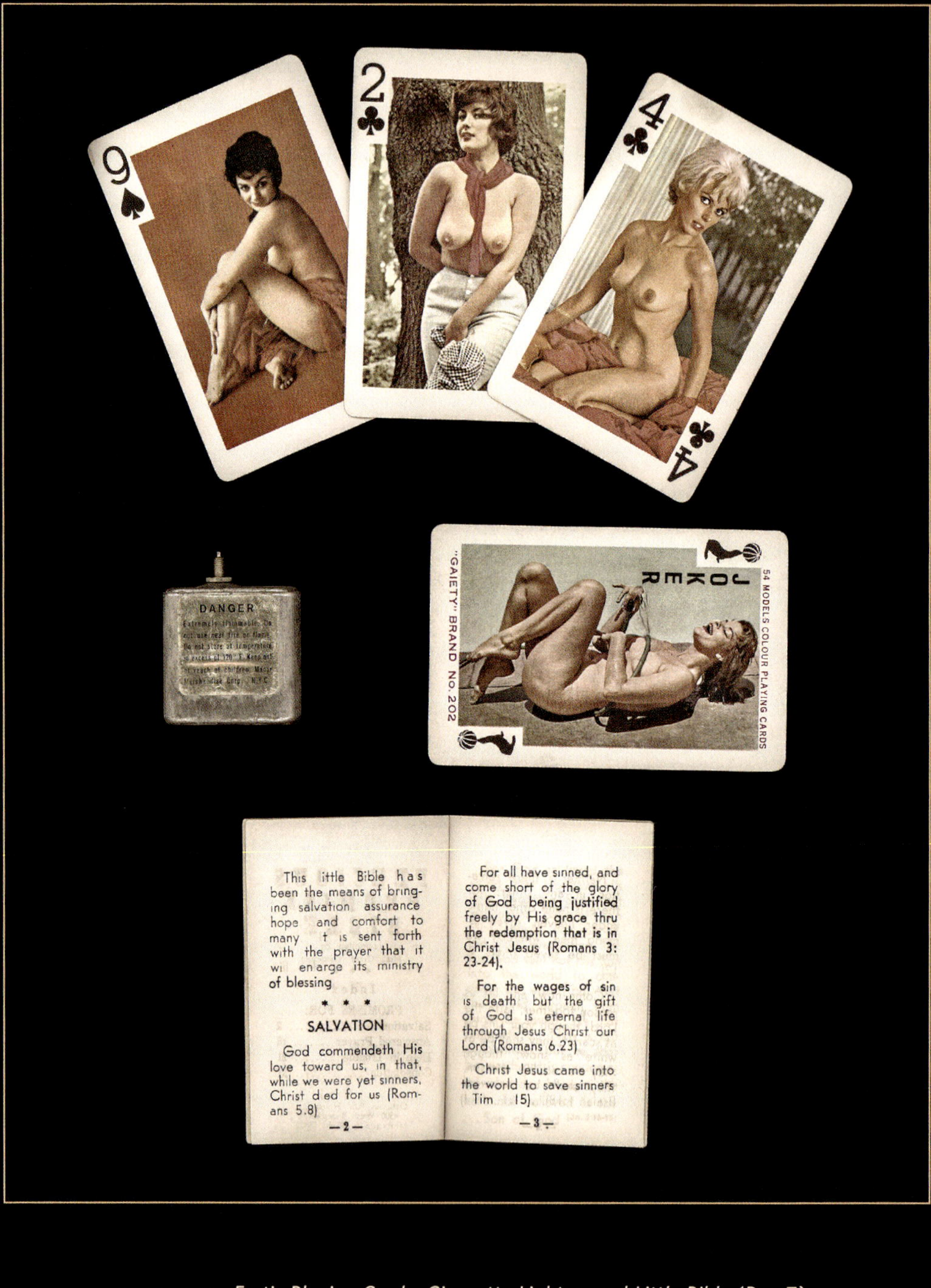

PLATE 0.41. *Erotic Playing Cards, Cigarette Lighter, and Little Bible* (Box 7).

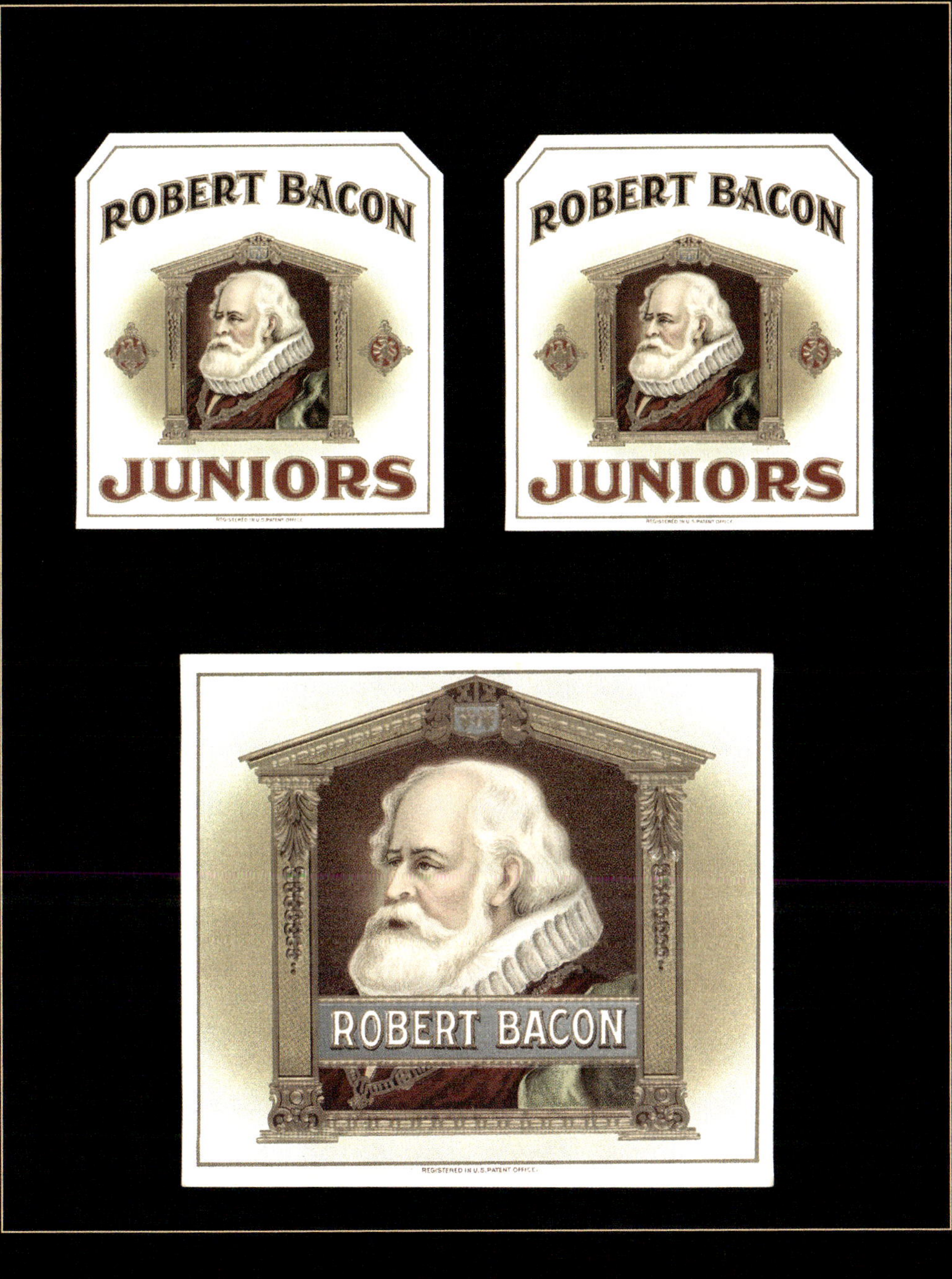

PLATE 0.42. *Vintage Robert Bacon Cigar Box Labels* (Box 7).

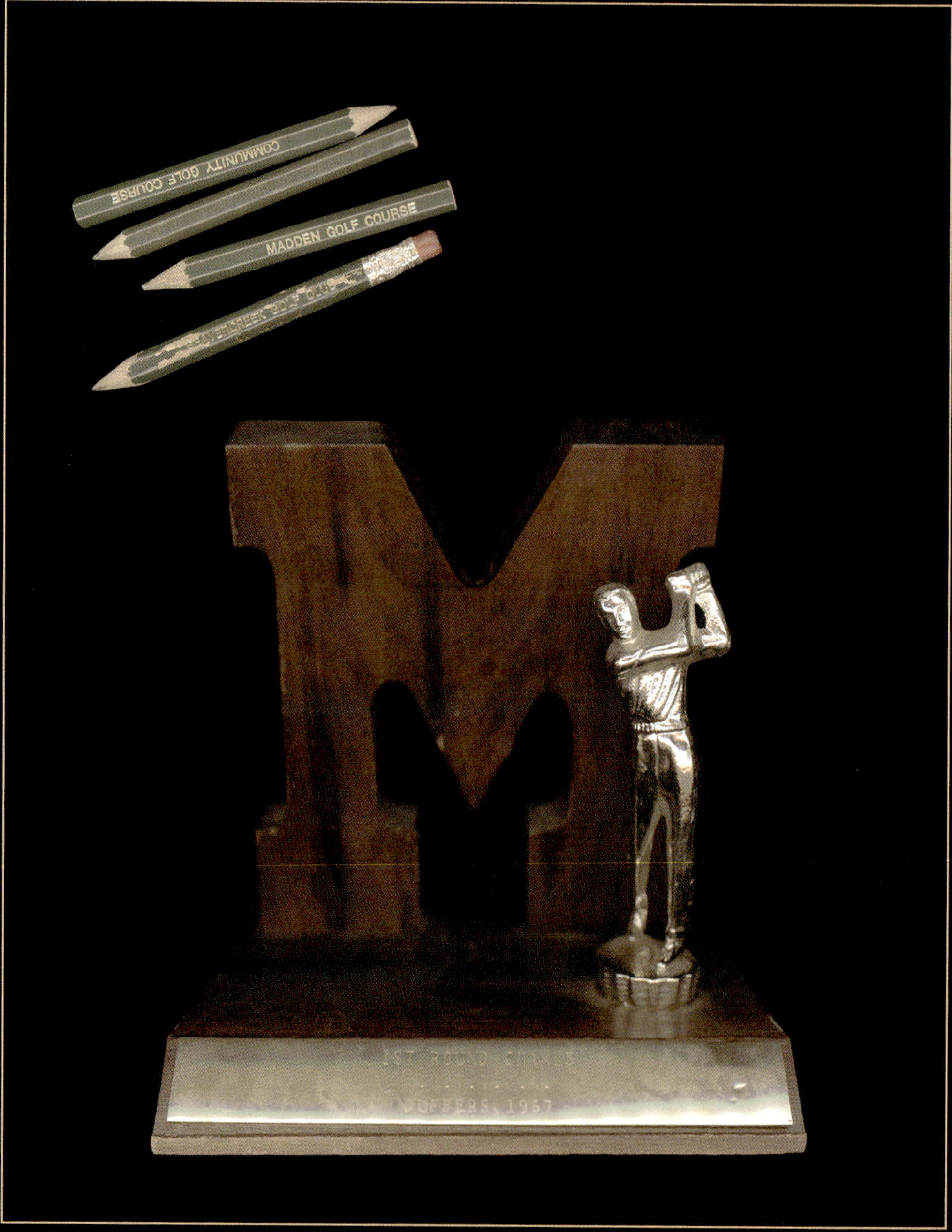

PLATE 0.43. *Golf Trophy and Pencils* (Box 7).

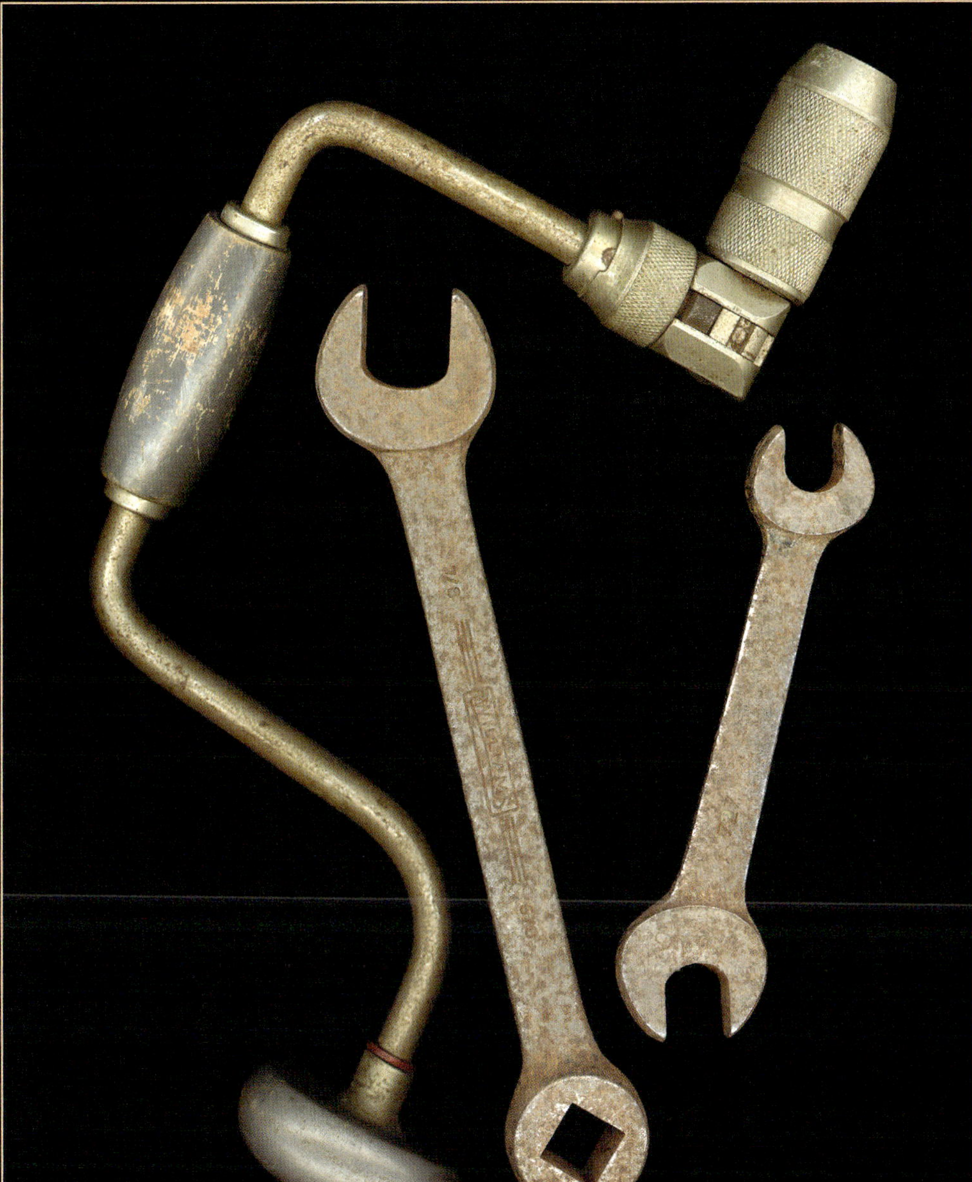

PLATE 0.44. *Drill and Two Wrenches* (Box 7).

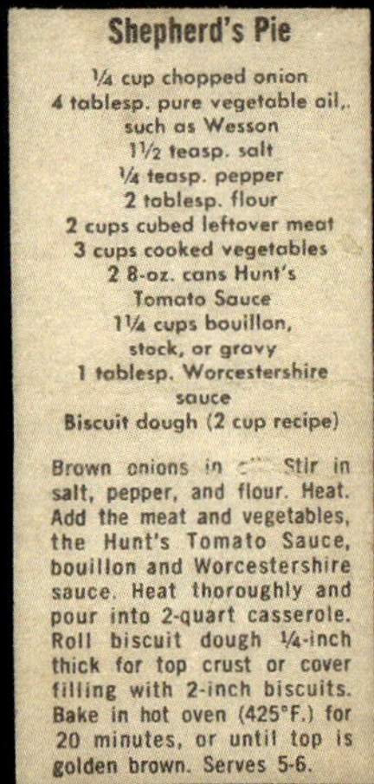

Shepherd's Pie

¼ cup chopped onion
4 tablesp. pure vegetable oil, such as Wesson
1½ teasp. salt
¼ teasp. pepper
2 tablesp. flour
2 cups cubed leftover meat
3 cups cooked vegetables
2 8-oz. cans Hunt's Tomato Sauce
1¼ cups bouillon, stock, or gravy
1 tablesp. Worcestershire sauce
Biscuit dough (2 cup recipe)

Brown onions in [illegible] Stir in salt, pepper, and flour. Heat. Add the meat and vegetables, the Hunt's Tomato Sauce, bouillon and Worcestershire sauce. Heat thoroughly and pour into 2-quart casserole. Roll biscuit dough ¼-inch thick for top crust or cover filling with 2-inch biscuits. Bake in hot oven (425°F.) for 20 minutes, or until top is golden brown. Serves 5-6.

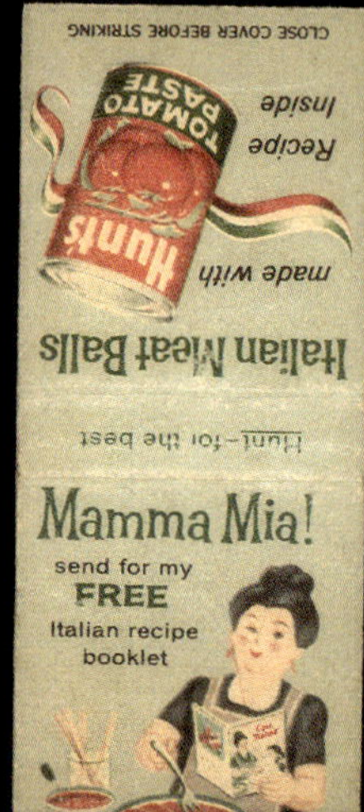

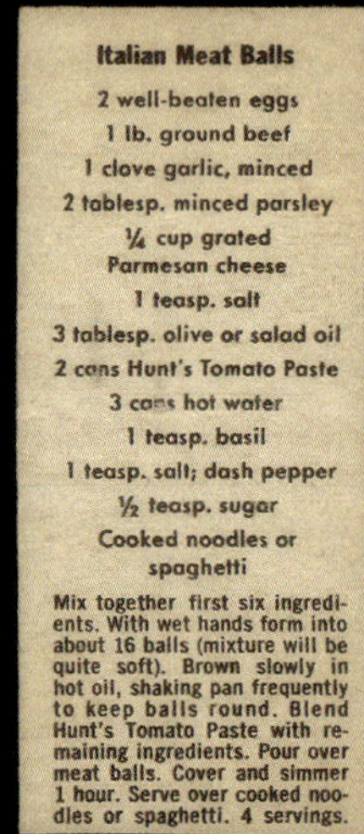

Italian Meat Balls

2 well-beaten eggs
1 lb. ground beef
1 clove garlic, minced
2 tablesp. minced parsley
¼ cup grated Parmesan cheese
1 teasp. salt
3 tablesp. olive or salad oil
2 cans Hunt's Tomato Paste
3 cans hot water
1 teasp. basil
1 teasp. salt; dash pepper
½ teasp. sugar
Cooked noodles or spaghetti

Mix together first six ingredients. With wet hands form into about 16 balls (mixture will be quite soft). Brown slowly in hot oil, shaking pan frequently to keep balls round. Blend Hunt's Tomato Paste with remaining ingredients. Pour over meat balls. Cover and simmer 1 hour. Serve over cooked noodles or spaghetti. 4 servings.

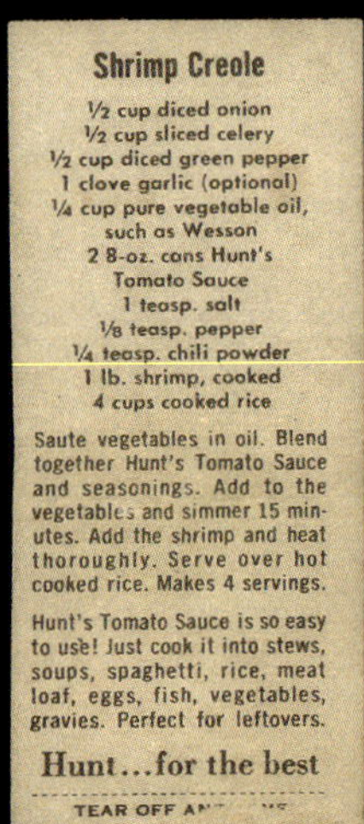

Shrimp Creole

½ cup diced onion
½ cup sliced celery
½ cup diced green pepper
1 clove garlic (optional)
¼ cup pure vegetable oil, such as Wesson
2 8-oz. cans Hunt's Tomato Sauce
1 teasp. salt
⅛ teasp. pepper
¼ teasp. chili powder
1 lb. shrimp, cooked
4 cups cooked rice

Saute vegetables in oil. Blend together Hunt's Tomato Sauce and seasonings. Add to the vegetables and simmer 15 minutes. Add the shrimp and heat thoroughly. Serve over hot cooked rice. Makes 4 servings.

Hunt's Tomato Sauce is so easy to use! Just cook it into stews, soups, spaghetti, rice, meat loaf, eggs, fish, vegetables, gravies. Perfect for leftovers.

Hunt...for the best

TEAR OFF AN[illegible]

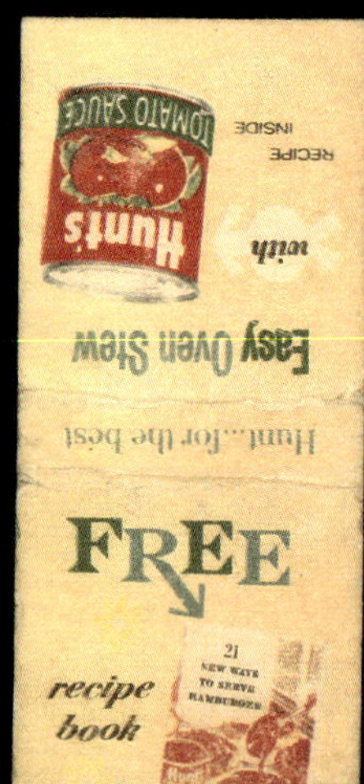

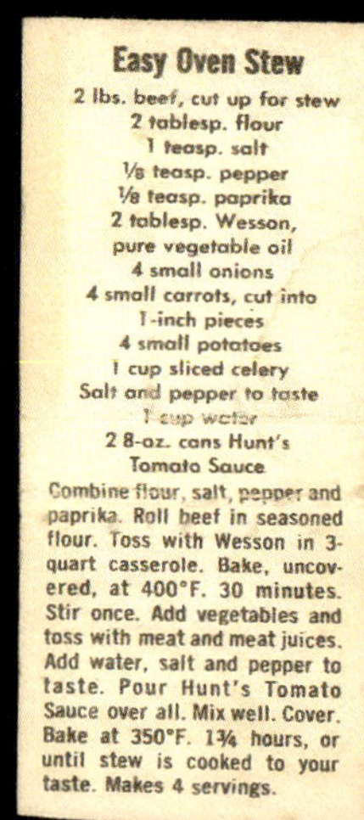

Easy Oven Stew

2 lbs. beef, cut up for stew
2 tablesp. flour
1 teasp. salt
⅛ teasp. pepper
⅛ teasp. paprika
2 tablesp. Wesson, pure vegetable oil
4 small onions
4 small carrots, cut into 1-inch pieces
4 small potatoes
1 cup sliced celery
Salt and pepper to taste
1 cup water
2 8-oz. cans Hunt's Tomato Sauce

Combine flour, salt, pepper and paprika. Roll beef in seasoned flour. Toss with Wesson in 3-quart casserole. Bake, uncovered, at 400°F. 30 minutes. Stir once. Add vegetables and toss with meat and meat juices. Add water, salt and pepper to taste. Pour Hunt's Tomato Sauce over all. Mix well. Cover. Bake at 350°F. 1¾ hours, or until stew is cooked to your taste. Makes 4 servings.

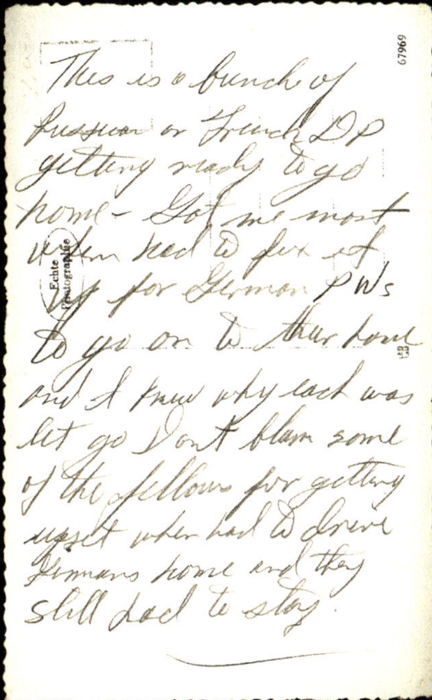

This is a bunch of Russian or French DP getting ready to go home - Got me most when had to fix it up for German PWs to go on to their home and I knew why each was let go Don't blame some of the fellows for getting upset when had to drive Germans home and they still had to stay.

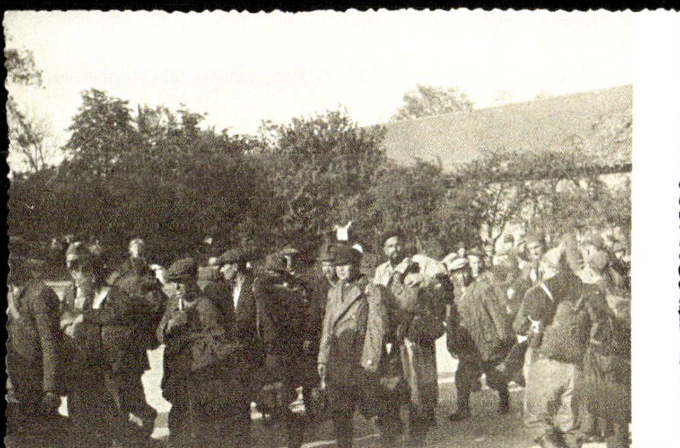

PLATE 0.46. *Photo of "Bunch of Russian or French DP" (Displaced Persons)* (Box 11).

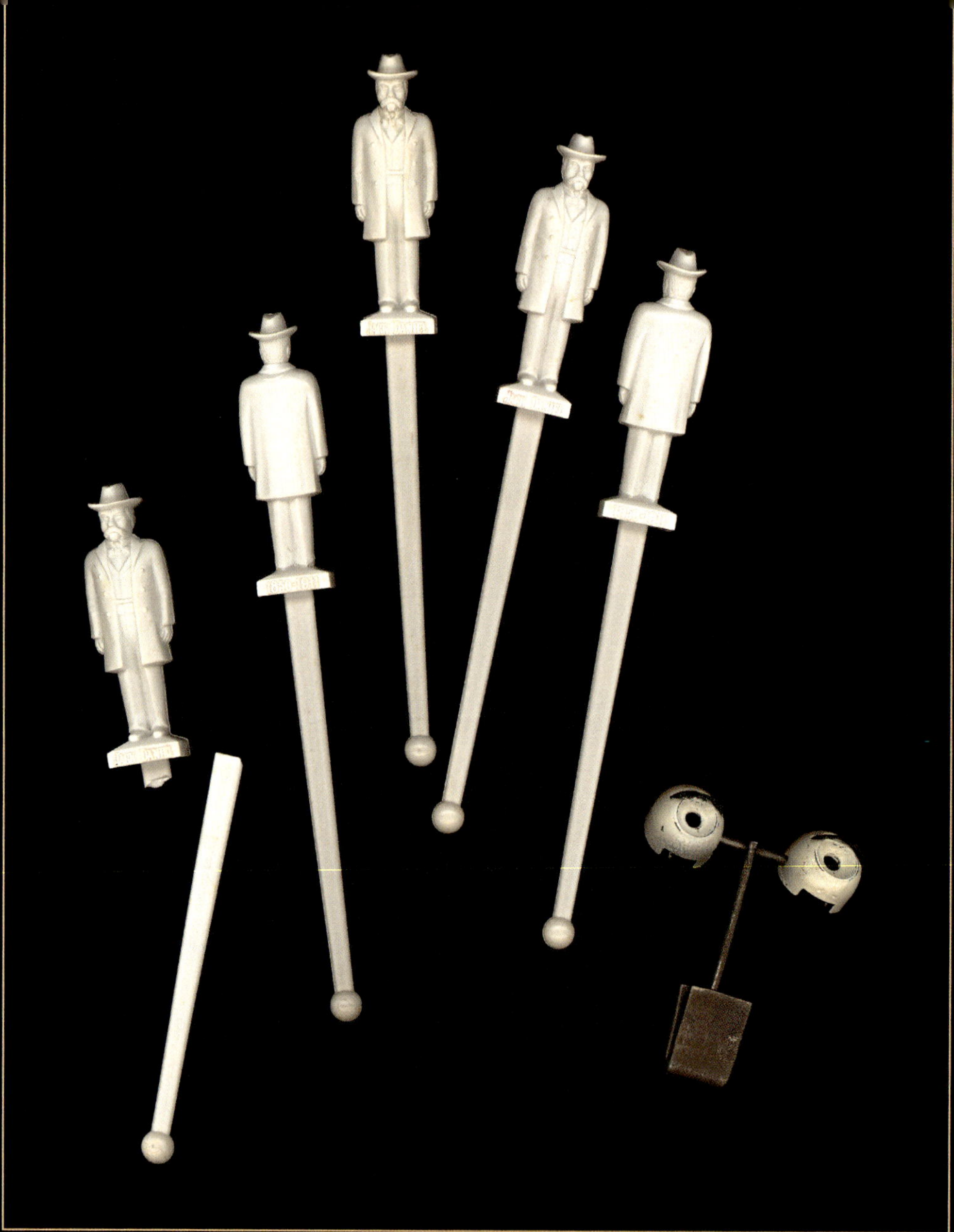

PLATE 0.47. *Whiskey Stir Sticks* (Box 11).

Daytimers Winter Special $1.75
Canada $1.95 35821

Daytimers Real Life

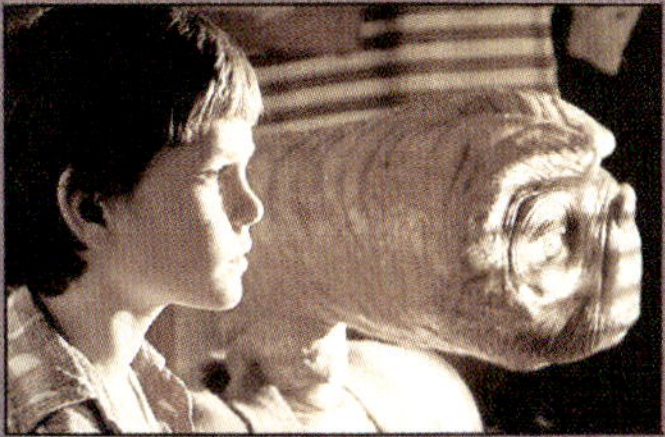

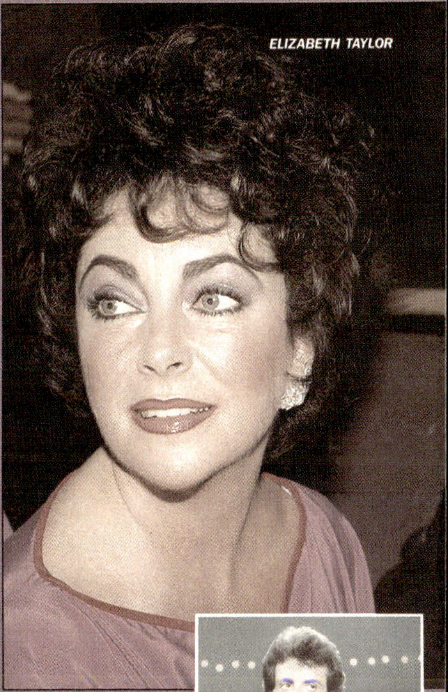

ELIZABETH TAYLOR

HOLLYWOOD'S YEAR OF DRAMA

from Many E.T.s!

E.T. Extra Terrestrial

E.T. ELIZABETH TAYLOR

RICK SPRINGFIELD: Exciting Talent

JOHN BELUSHI: Ending Tragically

RAQUEL WELCH: Extraordinary Turn

SYLVESTER STALLONE: Even Tougher

LUCIANO PAVAROTTI: Erstwhile Tenor

0 70989 35821 34

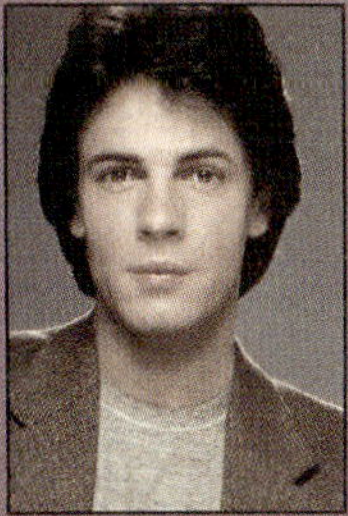

RICK SPRINGFIELD

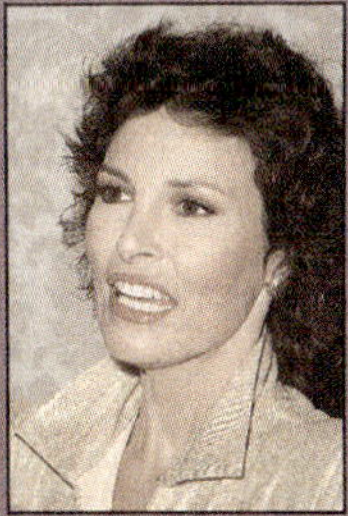

RAQUEL WELCH

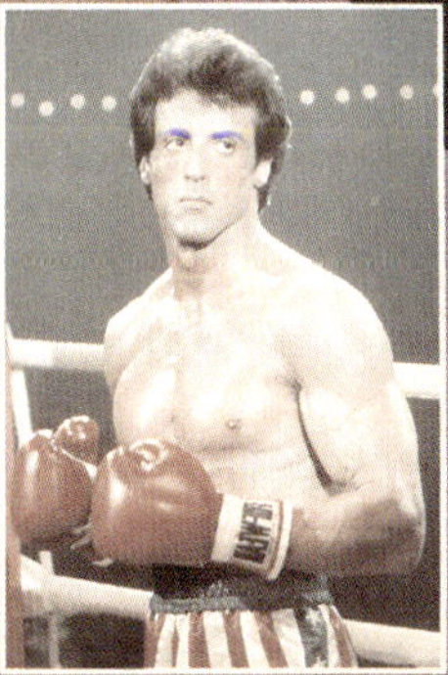

SYLVESTER STALLONE

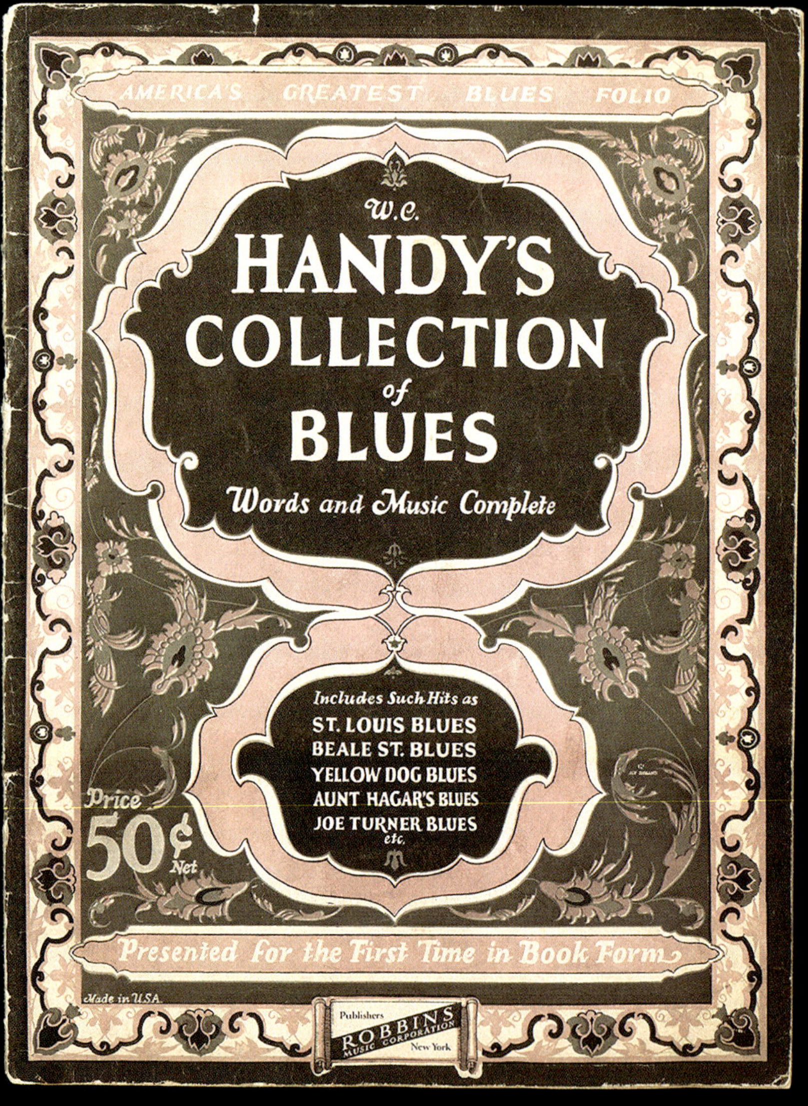

PLATE 0.49a. Handy's Collection of Blues, *cover* (Box 11).

PREFACE

The crude and primitive, stoical yet impressible philosophy of a great race gave us the "Blues," which term characterizes a funeral and melancholy type of music embracing weird and haunting strains, strange radical movements and harmonies, and uncanny effects.

A marked vogue for "Blues" exists throughout the land, more than a mere "craze," "Blues" music bids fair to definitely earn for itself a permanent niche in Music-dom. Its plaintiveness, subdued sadness and appealing naivete have won for this type of characteristic music a popularity that will endure.

To W C Handy has been given, rightfully, the title of "Father of American Blues." His genius created it, his enthusiasm fostered and nurtured it his "Blues" masterpieces immortalized it. From his brain,—one of the most fertile of the Race,—he evolved such undying Blues' gems as are included in this epoch-making collection.

This is the first time an attempt has been made to incorporate in one volume the only authentic and characteristic of the "Blues" classics. Now the music lover can have, in convenient form, such renowned master-works as "St. Louis Blues," "Beale St. Blues," "Yellow Dog Blues," "Aunt Hagar's Blues," etc.

Here, indeed, is an important addition to the music library,—a publication that, in itself, is virtually a history of the growth and progress of one of the most important eras in American musical history

The additional numbers herein contained were written by Mr Handy in collaboration with Mr Walter Hirsch, a well-informed student and writer of "Blues" music.

—THE PUBLISHERS.

PLATE 0.49b. Handy's Collection of Blues, *interior, Publisher's Preface* (Box 11).

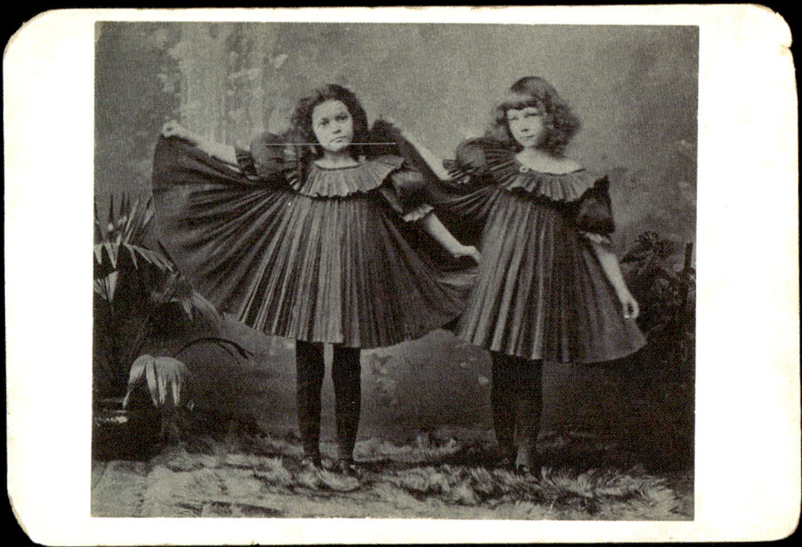

PLATE 0.50 *Formal Photo of Two Young Girls in Pleated Dresses* (Box 11).

READING THE JUNK DRAWER PHOTOGRAPHS

CHAPTER 1

WHAT WE LEAVE BEHIND

MARY BERGSTEIN

Barbara Von Eckardt is a philosopher and cognitive scientist as well as a photographer and conceptual artist. As both photographer and philosopher, she has created the images in this volume. In her rather quiet, even self-effacing, work, Von Eckardt queries what Ernst Gombrich (reworking Alois Riegel's fin-de-siècle concept) famously called "the beholder's share."[1] My own contribution here is to ask: what happens to the imagination of the beholder in *Junk Drawer*? How and what do Von Eckardt's *Junk Drawer* photographs communicate? Her pictures of indigent secondhand objects and neglected vernacular photographs ("snapshots") from junk drawers constitute the subject of this book and of this chapter.

We twenty-first-century critics, including James Elkins, who is known as one of the most influential art historians of the past forty years, seem never to tire of inquiring as to what photography really is.[2] Junko Theresa Mikuriya, herself a philosopher-photographer, recently considered the intellectual difficulty of coming to terms with photography in her book *A History of Light* (2018): photography, she posits in the Introduction, "is treacherous—at times it hides behind its object of depiction, other times concealing itself underneath its bedazzling technical splendor." Mikuriya adds that "Any attempt to write a history or theory of photography would have to address the challenges presented by the ubiquity of the photographic image and the changing forms of its technological manifestations."[3] Clearly, photography is not just one thing. Hagi Kenaan has stated recently in *Photography and its Shadow* (2020), "The history of photography is not a chronology of a given, essentially self-same, pictorial medium; but rather it is an account of a dialectical process that allowed photography to negotiate and sustain an identity."[4]

This is precisely the quandary of cross-disciplinary culture in which Von Eckardt's newest work participates. All this imaginative "looking" promises a transdisciplinary adventure in the abject and forgotten objects of the recent personal past. Of this material, what do we keep present in our impassioned visual imaginations? What gets left behind? When the substance of photography is questioned, as by Mikuriya, how can we then approach the ethical issues that Von Eckardt grapples with, in the act of publishing someone else's personal photographs? She states that she first felt "another, more negative, reaction: dismay" at the very idea that such things should be published and even sold. If such pictures participate in the roiling depths of what Christopher Bollas has called the "unthought known," then what business do we critics have in publishing and commenting upon them as though they were objects for sale in a consumer catalog?[5] Or perhaps it is simply the case that all images belong to everyone, and their reproductions must not be bartered. The beholder, consciously and not, must supply his or her own meaning in the wake of the uncertainty introduced by the image.

Among artists and art historians it is now commonly agreed upon that, rather than abiding by a chronological parade of culturally accepted artistic "masterpieces," the historian, the theorist, and, of course, the artist ought to examine, instead, "everything." This "everything" includes even the most vulgar and decrepit evidence: discarded materials and tools, vernacular depictions of sentimental topics, and conscious and unconscious designs from the everyday world. "Everything" includes rejected portraiture and genre scenes, images made by chance and discarded, as it were, by chance. Objects hiding in plain sight, therefore, ought to be considered just as apposite for consideration as the most aesthetically and historically charged antiquities conserved in art museums. Such relatively neglected, or even repudiated, objects (whether in fact hiding in plain sight or lingering in obscure historical shadows) can be as compelling to the cultural historian as the most satisfying work of art, or the monumental productions described in celebrated ekphrases from antiquity, such as the Shield of Achilles from Homer's *Iliad*, which depicts none less than the earth, sky, and sea, the sun, the moon, and the astronomical constellations of stars. The ekphrastic material at hand, together with fine art and its attendant literature, is gathered under the rubric of what we call "visual culture." Visual culture is everywhere in the historical past and the present, like the air we breathe or, as David Foster Wallace might have put it, the water we (we as fish, that is) swim in.[6] In psychoanalysis and the optical unconscious, visual ideation plays a large part, indeed, in the "unthought known," that is, what we know without thinking about consciously in verbal language.

American junk drawers, the working containers of Von Eckardt's photographs, are transitional zones—a kind of holding territory for objects neither kept and cared for, nor completely canceled or thrown out. In *Junk Drawer*, the primary referent objects tend toward abject insufficiency, and the artist is not particularly interested in enhancing their status as models or subjects of the camera's gaze, or framing them in heroic or tragic terms. Von Eckardt, through her keen, and admittedly subjective, intellect, selects and rearranges things into patterns or groups in each box according to what may appear to be arbitrary criteria. Part of her work as a photographer in *Junk Drawer* is that of a willing secondhand curator of inadvertent collections. She accepts the repudiated objects and images that have accidentally come her way by means of other (anonymous) people's assignments of this material to junk drawers, which, as repositories of discarded things, generate an aesthetic not far from that which is evoked by ruins or debris. Von Eckardt then approaches her subjects with a degree of scientific intensity, if not objectivity, in observation. The objects she deals with photographically include at least two distinct categories of small things, "found" photographs of people (which interest me the most) and small semi-ruined awards or keepsakes of various sorts of manufacture.

Von Eckardt's project is to a great extent about inadvertent collecting. Her groups of accidentally, or inadvertently, collected representations are what A.O. Scott calls "the useless stuff that form[s] the infrastructure of memory." Scott's essay "Our Collections and the Passage of Time" is primarily a review of Joachim Trier's 2022 movie *The Worst Person in the World*. A character called Aksel, who is a young man close to death in Trier's film, states, "I've spent my life doing that—collecting all that stuff." But the objects in his collection are of little consolation to him or to the film's spectators. Are gathered objects and images still as precious now as they had been for people living in earlier historical periods? Scott remarks that, for Americans born in the last two decades of the twentieth century, the so-called "millennials," shopping (collecting) no longer consists of the handling and gaining of desirable things. Rather than rifling through tables or drawers of goods, shopping as an aspect of collecting now consists of staring at a screen and clicking on an icon. Collecting has become an activity that requires fantasizing about images rather than engaging in the tactile appraisal and selection of goods.[7]

Von Eckardt asks her audience how to photograph (and view) ruined objects of small size and inconsequential value. One answer may reside in Marcel Proust's writing about everyday objects and their aesthetic in his youthful essay "How to Open your Eyes" (1895). Proust, in this essay written in his mid-twenties and dedicated to the painters Jean-Baptiste Chardin and Rembrandt, asks the reader to envision a melancholic young man sitting at his breakfast table in a state of bored malaise.[8] The only aesthetic comfort the man can think of at that moment is to imagine the ideas of beauty depicted in the great masterpieces of the Louvre, or certain princely *objets de virtu*. Proust would ask the young man to follow him to the section of the Louvre where the smallish pictures by Chardin are displayed. The author would have him stop in front of these works to look at the rendition of objects that were less than beautiful, even ugly, such as "a shiny saucepan lid, containers of every shape and material (salt cellar, skimming ladle), sights that you shrink from, dead fish lying on the table (The Ray [1728]), and sights that sicken you, glasses half-emptied and too many left full (Fruits and Animals)."[9] Proust explains that if all these scenes now strike us as beautiful to look at, it is because Chardin found them beautiful to render in paint, and that was principally because Chardin found them fascinating to look at. Thus, these lowly objects are brought to our highest level of awareness: "Your awareness, being too sluggish to reach down for such pleasure, had to wait for Chardin to take hold of it in you and raise it to a conscious level."[10]

Von Eckardt's photographic project likewise speaks to us of the melancholy aesthetic of everyday life. She, like Chardin, brings banal, trivial, unconscious materials to the surface. The following passage from Proust on Chardin seems appropriate to quote: "In rooms where you see nothing but pictures of other people's banality and the reflection of your own boredom, Chardin enters like light, giving each thing its color, summoning from the eternal darkness that had shrouded them, all the creatures of still or animate life together with the meaning of each form, so striking to the eye, so obscure to the mind."[11] Pictures "of other people's banality" are what Von Eckardt gathers and analyzes in *Junk Drawer*. The ultimate meaning of such pictures "so obscure to the mind" remains perennially open-ended in her work. Does Von Eckardt find her own collection of mundane trifles beautiful? Does it matter? The point is more that she shows us how to open our eyes to the detritus of our everyday lives without falsely beautifying or heroizing the materials that come our (her) way. It may be pertinent to divide Von Eckardt's junk from *Junk Drawer* into two categories, two tribes of objects with affinitive distinctions grouping them together: first, photographs of vernacular snapshots, which I shall discuss below, and second, digital photographs of junked objects that were meant to be keepsakes, special awards, or prizes. The collection includes photographs of photographs of people, professional portraits and homely snapshots alike. This brings me to the general conundrum about publishing photographs of people who are or were alive. It is an ethical dilemma, at least in my view, that Von Eckardt alludes to in her artist's statement, and that permeates her work.

Let me explain myself. About twenty years ago, curator Margit Berner showed me some things in the Natural History Museum of Vienna that were unforgettable, including some "anthropological" photographs of Jewish people (collected under the rubric "Jews and Jewish half-breeds") from the city of Tarnów in Western Galicia who were scheduled for deportation. Berner realized immediately that her accidental discovery of these photographs from 1942 (black-and-white standardized headshots, with anthropometric measurements) was of historical importance. These images were made without the subjects' consent and under conditions of abuse (such as the forced shaving of traditional men's beards before the photographs were taken) and terror, as the subjects of these portraits had no hope of survival. Berner told me that almost all of these people were murdered soon afterward.

At that time, in 2004, she explained to me the deeply problematic aspects of exhibiting such pictures, and how, for the time being, she had resolved not to show them, lest someone in the general public recognize his or her family member who had been deported and murdered by Nazis. Should these photographs be conserved in a museum for historical posterity? Or destroyed (possibly burned) in honor of the millions of victims murdered under the Nazi regime? Berner has dealt bravely with difficult material throughout her curatorial career, but to whom do these photographs belong? Do they belong to the progeny and survivors of these individuals who were examined, measured, and documented in the Tarnów Ghetto? Or do they belong to everybody? Berner's bilingual book (*Letzte Bilder*) *Final Pictures: The 1942 "Race Study" of Jewish Families in the Tarnów Ghetto* was finally published in 2020. There would never be a tasteful way to display pictures of people scheduled for murder, but here the photographs of individuals are arranged by family groups. In the words of Berner, these are photographs of people "who were supposed to be forgotten forever."[12]

In 2016, I wrote a little memoir "Hotel Michelangelo" about a found Polaroid photograph of an anonymous nude figure that had been abandoned ("left behind") in a hotel in Milan.[13] By this time, I had already been sensitized, in the Viennese Natural History Museum and elsewhere, to the ethics of publishing or exhibiting pictures of others. The fetishization of such Polaroid photographs, like the one found in Milan, had already become a Warholian tradition at the time of its making. The gender of the body here was not discernable, and it was not clear to me as to whether the subject was awake, asleep, dead, or alive when the photograph was made. On principle, I did not publish the mysterious Polaroid in question, a decision I did not regret. But times have changed. Now, in the days of the horrifying Russian war in Ukraine, we witness uncensored visual materials that shock even our most desensitized twenty-first-century expectations. We encounter images of human cadavers on a daily basis. I witnessed a Ukrainian woman dying in childbirth, carried on a stretcher in a videotape on my American news channel. Hours later, after she and the baby died, television audiences were shown her empty blood-soaked mattress. It was the grimmest and saddest, most physically intrusive memento mori imaginable. Shouldn't this footage have been censored, as it might have been in the past? Is it more respectful to the subject to censor the immensity of her suffering or to display it? To censor her death and the death of her newborn child? The ethics of (journalistic) narrative photography are strained in examples such as this.

Non-art snapshots of men, women, and children, made to remember certain moments in time, have been positioned under the category of "vernacular photography." Douglas R. Nickel author of *Snapshots: The Photography of Everyday Life, 1888 to the Present* (1998), was one of the first photo historians to take "found" photographs seriously.[14] In 2000, Geoffrey Batchen wrote "Vernacular Photographies," stating of such pictures that, "these ... artifacts represent the troublesome field of vernacular photography: they are abject photographies for which an appropriate history must now be written." Such photographs constitute what Batchen characterized at the turn of the twenty-first century as "the popular face of photography, so popular that it has been largely ignored by the critical gaze of respectable history."[15] Such "low" photography includes the kinds of photographs that were to be found in domestic situations, such as in junk drawers, discarded family photo albums, or boxes.

These were the objects that were not to be kept nor burned, as they didn't merit the trouble of either choice, or of making a choice, whether in public or in private. Today, the Internet at large provides some chat on such choices: the person browsing the Internet encounters myriad suggestions of what to do with old family or personal photographs, rather than mutilating the images, burning them, or throwing them away to languish in trash bins. But the ghostly double (the photographic image) dissolves back into the ether of the imagination, rather than suffering pain or abandonment, as in an act of sympathetic magic.

Throughout the twentieth century, in Europe and America, portrait photographs have served as powerful fetishes for sympathetic magic. Photographic portraits in particular are endowed with enormous value in everyday life. People will frequently kiss these photographs; and sometimes people will burn them. Photographs of mothers and grandmothers travel with their children in the process of immigration. Yet, photo portraits are occasionally injured or destroyed to mark, or even to cause, the termination of an affective relationship with the subject. Photographs stand in as surrogates for their human subjects in the lives of their collectors.

In *Photography and Science* (2009), Kelley Wilder, who has a background in the history of science as well as the history of art, emphasizes that, "the sheer transparency of photography as a physical object is what is crucial to creating photographic records."[16] In Wilder's view, transparency could be called one of the iconographic traits of the photographic record. This "photographic disappearing act," working together with neutral grounds, among other factors, creates effective "specimen photographs," by isolating the object of the photograph for close looking. In modernism, specimen photographs are like "portraits" of objects, which appear to communicate directly.[17] Such "specimen portraits" encourage the observer to assume (consciously or not) that they are looking directly at the primary referent object, and interpreting it ab initio, and per se, rather than as a printed or projected photographic representation of the primary referent.

Turning to Von Eckardt's Box 11, we find a memento not easily forgotten. Stamped "Echte Photographie 67969," it was originally inscribed with a message on the verso in pencil: "This is a bunch of Russians or French DP [displaced person] getting ready to go home. Got me most [information] when told to fix it up for German PWs on the other hand knew why each was let go. [I] don't blame some of the fellows for getting upset when [they] had to drive Germans home and they still had to stay." What we see in the photo (PLATE 0.46) is a group of people walking from right to left with backpacks and other scarce luggage against a background of trees and an abstract view of a large low wall. These must be the displaced persons in question, fleeing some outdoor site in non-military garb. The photograph is not the work of a professional photographer, but rather someone making a photo for his or her personal wartime recollection, using a small portable camera equipped with a good lens and packed with a fast film. The most popular camera in Germany and throughout Europe at that time, and the one that was used to make this snapshot, was the Leica. Early Leica cameras bear the initials "D.R.P.," which stands for Deutsches Reichspatent, the name for German patents before 1945. This is probably a reference to the "Rollfilmkamera" patented by Ernst Leitz in 1923.[18]

The nationality of these DPs is not discernable to me in iconographic terms. Are they Russian? French? They could be peasants, Jews, deserters, or discharged soldiers from any army. The photograph and its inscription dates from about 1945, the close of the Second World War. Some of the men photographed here might have been (or might still be) recognizable to an individual looking for evidence of the destiny of a particular displaced person. But this photograph was apparently the property of an American soldier, a personal souvenir that ended up in an American junk drawer some six decades later. The photograph itself requires historical interpretation. The element of time marching forward and a certain sense of postwar forgiveness pervade the ensemble of text and image. Again, as with the anthropological portrait photographs that Margit Berner showed me in Vienna, we may have some misgivings about exhibiting photographs of displaced persons, who may or may not have found their way home after the war.

In capturing the loneliness of American postwar cities and suburbs, their desolate sorrows, conscious and more likely unconscious, their junk boxes and their obsolete mementos, a film from 1964 about extreme psychological displacement comes to mind. *The Pawnbroker*, directed by Sidney Lumet and starring Rod Steiger, depicts a middle-aged Jewish man broken by Nazi brutality, having witnessed the murder of his wife and children, languishing in a Long Island postwar suburb of the most drab, desolate kind. *The Pawnbroker* is shot in black and white, and memories, which take the form of dramatically composed still photographs, appear intermittently in flashes, though too rapidly for the viewer to take them into conscious critique. Consciously or not, these intervening image blasts are present enough to disclose the memories that haunt the pawnbroker's everyday existence.

In Box 6, Von Eckardt gives us a different kind of haunting. The small black-and-white snapshot, dated February 1963 (PLATE 0.36), is a nocturnal portrait of two people that slips quite unwittingly into the realm of the Freudian "Uncanny" (*Unheimlich*).[19] A little girl happily disguised as a Roma fortune teller is seated at a small table for consultation in the darkness of the backyard of a rural or suburban home. How do we know she is playing the role of a fortune teller? We do not know, but there is a tremor of ambiguity that emanates from this little photograph. Fortune-telling is a mysterious business; divination is always a double-edged sword. The innocuous little girl's costume of headscarf and long skirt allude to a particular type, namely a Roma or Sinti woman or girl. Her companion at the table is a large-scale adult woman in a glowing white dress seen in a side view, like one of Michelangelo's Sibyls from the Sistine Chapel ceiling, perched precariously on a folding chair. This second figure dominates the apparently impromptu composition and seems far too big in proportion to the smiling child. It is worth mentioning that the child and adult are both playing theatrical roles here, the child as soothsayer and the adult woman (likely the too-large mother) as her powerful client. The traditional mother-child formula is thus upset. This small-scale chiaroscuro image from a junk drawer looks uncannily familiar, as well as strangely haunting, but its ultimate meaning can only be supplied by the beholder.

As in Diane Arbus's disturbing photographs of children taken in almost the same time period, we wonder whether the innocence of childhood can or must haunt the adult spectator. The quality of feeling here is one of absurdity at cross-purposes with a hovering anxiety, creating a deep tremor of ambiguity. The landscape environment itself may be the true protagonist, as an overall darkness pervades the small, intimate scene. The atmosphere is represented by a uniform or dappled dark gray sky. There are a few scratches on the skin of the photograph, added post-facto, as if in anger. But these marks are not necessarily angry: according to the beholder, the scratches could be read as an electrical disturbance before a storm in a dark gray, monotonous sky. These presumably accidental damages participate in what we might call the iconographic puzzle of the image.

Recently, cultural historians have looked back about a century, using early psychoanalytic writings as a springboard from which to address twenty-first-century issues. Historians and critics have been captivated by concepts and aesthetics from the beginning of the twentieth century, from just that time and place that we casually locate as "Vienna 1900." Vectors of meaning that have plotted back to that point in time-space edge into the thinking about several difficult new notions. One of these currently fashionable topics is the aesthetic that Freud called the "Uncanny" in 1919.[20] In our age, the Freudian Uncanny is applied not only to literature but also to diverse fields such as architecture theory, film studies, and radical philosophy. We need not go as far as Anneleen Masschelein, who called the Uncanny a "late-twentieth-century theoretical concept" rather than an early twentieth-century psychoanalytic aesthetic category.[21] Instead, the Uncanny has now remained one of the most fascinating, if malleable, ideas in psychoanalysis, and one of the most difficult ideas to come to terms with in the study of aesthetics.

Von Eckardt's found photographs illuminate the Uncanny as a feeling of something dreadfully familiar, or even infantile, as well as profoundly mysterious. As a field of visual studies, the Uncanny, in the words of contemporary thinker Nicholas Royle, "is a province still before us, awaiting our examination."[22] Von Eckardt tacitly engages with that call for examination as she revisits and examines these concepts visually, rather than textually, in her deeply pondered junk drawers. As a philosopher and cognitive psychologist, one might expect Von Eckardt to investigate the Uncanny in terms of brain science or the philosophy of cognition. Instead, she invites the observer to experiment with her collections of images, and there is an abundance of visual material at hand to trigger the imagination. When disparate images of abject objects, such as those left behind in the junk drawers, are inspected in purely visual terms, as they are by Von Eckardt, they prick the beholder with optical allusions to unconscious ideation, to that which is hidden, forbidden, forgotten, or taboo.

Walter Benjamin famously proposed that early twentieth-century photographic practices made present a zone that he called an "optical unconscious," a mode of visual awareness somehow parallel to psychoanalysis, slipping behind the scene (or the seen) to reveal what has been previously denied, including images hidden in plain sight, and invisible views, hidden in physical space or in the rapid unscrolling of photographic or cinematic time.[23] Benjamin first introduced the concept of the "optical unconscious," so present to current art historians and theorists, in his *Little History of Photography* (1931). The concept of optically unconscious vision, which was developed by Rosalind Krauss in her book *The Optical Unconscious* (1993), is operative in *Junk Drawer*, where the unconscious ideation of the artist (Von Eckardt) and her beholders are called into play. We may also examine photographic and three-dimensional detritus for the unconscious intentions of its makers throughout the history of visual culture. I and others who write about visual culture employ terms like "uncanny" and "optical unconscious" with frequency and conviction, but these topics are still somewhat fragile, haunted, frightening, and uncertain in the 2020s. In *Photography and the Optical Unconscious* (2017), co-editors Shawn Michelle Smith and Sharon Sliwinski state that even in the third decade of the twenty-first century, "the optical unconscious remains elusive."[24] The optical unconscious, of course, resides in Bollas's "known without knowing."[25]

The idea of an uncanny double arises in Von Eckardt's work, as is illustrated in PLATE 0.50. Standing against a generalized studio backdrop, on a fur rug, are two girls identically dressed and posed by a professional commercial photographer. Around seven or eight years old, they are wearing circular pleated dresses, probably designed and made around 1900, with hyper-pleated round skirts, round pleated collars, and puffy pleated sleeves. The dresses are cut in a remarkable, bold design, apparently executed with meticulous craftsmanship. Although the girls are wearing identical dresses, they are not to be mistaken for twins, since the child at the viewer's left has dark hair, and the other girl might be blonde. The shapes and inflections of their eyes, nose, and mouths differ, too. The emotional tenor of this anonymous image is quite silent, and thus the photograph ought probably not be classified as a "portrait" in the art-historical sense nor in the tradition of social custom. The girls may well have been employed to model the dress for a tailor, rather than to portray their own personal characteristics. Each girl duplicates the other's femininity, and the doubling effect (one plus one; one and then the other) is startling to any viewer, immediately suggesting an uncanny doubling. Innocent children are sometimes viewed as uncanny or sinister insofar as they do not reveal what they may know on a preverbal level.

Here, however, neither girl is quite the Doppelgänger of the other. They do not witness each other, nor are they mirror images—in fact, there are no mirrors or reflections represented in this photograph. Instead, the girls exist in space side-by-side, like impermeable works of decorative art, like identical Tiffany silver beakers or coffeepots, objects posed and put in place, which are interesting for the shapes of their bodies and their formidable decorative cladding. They exist for the viewer as an exercise in repetition. They look something like children disguised as inanimate objects, perhaps indicating the muffled presence of a secret or a mystery. The picture in question is distant in time and space. We must not forget that this is the photograph of a photograph. Historical distance is operative in this picture, as the girls are both much older (historically) and much younger (in terms of human development) than we adult viewers are in the 2020s.

A perplexing trope in European thinking around 1910 maintained that women not only age in photographic representation, but they can also become younger. The radical architect Adolf Loos wrote about this in his treatise of 1908, *Ornament and Crime*: "Place the photographs from the last twenty years of a woman's life side by side. And she will exclaim: 'How old I looked twenty years ago!' And you, too will have to admit: she looks youngest in the last picture."[26] In a similar vein, Proust rhapsodized on an old photograph of Odette in the fifth volume of *In Search of Lost Time*: "a little snapshot taken at Nice... though a woman of fashion twenty years younger, she looked (for the earlier a photograph, the older a woman looks in it) like a little maidservant twenty years older."[27] When was the original photograph of the matching girls made? We can detect a manufacture early in the twentieth century, say 1910 or 1920, in the workshop of an anonymous studio photographer. But there is a special resonance here in this picture for artists and viewers in the present, especially those who are of the same postwar generation as Von Eckardt. We find an inspiration, or inspired memory, after the fact.

Indeed, my first feeling upon seeing this picture was one of déjà vu, flashing back to Arbus's photograph *Identical Twins, Roselle, New Jersey* (1967), which was in the back of my mind, that is to say, flourishing in the Freudian preconscious. This is an example of what I would call "reverse influence," residing in historical memory—namely the direct influence of a more recent photograph on an older one in the mind's eye of the beholder. As an art student in the 1960s, I resented Arbus's work for what I considered its clanking intrusiveness and pessimism. But as Judith Butler wrote in her 2004 essay on Arbus, "There are reasons to be permanently skeptical of any effort to excise the negativity from Arbus." Butler commented that "Arbus's photographic gaze seems inappropriately fascinated by human distortions, playing on spectacle, pandering to the unseemly desire to gawk at what might seem aberrant, to peer, to invade."[28] But, over twenty years later, our notion of the real world has expanded to include disabled or altered bodies and unusual states of mind. Negativity and fatigue are tangible in the everyday world of any thoughtful observer and need not be banished from the pictorial space.

It is not so strange, after all, to begin with Von Eckardt and end with Arbus. Arbus's work seems to reside in the preconscious histories of several of the vernacular pictures selected by Von Eckardt, as in that of the little fortune teller and her mother from 1973. Jeff Rosenheim of the Metropolitan Museum, who wrote a definitive study of Arbus, *Diane Arbus: In the Beginning* (2016), summed up the impact of Arbus's work: "It's a transformative experience having seen an Arbus work.... [y]ou do look at the world differently. You can't not."[29] An Arbus-informed person like photographer Von Eckardt, and many of us who are interested in the American photography of the later twentieth century, already look at the world through an ironical postmodern view with an inner eye to the Uncanny. We are therefore already in place to receive the optically visible, but somehow unfathomable familiarity of *Junk Drawer*.

1. Ernst Gombrich, *Art and Illusion: A Study in the Psychology of Pictorial Representation* (Pantheon Books, 1960), 182–202.
2. James Elkins, *What Photography Is* (Routledge, 2011).
3. Junko Theresa Mikuriya, *A History of Light: The Idea of Photography* (Bloomsbury, 2018), 1.
4. Hagi Kenaan, *Photography and Its Shadow* (Stanford University Press, 2020), 11.
5. Christopher Bollas, *The Shadow of the Object: Psychoanalysis of the Unthought Known* (Columbia University Press, 1987), 246ff.
6. David Foster Wallace, *This Is Water: Some Thoughts Delivered on a Significant Occasion, about Living a Compassionate Life* (Little, Brown and Co., 2009).
7. A.O. Scott, "Shelf Life: Our Collections and the Passage of Time," *The New York Times*, Feb. 27, 2022, 38.
8. Marcel Proust, *Chardin and Rembrandt*, trans. Jennie Feldman (David Zwirner Books, 2016).
9. Proust, *Chardin and Rembrandt*, 12.
10. Proust, *Chardin and Rembrandt*, 13.
11. Proust, *Chardin and Rembrandt*, 13–14.
12. Margit Berner, (*Letzte Bilder*) *Final Pictures: The 1942 "Race Study" of Jewish Families in the Tarnów Ghetto*, trans. Jeffrey S. Chase (Bilingual edition) (Hentrich und Hentrich, 2020), 17.
13. Mary Bergstein, "Hotel Michelangelo," *Afterimage: The Journal of Media Arts and Cultural Criticism* 43, no. 6 (2016): 9–12.
14. Douglas R. Nickel, *Snapshots: The Photography of Everyday Life, 1888 to the Present* (San Francisco Museum of Modern Art, 1998).
15. Geoffrey Batchen, "Vernacular Photographies," *History of Photography* 24 (2000): 262–71 (262).
16. Kelley Wilder, *Photography and Science* (Reaktion Books, 2009), 88.
17. Wilder, *Photography and Science*, 88.
18. I am grateful to the late Marcin Gizycki (1951–2022) for sharing his knowledge of the history of cameras and photographic techniques with me for the past three decades.

19. Sigmund Freud, "The Uncanny" [1919], in *The Complete Psychological Works of Sigmund Freud*, trans. Alix Strachey (Hogarth Press, 1955), 217–56.
20. Sigmund Freud, "The Uncanny" [1919].
21. Anneleen Masschelein, *The Unconcept: The Freudian Uncanny in Late Twentieth Century Theory* (State University of New York Press, 2011), 4.
22. Nicholas Royle, *The Uncanny* (Manchester University Press, 2003), 26–27.
23. Walter Benjamin, "Little History of Photography," in *Illuminations*, ed. Hannah Arendt (Schocken Books, 1968), 217–51 (223).
24. Shawn Michelle Smith and Sharon Sliwinski, Introduction to *Photography and the Optical Unconscious*, eds. Smith and Sliwinski (Duke University Press, 2017), 4.
25. Christopher Bollas, *The Shadow of the Object: Psychoanalysis of the Unthought Known* (Columbia University Press, 1987), 281ff.
26. Adolf Loos, *Ornament and Crime: Thoughts on Design and Materials*, trans. Shaun Whiteside (Penguin, 2019), 94.
27. Marcel Proust, "The Captive," in *In Search of Lost Time*, vol. 5, trans. C.K. Scott Moncrieff and Terence Kilmartin, rev. D.J. Enright (The Modern Library, 1999), 267.
28. Judith Butler, "Diane Arbus: Surface Tensions," *Artforum 42*(6): 118.
29. Butler, "Diane Arbus," 118.

CHAPTER 2

ESTATE CURIOSITIES

DANIEL CAVICCHI

FOUND OBJECTS, LOST MEANINGS

At the end of Rolf Potts's *Souvenir*, he recounts the death of his Aunt Lynda, about whom he had fond memories as a child. When it came time to sort through her belongings, it was only after the immediate family had taken or distributed what they had deemed the most valuable that he was invited to examine the remaining items. Her kitchenware and handmade quilts were gone. He was faced with leftovers, the items without much practical utility or resale value: photo albums, brass figurines, alabaster carvings, and picture postcards. "Looking at those items," he explains, "I was struck by how much of what we collect in life ultimately becomes depleted of meaning. Without any sense for the memories or desires that led Lynda to save these keepsakes, they felt like a sorrowful menagerie of lost objects." Potts ended up taking an alabaster elephant, which he displays in his home as "a reminder that the things we own, like life itself, can only be appreciated in real time, on ephemeral terms."[1]

While Potts's encounter with his Aunt Lynda's discarded belongings makes a specific point about the role of highly personal and often irretrievable memories in shaping the significance of souvenirs, it also raises interesting parallel questions about how, exactly, to make sense of such belongings when their owners are absent, and the objects' meanings are lost. This is not an uncommon situation; family members responsible for the affairs of the deceased often have to work through rather complex feelings of bewilderment and rediscovery while trying to gather, reorganize, and divest the stuff of another person's life.[2] Indeed, if, as several scholars suggest, such stuff forms for its users a kind of "intimate geography,"[3] "personal sceneography,"[4] or "a stable ecology of memory cues,"[5] the loss of that intimacy and its cues can make encounters with objects feel like wandering in a strange landscape, uncertain of what one is experiencing.

The discarded belongings in Barbara Von Eckardt's *Junk Drawer* photographs evoke similar feelings of loss and depletion. Like Potts's "menagerie of lost objects," the photographs depict random things, estate leftovers acquired through online marketer eBay that have little to no provenance or context. We are confronted with arrays of keychains, matchbooks, snapshots, playing pieces, military insignia, tools, cheap jewelry, recipe clippings, and magazine images. The items are personal belongings and thus suggest the unity of a person's life experiences and interests. However, there is also a disarming entropy to it all. While themes such as military service or family emerge in some of the photographs, others juxtapose wildly diverse odds and ends (e.g., a pencil stub, a pair of baby moccasins, miniature toys). Items sometimes appear carefully placed; at other times, they are scattered, partially out of frame, as if carelessly tossed.

The question of the capacity of objects alone to sustain or transmit meaning is a challenge faced by any curator, archeologist, or historian. As Steven Lubar has explained, "artifacts have stories" and animating objects is "a complex dance of showing, watching, listening, discussing, teaching, and learning."[6] Even then, while museums and collectors make every effort to preserve objects and their meanings, there is no guarantee that collected objects will be understood in the same way over time. After all, objects can facilitate forgetting, as well as remembering.[7]

The potential meanings of the *Junk Drawer* items are further complicated by the fact that they are not obviously significant, historically or socially; not only are they the personal remains of an anonymous individual, but they are also remains of those remains. As Daniel Miller and Fiona Parrott explain, objects after death are often used to mediate between ideal and actual memories of the deceased, and what is leftover to be donated, or given away outside the circle of close relatives and friends, is often what is considered "non-ideal."[8] In other words, the *Junk Drawer* items, acquired from eBay, are likely objects that are mundane keepsakes and ephemera, often mass-produced, what historian Wendy Woloson calls "crap."[9] As a social category in capitalist society, crap has a rich history that can lend insight into broader cultures of consumption, but particular, mass-produced items are more enigmatic. It can be especially difficult to decode individual emotional attachments to things that are materially identical and whose meanings are primarily elective.[10]

Ebay especially ruptures the ability of discarded or remnant objects to hold and transmit meanings. Woloson cites the role of eBay and other online sites as erasing "information asymmetries about price and value," thus providing an easy means for collectors to divest their objects and for others to acquire them.[11] This rapid turnover affects how objects are invested with meaning, both enhancing their role in socially shared nostalgia while also accelerating their accumulation of personal associations over time. Citing the example of savvy collectors purchasing generations' worth of family photographs on eBay, Henry Jenkins summarizes that "the digital has led to new systems for appraising and circulating goods, new configurations of knowledge and interest, new communities of fans and collectors, and thus new forms of historical consciousness."[12]

And yet, despite these ruptures of meaning—and the fact that in the *Junk Drawer* photographs we are dealing with things whose resonant associations in everyday life were idiosyncratic and have thus reasonably faded—the depicted objects do still fascinate. Literary theorist Bill Brown has identified the breakdown of a thing—that is, the cessation of normal use and expectation, as the very reason that things seem suddenly to become evocative.[13] They cease to act as objects, defined in relation to us as subjects, and instead function as things, existing in themselves.[14]

And indeed, isolated and highlighted in the *Junk Drawer* photographs, the patina and fractal outlines of tools and keys emerge in new ways, the repetition of matchbooks or whiskey stirrers points to their differences in wear and tear, and photographs of individuals and couples become sepia-toned abstractions, relics that refer to pastness rather than to any particular past.

Even then, a thing's meaning is hard to pin down. What did the photographed keys, for instance, open, if anything? Who stamped them in the first place, and in which factory, when? And how exactly did they end up, parted from their locks and ignitions, on eBay? Matchbooks are a common utility item in a household for lighting candles and cigarettes, but also, historically, have had significance in public etiquette between men and women, as well as in advertising and personal collectibles.[15] How were these particular matchbooks situated in the matchbook industry? Are the books shucked of matches or still full? What did the various *Junk Drawer* matchbooks signify to the people who kept them? Overall, in other words, how might we tell the biographies or itinerancies of these objects?[16] We can only make reasonable guesses, and the objects' elisions and absences set the terms of such conjecture.

Anthropologist Barbara Kirshenblatt-Gimblett has noted that the ethnographic object, extracted from its origin for display as a piece of art in a museum, functions as a "split-sign," which "exposes the signifier and defers the signified."[17] Its display is part of a "theater of secrecy," in which meaningfulness takes precedence over meaning, a "paradox of showing secrets without revealing them."[18] Kirshenblatt-Gimblett focuses on instances of "overcoded" formal art in which the withholding of determinative meaning is intentional, as a form of pleasure. The same disconnection from meaning can be true of discarded belongings, but for them the splitting of the sign is unintentional, the byproduct of abandonment. Junk drawer items, like ritual artifacts isolated for a museum viewer's gaze, are intensely expressive while also confoundingly unspecific.

LOST OBJECTS, FOUND MEANINGS

At first glance, the *Junk Drawer* photographs suggest a collection, and the world of collecting is one entry point into making sense of the depicted objects. However, the literature of collecting deeply emphasizes ownership, as well as its creative corollary, authorship. From early theories by Walter Benjamin and Jean Baudrilliard to revisions by Werner Muensterberger, Susan Pearce, and Majorie Swann, as well as more recent investigations by Lincoln Geraghty and Henry Jenkins, the people who care about, gather, sort, and display things are often given a special authorial role over those things' meanings, and those things, in turn, are made special by the investments made in them.[19] Given the absence of those investments, each set of *Junk Drawer* items, while collected together and on display, function less like an intentional collection than a menagerie, a modern cabinet of curiosities.

Cabinets of curiosities, from European *Wunderkammer* in the sixteenth century to early museum displays in the Victorian era, gathered a plethora of objects on a set of shelves or in an elaborate cabinet with drawers and compartments. Audiences were invited to explore their contents, often without direct information or guidance. The objects within were often placed according to idiosyncratic or esoteric schemes, which were not immediately intelligible and privileged close attention and discovery.[20] Cabinets of curiosities influenced or echoed a number of similar forms: Romantic-era publications of diverse articles and reprints, called "cabinets," "museums," and "miscellany";[21] the eighteenth-century peddler's wagon of random goods and cures, which led to the "omnium gatherum" of later variety stores and mail order catalogs;[22] and scrapbooks and commonplace books, which compiled snippets and fragments of one's experiences.[23]

All of these forms of display depended on the dynamics of encounter, emphasizing first novelty, and second variety, or, in the words of Adalgisa Lugli, "marvel" and "accumulation."[24] Cabinets of curiosities, for example, were built around the idea of captivation in terms of, first, acquiring never-before-seen objects and, second, highlighting their oddity and collective volume to fixate attention. Encounters with such collections of objects could lead to confusion. Potts notes that early cabinets of curiosities, derived from the personal souvenirs of the wealthy, bewildered everyday visitors, who "weren't really sure what it was they were seeing."[25] But, just as often, that lack of understanding could lead to fascination. Stephen Greenblatt refers to this particular response as "wonder," or "the power of the object displayed to stop the viewer in his tracks" even with little or no knowledge of it.[26] Lugli goes further, describing such wonder as "an intermediate, highly particular state akin to a sort of suspension of the mind between ignorance and enlightenment that marks the end of unknowing and the beginning of knowing."[27]

As recognizable everyday objects, the *Junk Drawer* items are not necessarily novel and wondrous, but they still offer a number of intriguing gaps in sense, or curious puzzles to solve. The objects' haptic qualities—texture, weight, temperature, malleability—are palpably missing. Upon encounter, it is difficult not to imagine the feel of the matting, rag content, and wearing of the paper of some of the older postcards and photographs, or, say, the coldness, rigidity, or interplay of the metal parts of the combination box door or some of the jewelry pictured. The objects are static and do not emit sounds of movement or handling, so one can only imagine the likely clink of metal or glass and the rustle of paper. In fact, the objects are accessible only through viewing stylized photographic images, quite similar to those objects encased for viewing in a museum display cabinet; they invite scrutiny by withholding experience, provoking desires by "evacuating" the possibility of those desires' fulfillment.[28]

The objects' mystery is further enhanced by lack of information about their origin. They are familiar mass-produced items with typical uses and associations, but, as noted, they are also leftover personal effects, but with those private investments and stories tantalizingly withheld. Thus, the objects have a kind of semiotic privacy, proffering secrets that cannot be truly known except with conjecture from the outside, which invites not simply looking but a more suggestive looking-in, based on anticipated revelations.[29] The various family photographs obviously fall into such a category of semiotic privacy, pointing to key life moments and experiences; likewise, the jewelry remnants hint at bodies, gifts, and relationships, and trinkets suggest trips, landscapes, and encounters.

Aside from novelty, the variety of items in cabinets of curiosities and other menageries created its own "allure of heterogeneity," as Woloson put it, in which "each omnium-gatherum was its own new thing: a novelty made up of other novelties."[30] Variety could excitingly create the possibility of new equivalencies, associations between incongruent objects. Patrick Mauries has noted that a cabinet of curiosities "cramming together so many objects within such a confined space had the effect of creating a dizzying foreshortening of the perception."[31] Caitlin DeSilvey, working with discarded remnants of a farm homestead, bases her conclusions on the ways that "fragmentary objects and documents are brought into focus through their juxtaposition with each other," which afford a "recuperation of obsolete networks of use and affinity."[32] Orhan Pamuk, too, put this effect to stunning use in an entire museum in Istanbul devoted to the ordinary objects of the city's residents. "What I found most enthralling," he explains, "was the way in which objects removed from the kitchens, bedrooms, and dinner tables where they had once been utilized would come together to form a new texture, an unintentionally striking web of relationships."[33]

The *Junk Drawer* items similarly exhibit such contingent relations in a variety of ways. In Box 2, for example, there is a photograph with a box of Diamond brand wooden matches, three Scrabble pieces, two keychains (a mini-horseshoe and a gelatinous dolphin), and a single key (PLATE 0.05). The lighting highlights the similarly bleached wood of the matches and the Scrabble pieces, while the metal objects recede. In Box 3, eight metallic toy soldiers, rubbed of their white or red paint and much of their detail, are luminous, as if in a film negative, while an adjacent black-and-white photograph of two soldiers, standing in a European square, provides a surprising reversal—they are detailed real soldiers, in an actual place (PLATE 0.12). Scattered keys in Box 5 reveal an astonishing variety of teeth; the circular shapes and differently sized holes of the key heads punctuate the surface (PLATE 0.21). Throughout the boxes, gold and silver jewelry chains snake across the black background, encircling smaller objects, crisscrossing in spontaneous patterns. Juxtaposed with printed fonts on advertisements, the homogeneous scrawl of handwriting becomes linked. While different in content, family photographs, postcards, clippings, and notebooks resonate materially across the boxes: all are rectangular shapes on printed paper or cardboard, pocket-sized, evenly framed, with faded sepia tones and slightly damaged edges.

Of course, while the novelty and variety of seventeenth-century cabinets of curiosities could provide a sense of decontextualized encounter with objects, such an encounter was always contrived; it did not take place in a vacuum. Many European cabinets of curiosities, for instance, were culturally meaningful in the first place because they usefully exhibited a collector's idiosyncratic interests, as well as their wealth, access, and knowledge.[34] Cabinets routinely employed architectural techniques that widened the visual field and enhanced the visual perception of objects, facilitating revelation through enclosures, drawers, and doors.[35] And, as is obvious to any curator, the purposeful organization of things in cabinets could differently affect the things' potential meanings.[36] Eighteenth-century peddlers exploited this effect, for instance, juxtaposing fine objects and junk to instill profitable equivalencies or using the conceit of "spilled" contents to convey an abundance of goods and the promise of ownership.[37]

At the same time, encounters with the objects in cabinets of curiosities were shaped by the variable of reception. While friends, visitors, guests, and patrons were expected to marvel at the cabinets' gathered objects, their responses emerged from their own sense of the marvelous. While there are not many studies that address the responses and reactions of cabinet visitors, there is some indication that interpretation was never a simple affair. In 1714, for example, when Peter the Great used his cabinet collections, including a range of anatomical specimens, to establish a public museum, the reaction was tepid: "Russians of the Petrine period saw it a frightening and dangerous place, a place where the dead, denied their rightful Christian end, might plausibly return to exact their vengeance upon the living."[38] In 1740s Paris, visitors invited to French cabinets were expected to demonstrate a "connoisseurial eye," developed through educated acquaintance with the practices of collectors and dealers, as well as auction catalogs.[39] Some travelers, who, by the mid-eighteenth century, had experienced multiple cabinets of curiosities, reported boredom.[40] Overall, documented changes in the understanding of cabinet objects—including horns,[41] hummingbirds,[42] and taxidermy[43]—indicate how perceived meanings could be fluid, shaped and reshaped by new classes or generations of visitors.[44]

The same contextual factors affect the *Junk Drawer* items. It is not entirely clear how each photograph was arranged, but the objects were obviously not received from eBay as depicted. The items are clustered into virtual "boxes," based on separate estate sales, which implies the objects in each box represent individual owners and thus lives. Types of items (photographs, jewelry, eyeglasses buttons, keys) have apparently been sorted together, while other items (trinkets, washers, cases, bits of metal) appear to be true miscellany. Akin to a museum display, all of the objects are well-lit on a light-absorbing black background, highlighting their individuated material qualities. They are not, for instance, presented in an everyday home environment or in reconstructed kitchen drawers, which might direct one's attention from the objects to situational meanings. The photographs are presented as part of this book, offered as a subject of scholarship, which espouses certain values associated with study, such as dispassionate analysis or intellectual dialogue. The goal is not comedy, say, or propaganda.

Still, how might a contemporary viewer respond to these discarded objects as presented? If eighteenth-century viewers of curiosities are any indication, even the best-laid plans for staging meaning can be misunderstood, elided, or even rebuffed. And the framing in this case only goes so far in overcoming the fact of the objects' meanings being minimally suggested, hidden, "split." Indeed, as with cabinets of curiosity and their visitors, a lot rides on the dynamics of an actual encounter between the *Junk Drawer* items and a viewer.

ENCOUNTERING THINGS, MAKING MOVES

Explaining the nature of human encounter with things has shaped study in a wide range of disciplines, including archeology, history, museum studies, and arts criticism. Reception theorists in the arts have talked about the ways that a reader realizes a text,[45] how a listener derives pleasure from hearing a piece of music,[46] or a museum visitor understands unfamiliar objects from other cultures.[47] Most recently, theorists of "new materialism" have more generally emphasized the ways that things and humans may "entangle" in mutually constitutive processes.[48]

The differences between these diverse approaches to human-thing encounters are beyond the scope of this essay, but, in general, they usefully point to the experiential dynamics of engagement with things. For instance, one general approach, from ethnomusicologist and linguist Steven Feld, may be useful for thinking about the *Junk Drawer* photographs. Responding to what he saw as overly prescriptive formalism in the semiotics of art, Feld wrote in detail about the experience of hearing music, which he understood as a particular kind of aesthetic encounter involving a "juxtaposition—in fact an entangling—of a dialectical object and a situated interlocutor." The juxtaposition is dynamic and multidirectional, shaped by the object's musical and extramusical codes and by the hearer's split-second "interpretive moves," involving a mental sorting that is locational, categorical, associational, reflective, or evaluative.[49]

Interpretive moves offer a starting place for talking about encounter. With reference to Box 5, for instance, what would allow a viewer to know, at first sight, what any of the objects in the box are (PLATES 0.18–0.27)? For one, this would likely involve placing the items in a wider field of subjective reference, including varying degrees of understanding about, say, photography, portraiture, locksmithing, the Bible, or tourism. Anyone looking at the items would probably sort them, too, into general classes of things: objects that look like they are made of paper versus those made of metal, for instance, or according to other categories of size, weight, or color. Those decisions, in turn, would help identify the items in more established terms, as portraits, tools, jewelry, printed matter, toys, etc.

Most viewers will associate given items with like or unlike items. The keys of Box 5 (PLATE 0.21), for instance, might recall other collections of keys, or similarly small, flat, metal objects, like washers or nails, that might be strewn on a surface. Postcards (PLATES 0.18, 0.23, 0.25), with their standard form dictated by the U.S. Postal Service, are easily related to other postcards, stamps, or messages, but also to any letters or messages to loved ones. A viewer might also link the items to time. Twentieth-century dates (1913, 1958, etc.), references to wartime military service, outdated fashions, and other indications of bygone practices (like smoking paraphernalia or photographic slides) are likely to evoke associations, memories, or feelings linked to specific chronological periods.

Feld's model suggests, too, that a viewer will engage in reflective moves that relate the items to broader ideas and questions about identity, society, or behaviors. The first photograph of Box 5 (PLATE 0.18), for instance, is of a young man who, as if in a frontispiece, appears to be the owner of the subsequent materials. But, to the contrary, those materials refer to multiple people: the Bible is addressed to "Roy" (PLATE 0.19), but the postcard is addressed to "Esther" and signed from "Florence" (PLATE 0.23). All this, in turn, might make one wonder about the gendering of objects or the assumption that the box has a single owner at all. Are the East Asian-themed items (the small containers and the plate in PLATE 0.26) related to American military service overseas? If so, how might that suggest debates on war trophies or, more generally, tourist merchandise? The first postcard ("For the whole damn bunch of yez") (PLATE 0.18) is humorously grudging and not typical of postcard greetings. One might introduce moral assessments about religion in response to the Bible (PLATE 0.19), or about sexuality in response to the cancan girl image (PLATE 0.25). In general, one might react to the fact that every item in the photographs is a washed-out orange, brown, or sepia—the things just look old and faded rather than colorful and vibrant. For some, that might be soothingly nostalgic or signal historical interest; for others, it might just be depressing.

These potential interpretive moves on the part of viewers are inflected by the items themselves and their arrangement in Box 5. None is simply an inert thing with an established meaning to be apprehended; as Feld suggests, a perceived object already holds multiple and sometimes contrary realities in tension.[50] The New Testament Bible (PLATE 0.19), for instance, is not a single thing but socially coded in multiple ways, all of which are tied to diverse histories, theologies, debates, and meanings of Christianity. These meanings will emerge and shift in response to any viewer's own associations, experiences, and assumptions. At the same time, the circumstances of encounter—in this case, arrangement and presentation—also can influence a viewer's interpretive moves. As already noted, for example, the material qualities and abstract patterning of the keys are at least as interesting as what they might access. Matchbooks have multiple purposes for lighting flame, and a shallow metal tray can hold just about anything that will fit in it, but putting them together strongly suggests the practice of smoking.

For Feld, all this is constrained by the role of contextual framing, which directs the possible meanings of any encounter. For example, an encounter with the *Junk Drawer* photographs at the moment of this writing took place in 2022, bringing to bear all the knowledge, assumptions, and prejudices of that time, along with various degrees of distance between 2022 and the perceived times of the objects' origin and use. Tie-pins, World War II, smoking, slides, even Star Trek may carry certain meanings now that they may not have in the past and vice versa. Yet, too, there are continuities. Right now, the items are generational; while not necessarily associated with 2022, they are the sort of thing that someone alive today still may see, or may have seen, around the homes of parents or grandparents. Soon, the items will cease to have such an experiential quality.

Viewers make evaluations of the items that assess their quality or place them into hierarchies in relation to each other. My initial encounter with the photographs in Box 5 involved similar sorts of sorting. As someone familiar with the world of images, I immediately sought to classify the different kinds of photographs: prints or slides, those taken professionally in a studio (like most of the portraits), and home snapshots (such as the photograph of Polly the dog in PLATE 0.20). These were entirely different than the idealized promotional images of, say, La Fonda Motel and Trailer Park (PLATE 0.23) or the Ghost Town in the Sky amusement park (PLATE 0.25). Some of the images brought up personal associations. I remembered sitting awkwardly as a teen, my stance carefully arranged by a photographer, for a family portrait in a local studio. While it did not involve cancan girls, I visited a regional Wild West amusement park several times as a child, and memories of that park, including staged shootouts and a sheriff's jail, came to mind when looking at the unused stationery for Ghost Town in the Sky (PLATE 0.25). The photograph highlighting the keys (PLATE 0.21) referenced my own piles of random keys at home, inherited from a previous homeowner. More powerfully, though, their intersecting forms brought to my mind similarly formatted scenes of tiny floating creatures, such as my memory of a newspaper illustration at Halloween of ghosts swarming above a haunted house, or National Geographic photographs of strange deep-sea fish swimming in the darkness and caught by an underwater camera's light.

I reflected, too, about what was in the box. Why, for instance, were there slides of scenes from two movies (*Friday the 13th* and *Star Trek: The Motion Picture*) released around 1980 (PLATE 0.27)? Carousel slides were a popular form of private photographic storage and display in the 1960s and 1970s, typically used for family snapshots and sometimes sold by tourist sites as souvenirs. They were something my own family used regularly when I was growing up. Were the slides of *Friday the 13th* and *Star Trek* souvenirs, say, from a trip to Paramount Studios, which produced both films? The handwritten identification of the films' titles suggests the items were for promotional use—or were they some kind of fan paraphernalia, received through the mail? Overall, such entertainment collectibles are very unlike the others in the box, which mainly appear to have come from much earlier in the twentieth century and have to do with more localized events and travel. How did they end up here? All these memories, impressions, and judgments entangle specific qualities of the photographed objects with my own experiences and attitudes.

In a decidedly unscientific survey, I asked seven family members and friends to look at the entirety of the *Junk Drawer* photographs and tell me what came to their mind. They were aware of the premise of a "junk drawer gallery" at the header of the web page I shared but had no other information about what the objects were or how they were assembled. What they reported, in response to the entire collection, exhibited a variety of interpretive moves and frames. Several wanted to immediately locate the objects somehow by asking, "How were these curated?" or "Who grouped these together?" Repeated phrasing included associating the objects to like objects in one's own experience ("Oh, we have this!," "[A] Mary Poppins bag," or "This reminds me of the stuff I find in Nana's house"), or to general fields and categories ("Elderly," "This guy is Italian," "Army, Army, Army, family," "they were travelers, it looks like," or "I see a lot of military history, saved newspaper headlines ... high school mementoes, also some baby stuff"). Not being able to identify something caused confusion. Studying the whiskey stirrers, one person admitted, "I don't know what those are; they look like they might clip onto something, but I don't think they do." Another, passing over the cigar box labels (PLATE 0.42), said simply, "I don't know who Robert Bacon is." One person lingered over the "For the whole damn bunch of yez" postcard (PLATE 0.18), seeking to interpret the handwriting. She was doubtful: "I don't think that's what it says."

For some people, evaluation was a main entry point, with comments shaped around whether or not they liked the depicted object, or found it "cute," "interesting," "creepy," "understandable," etc. Judgments included "these are things children wish their parents had burned," "this is a great photo," or "Blossom Time—that's a terrible name for a play." For one respondent, the older familiar objects were the most compelling, adding, "when it gets to more recent objects—mass produced, made of plastic—I find those not interesting at all." Overall, some reacted to the title of "junk," questioning whether it was too dismissive of a term.

Reflections about ideas and themes also emerged as viewers spent time with the boxes, and they began to ask, "Why keep this stuff?" Some moved from the photographs to broader issues of religion or the arts: "Not sure what the racy playing cards are all about, but it looks like they found salvation"; "There are baby shoes—that makes me think of the six-word short story by Hemingway." Overall, metalanguage about the experience of looking was also common. Some narrated their own movement through the photos, with commentary like: "Now we're getting into color photos, which we haven't had before," or "My instinct is to fill in the gaps."

The responses of these particular viewers suggest both a variety of impressions (especially in terms of associations and evaluations) and the repetition of shared themes (especially in terms of categories and reflections—war, family, old versus new, me versus them). Those responses have much to do with the identities of the individuals involved (American, white, middle-class, educated, of different ages, genders, and opinions), as well as the framing of the photographs (composition, lighting) and the circumstances of the encounter (photographs on a website, shared by a professor and by someone closely related). In general, those who encountered the *Junk Drawer* photographs reported thoughts in line with Feld's model: they entangled themselves, as socialized individuals, with the things depicted in the photographs, as well as with the photographs themselves.

SPLITTING SIGNS, MARKING PHASES

While the reactions and thoughts of actual visitors to seventeenth-century cabinets of curiosities are not well documented, we do know that the things displayed did not remain. The relics, taxidermy, and other oddities of private collections over time were donated to early museums, where they were reinterpreted as specimens and artifacts rather than as marvels and status symbols, or they were discarded, broken up, or resold, changing how the things were used and understood. Of course, those curiosities also came from somewhere previous to their display on a shelf. Many of the items in European cabinets were removed from natural environments or stolen from Indigenous communities in the Americas, Asia, and Africa, where the objects were not curious but rather integral to local systems and cultural institutions. These meanings have not disappeared; repatriation demands and efforts at transculturation by colonized peoples exemplify how objects' meanings are not easily erased and may remain, multiple and contested, across time and space.[51]

Anthropological theorists of things have long noted the ways that objects may be understood as having their own biographies based on patterns of classification and reclassification. Igor Kopytoff's influential work introduced the notion of the phases involved in objects' journeys through the world from owner to owner and context to context, where each phase imbues and layers an object with meaning. Kopytoff notes, in particular, that objects can have life histories in which some potential aspects of those histories are heightened over others; the presentation of these differences is culturally constructed and informed at different phases of an object's life.[52] House museums, for example, might place a family's utilitarian objects (pots and pans, curtains, chairs, writing desks, etc.) into an inhabitable still life where the objects are transformed from tools to symbols, offering visitors not an opportunity to cook, sit, or write but to appreciate the objects' authenticity and understand history.[53] Similarly, at museums that explore trauma, visitors are asked by curators to consider displayed "ordinary" objects, such as shoes, a tricycle, or a hat, that have been recoded as witnessing or surviving trauma, moving those objects far from their previous roles and associations.[54]

Arjun Appadurai, in dialogue with Kopytoff's ideas, has suggested that "the corrosion of history only supports and intensifies the inherent tendency of things to move on to some new state in their social lives."[55] But by what mechanisms do we identify that new state? While Appadurai does not specifically identify how a new state emerges, he does echo Bill Brown's argument about objects' heightened visibility when they break down.[56] Appadurai repeatedly points to situations in which things' constant movement through social space and time may be seen to stop or freeze. In fact, he defines things fundamentally as perceived stoppages, that is "congealed moments in a longer social trajectory," "momentary aggregations of material," or "photographs that conceal the reality of motion."[57] Working in the slightly different context of archeological analysis, Philipp Stockhammer has sought to explain what he calls the "changeability" of a thing, focusing on human perception, or "objectivation"—through naming, categorization, and evaluation—as the catalyst for things having new "effectancy," enabling or hindering human action.[58]

Each of the *Junk Drawer* items has its own life history, which may, in part, be built on a series of identifiable social and contextual changes over time, from creation to distribution, exchange, ownership, display, investment, use, sorting, discarding, re-exchange, resorting, reuse, and reinterpretation. But, as Appadurai and Stockhammer suggest, what's key is that each of those changes involve more nuanced moments of perception, when the thing is frozen momentarily and categorized, named, realized, and reacted to. In that sense, consideration of the objects now collected and photographed as part of Von Eckardt's *Junk Drawer* series also has the potential to mark the start of a new phase in each of their biographies, a moment in which specific new meanings, or rearranged emphases, may emerge.

The emergence of new meanings is especially pronounced in the case of the *Junk Drawer* items because of their unique social situation. Discarded from an estate and placed on eBay, the items are without the usual frameworks of significance afforded personal belongings. There is no accompanying text or any identifying cues of provenance or value; most viewers will not know the details of the personal circumstances or nature of the longing associated with the items. Such absences indeed point to an emergence that is less about discovery, or learning what the items already are, and more about entanglement, or a situated constituting of the items and their meanings. An encounter with the items is apt to function more like an inflection point in the lives of those things rather than a continuity. It is hard not to dwell on the fact that much of the *Junk Drawer* project offers new images of images, using re-representation to subtly invite resignifying.

Still, not all meanings are possible or likely. The presentation of the *Junk Drawer* items first of all suggests reading them with semantic intention.

They are artfully arranged and photographed, rather than found damaged in the street or covered in grime in a trash bin. Even if someone were to struggle to find meaning in a random key or a box of common wooden matches, they would be unlikely to dismiss the entire set of objects as invaluable or insignificant because someone (Von Eckardt) has already gestured to them meaningfully, gathering the things for sharing and preparing them for an audience. The things' pastness itself invites viewers to think about certain ideas: time, personhood, history, the material people acquire and leave behind. And as suggested by the previously mentioned responses of those I invited to look at the collection, there are certain shared meanings, or types of disagreement, that might emerge among viewers of the same culture or generation.

These tensions shape the bounds of encounter in this shared phase of the items' life histories. It is not clear what will happen to the items and their photographs in the future. Will the photographs become part of a museum exhibit? Will some of the items be recognized and reclaimed by family members previously uninvolved with their relatives' estates? Will everything be left hidden in Von Eckardt's closet as she embarks on a new project? Will the objects be separated and sorted in new ways, or tossed out, individually or as a group? Each potential change will involve a different encounter between a thing, or things, and a person, or people, in which each material item, momentarily suspended as a split-sign, will again become an object, entangled and rich with new significance.

1. Rolf Potts, *Souvenir* (Bloomsbury Academic, 2018), 107–9.
2. Mary Ellen Bell and Susan E. Bell, "What to Do with All this 'Stuff'? Memory, Family, and Material Objects," *Storytelling, Self, Society* 8, no. 2 (2012): 63–84.
3. Dydia DeLyser, "Collecting Kitsch, and the Intimate Geographies of Social Memory: A Story of Archival Autoethnography," *Transactions of the Institute of British Geographers* 40, no. 2 (2015): 209–22 (212).
4. Patrick Mauries, *Cabinets of Curiosities* (Thames and Hudson, 2002), 244.
5. Richard Heersmink, "The Narrative Self, Distributed Memory, and Evocative Objects," *Philosophical Studies: An International Journal for Philosophy in the Analytic Tradition* 175, no. 8 (2018): 1829–49 (1830).
6. Steven Lubar, *Inside the Lost Museum: Curating, Past and Present* (Harvard University Press, 2017), 152.
7. Marta Zarzycka and Jonathan Mogul, "Introduction: Souvenirs and Objects of Remembrance," *The Journal of Decorative and Propaganda Arts* 27 (2015): 7–11 (8). This was true, for example, of the vast collections of Queen Charlotte of Britain, which, after her death, were dismantled and reassembled by court stewards to promote her high taste rather than her intense boredom (Judith Pascoe, *The Hummingbird Cabinet: A Rare and Curious History of Romantic Collectors* [Cornell University Press, 2006], 80–82), or of the fate of gifted Indigenous items from the seventeenth-century *wunderkammer* of Johan Maurits, Dutch colonial governor of Brazil, which, when relocated in new collections and museums, lost their meaning as representations of Maurits's alleged "civilizing" influence and instead became generalized "Indian" exotica (Virginia Spenlé, "'Savagery' and 'Civilization': Dutch Brazil in the Kunst- and Wunderkammer," *Journal of Historians of Netherlandish Art* 3, no. 2 [2011]: 1–19 [9]).

8. Daniel Miller and Fiona Parrott, "Loss and Material Culture," *The Journal of the Royal Anthropological Institute* 15, no. 3 (2009): 502–19 (515).

9. Wendy A. Woloson, *Crap: A History of Cheap Stuff in America* (University of Chicago Press, 2020).

10. Henry Jenkins, *Comics and Stuff* (New York University Press, 2020), 18. Caitlin DeSilvey has written eloquently about her struggle to make sense of the "inscrutable remains" of a midwestern homestead, including "abject and devalued" objects: a spoon, a broken cup, balls of string; she does so only by creating "associative links" between the objects, American history, and the fading childhood memories of a family member ("Salvage Memory: Constellating Material Histories on a Hardscrabble Homestead," *Cultural Geographies* 14, no. 3 [2007]: 401–24). Marianne Hirsch addresses the use of conventional media forms, like the family photograph, to rebuild the affective force of trauma across generations, something that depends on both shared traumatic knowledge and familial connection; the photographs themselves may be rather formulaic, a banality that can heighten the intensity of postmemory (*Family Frames: Photography, Narrative, and Postmemory* [Harvard University Press, 1997], 21).

11. Woloson, *Crap*, 269. See also Dydia DeLyser, "Collecting Kitsch, and the Intimate Geographies of Social Memory: A Story of Archival Autoethnography," *Transactions of the Institute of British Geographers* 40, no. 2 (2015): 209–22 (212).

12. Jenkins, *Comics and Stuff*, 43. This rupturing, is, in part, why Von Eckardt finds the practice of selling estate leftovers on Ebay as disrespectful to the dead.

13. Bill Brown, "Thing Theory," *Critical Inquiry* 28, no. 1 (2001): 1–22.

14. Stephen Greenblatt ("Resonance and Wonder," *Bulletin of the American Academy of Arts and Sciences* 43, no. 4 [1990]: 11–34) makes a similar observation in his discussion about "wounded artifacts" exhibited in museums (19–20, 22).

15. Anna Jozefacka, "Protean Prompt: The Matchbook as Commercial, Private, and Cultural Reminder," *The Journal of Decorative and Propaganda Arts* 27 (2015): 196–213.

16. Igor Kopytoff, "The Cultural Biography of Things: Commoditization as Process," in *The Social Life of Things: Commodities in Cultural Perspective*, ed. Arjun Appadurai (Cambridge University Press, 1986), 68; Philipp W. Stockhammer, "Doing/Changing Things/Us," in *Exploring Materiality and Connectivity in Anthropology and Beyond*, ed. Martin Saxer, Philipp Schorch, and Marlen Elders (UCL Press, 2020), 36–50.

17. Barbara Kirshenblatt-Gimblett, *Destination Culture: Tourism, Museums, and Heritage* (University of California Press, 1998), 249–56 (254).

18. Kirshenblatt-Gimblett, *Destination Culture*, 256. For a description of Kirshenblatt-Gimblett's concept of the split-sign applied to scrapbooks, see Danille Elise Christiansen, "(Not) Going Public: Mediating Reception and Managing Visibility in Contemporary Scrapbook Performance," in *Material Vernaculars: Objects, Images, and Their Social Worlds*, ed. Jason Baird Jackson (Indiana University Press, 2016), 40–104 (81).

19. Walter Benjamin, "Unpacking My Library," in *Illuminations*, ed. Hannah Arendt (Schocken Books, 1968), 59–67; Jean Baudrillard, "The System of Collecting," in *The Cultures of Collecting*, ed. John Ellsner and Roger Cardinal (Harvard University Press, 1994), 7–24; Werner Muensterberger, *Collecting: An Unruly Passion* (Princeton University Press, 1994); Susan Pearce, *On Collecting: An Investigation into Collecting in the European Tradition* (Routledge, 1995); Marjorie Swann, *Curiosities and Texts: The Culture of Collecting in Early Modern England* (University of Pennsylvania Press, 2001); as well as more recent investigations by Lincoln Geraghty, *Cult Collectors: Nostalgia, Fandom, and Collecting Popular Culture* (Routledge, 2014), and Henry Jenkins, *Comics and Stuff* (New York University Press, 2020). Swann's research on collecting especially addresses how an overlap between categories of "author" and "collector," as well as "text" and "object," developed in early modern England.

20. See Swann, *Curiosities and Texts*; Patrick Mauries, *Cabinets of Curiosities* (Thames and Hudson, 2002); Daniela Bleichmar, "Learning to Look: Visual Expertise across Art and Science in Eighteenth-Century France," *Eighteenth-Century Studies* 46, no. 1 (2014): 85–111.
21. Judith Pascoe, *The Hummingbird Cabinet: A Rare and Curious History of Romantic Collectors* (Cornell University Press, 2006), 5.
22. Woloson, *Crap*, 20–21.
23. Christiansen, "(Not) Going Public, 40–104; Paul R. Mullins, "The Rhetoric of Things: Historical Archeology and Oral History," *Historical Archaeology* 4, no. 1 (2014): 105–9 (105).
24. Adalgisa Lugli, "Inquiry as Collection: The Athanasius Kircher Museum in Rome," *RES: Anthropology and Aesthetics* 12 (1986): 109–24 (110–11).
25. Potts, *Souvenir*, 43.
26. Greenblatt, "Resonance and Wonder," 11–34 (19–20).
27. Lugli, "Inquiry as Collection," 123. Such decontextualized encounter was eventually idealized in the exhibition of fine art, often in competition with the more didactic approaches of history museum displays (Lubar, *Inside the Lost Museum*, 180). Barbara Kirshenblatt-Gimblett even identified "confusion" as a source of pleasure among avant-garde music audiences, who embraced decontextualization as a means to encounter a performance directly, without the mediating frames of scholarly criticism (*Destination Culture*, 249–56).
28. Greenblatt, "Resonance and Wonder," 28.
29. Kirshenblatt-Gimblett, *Destination Culture*, 25; Mauries, *Cabinets of Curiosities*, 66.
30. Woloson, *Crap*, 28.
31. Mauries, *Cabinets of Curiosities*, 66.
32. DeSilvey, "Salvage Memory," 401.
33. Orhan Pamuk, *The Innocence of Objects* (Abrams, 2012), 52. Lawrence Weschler notes that Sir Francis Bacon, in 1594, was among the first to describe the effect of "singularity, chance, and the shuffle of things" among miscellanies (*Mr Wilson's Cabinet of Wonder: Pronged Ants, Horned Humans, Mice on Toast, and other Marvels of Jurassic Technology* [Vintage Books, 1997], 76). For a compelling theory about this effect, see Jane Bennett's more recent discussion about the "agency of assemblages" in *Vibrant Matter: A Political Ecology of Things* (Duke University Press, 2009), 20–38.
34. Lorraine Daston and Katharine Park, *Wonders and the Order of Nature, 1150–1750* (Zone Books, 1998), 266.
35. Celeste Mary Williams, "The Cabinet of Dr. Linnaeus: The Reemergence of the Wunderkammer as a Counterpoint to Established Museum Architecture," *Proceedings of the Association of Collegiate Schools of Architecture: Encounters Encuentros Recontres* 26 (2005): 218–26 (205), and Daston and Park, *Wonders and the Order of Nature*, 255.
36. Lubar, *Inside the Lost Museum*, 185.
37. Woloson, *Crap*, 22, 47.
38. Anthony Anemone, "The Monsters of Peter the Great: The Culture of the St. Petersburg Kunstkamera in the Eighteenth Century," *The Slavic and East European Journal* 44, no. 4 (2000): 583–602 (589).
39. Bleichmar, "Learning to Look," 96.
40. Daston and Park, *Wonders and the Order of Nature*, 276.
41. E.C. Spary, "On the Ironic Specimen of the Unicorn Horn in Enlightened Cabinets," *Journal of Social History* 52, no. 4 (2019): 1033–60.
42. Pascoe, *Hummingbird Cabinet*.
43. Steven Lubar, *Inside the Lost Museum*.
44. For a general overview of the changing meanings of museum objects, see Samuel M. Alberti, "Object and the Museum," *Isis* 96, no. 4 (2005): 559–71.

45. Roland Barthes, "The Death of the Author," *Aspen* 5 & 6 (1968); Wolfgang Iser, "The Reading Process: A Phenomenological Approach," *New Literary History* 3, no. 2 (1972): 279–99; Stanley Fish, "Interpreting the Variorum," *Critical Inquiry* 2, no. 3 (1976): 465–85.
46. Leonard Meyer, *Emotion and Meaning in Music* (University of Chicago Press, 1956), 43–82; Steven Feld, "Communication, Music, and Speech About Music," in *Music Grooves: Essays and Dialogues*, ed. Charles Keil and Steven Feld (University of Chicago Press, 1994), 77–95.
47. Gwyneira Isaac, "What Are Our Expectations Telling Us? Encounters with the NMAI," *American Indian Quarterly* 30, no. 3/4 (2006): 574–96; Ivan Gaskill, "Encountering Pacific Art," *Journal of Museum Ethnography* 21 (2009): 202–10.
48. *Museum Objects: Experiencing the Properties of Things*, ed. Sandra H. Dudley (Routledge Press, 2012), 1–15; Philipp W. Stockhammer, "Lost in Things: An Archaeologist's Perspective on the Epistemological Potential of Objects," *Nature and Culture* 10, no. 3 (2015): 269–83; Sonia Hazard, "Thing," *Early American Studies* 16, no. 4 (2018): 792–800; Martin Saxer and Philipp Schorch, "Introduction: Materiality and Connectivity," in *Exploring Materiality and Connectivity in Anthropology and Beyond*, ed. Martin Saxer, Philipp Schorch, and Marlen Elders (UCL Press, 2020), 1–14.
49. Feld, "Communication, Music, and Speech About Music," 86–87.
50. Feld, "Communication, Music, and Speech About Music," 84.
51. See, for example, Chip Colwell and Lindsay M. Montgomery, *Objects of Survivance: A Material History of the American Indian School Experience* (University Press of Colorado, 2019).
52. Kopytoff, "The Cultural Biography of Things," 68.
53. Barbara Appelbaum, "Criteria for Treatment of Collections Housed in Historic Structures," *Journal of the American Institute for Conservation* 33, no. 2 (1994): 185–91; Franklin Vagnone, Deborah Ryan, and Olivia Cothren, "The Anarchist Guide to Historic House Museums: Evaluation Methodology for Historic House Museums," *The Public Historian* 37, no. 2 (2015): 97–111.
54. Ran Zwigenberg, "Modern Relics: The Sanctification of A-Bomb Objects in the Hiroshima Museum," *Holocaust and Genocide Studies* 35, no. 1 (2021): 44–62.
55. Arjun Appadurai, "The Thing Itself," *Public Culture* 18, no. 1 (2006): 15–21 (16).
56. Brown, "Thing Theory," 4.
57. Appadurai, "The Thing Itself," 15.
58. Stockhammer, "Doing/Changing Things/Us," 39–43.

CHAPTER 3

GHOST STORIES

JOHN P. JACOB

The popularity of recent exhibitions and books of found photography suggests an end-of-an-era nostalgia among their audiences.[1] The transformation of the vernacular family photograph into an object of material culture affirms an end to visual communication as we have known it, and to memory as conditioned by nearly two centuries of domestic photography. In its new setting, the snapshot now stands for an idealized mode of remembrance under pressure from the digital camera's delete button, and for privacy under pressure from the pervasive use of imaging systems for public surveillance. It stands, that is, at the intersection of changing technologies, where the analog itself has become a rueful signifier of collective self-identity.[2] The attraction to such photographs, like that of our eighteenth- and nineteenth-century forebears to ruins, points to a transhistorical yearning, a yearning for the re-enchantment of images.

To yearn for re-enchantment is to acknowledge that images were enchanted in the first place, but now they are not. It is to acknowledge an age of the image that is different from our own, to which we retain some access, if only through our yearning.[3] Indeed, it is through our yearning that this other age makes itself known to us. The attraction to found pictures is its symptom in the contemporary observer. It points to a past age of non-differentiation between image and reality made more poignant by being irrecoverable. As the Rousseauean citizen recognizes the state of nature through his or her irrevocable separation from it, so we experience the non-differentiation from images as if from across a divide. Hence, the attraction of the snapshot, which points to a life that it alone substantiates and of which death is its sole condition. In this way, I argue that it points to a particular, of which it is the surviving agent, and to a purpose in which the viewer has a role to play.

The found photograph was unthinkable in the early decades following the invention of photography. First, photographers democratized portraiture, the declining costs of the new medium making visits to the portrait studio cheap and readily accessible. Then, in the late nineteenth century, the first generations of portrait sitters began to die. War accelerated the proliferation of photography. A flood of images, unprecedented and unstoppable, was set into motion by death. It would take generations to complete the passage from keepsake to commodity. Today, pictures circulate freely, entering our homes and our cultural institutions. The dead move among the living as lost and found pictures, inciting among some a deep attraction and among many a great unease. Our ambivalence is symptomatic of a repressed anxiety surrounding images concerning their destruction no less than their survival. That apprehension is renewed by the ghostly return of images, formerly intimate objects of affection and regard now circulating within networks of economic or aesthetic exchange.

The term "found photography" refers to a cultural practice of the late twentieth century whose subject and material were the images that constitute this flood. It describes the fate of such images, even when we find them in our own junk drawers and attics. In this essay, I write about discarded photographs.[4] "Found" implies that a thing has been lost and subsequently recovered, but what is at issue with family pictures is their disposal. My thesis is that we sometimes receive images as persons, not merely as things, in an encounter that is transactional. Something of the subject's particularity sticks to it, and from time to time will speak to me as I peruse the bins at the flea market. Indeed, how else to describe the bizarre attraction of discarded photographs, which we can purchase, collect, and mingle with our own family pictures? The photograph's life, set into motion by death, defines our own age of the image. Whispering their secrets and rattling the mystic chains of recollection, the flood of images is nothing less than a haunting.

The disposal of images is a frightful, superstitious matter. Disposal marks the end of ritual, of the continuity expressed by passing family photographs from one hand to another. It initiates a transformation, but to what? Roland Barthes wrote that disposal marks the end of the perishable thing: "The only way I can transform the Photograph is into refuse: either the drawer or the wastebasket."[5] This assertion raises two questions, the first concerning the anxiety aroused by such an act, and the second concerning the afterlife of the photograph that survives it. The household drawer is the place to which photographs are relegated when we do not fully recognize ourselves or a loved one in them. It is the space of forgetting images that we encounter as fragments of a self, whose failure to represent wholly we regard as making them too disruptive for public use, but not so unsettling that we are compelled to destroy them. Art historian Carol Mavor described the drawer as, like the photograph itself, "a space between life and death."[6] It is a holding space, halfway between the album and the wastebasket.

The album and the drawer are exemplary sites of encounter with the photograph for understanding the photograph as souvenir, which is the first of four metaphors I shall introduce to explore the operations of the photograph in such encounters. As a metaphor of use, the souvenir encompasses both the context of origin of the snapshot, its social event, and the limit case, its photographic event. A limit case, philosopher Barry Miller wrote, differs from the series or class of things that it is, as he showed with the example of speed.[7] The maximum speed, the speed of light, is the logical or conceptual completion of a series of possible speeds.

As such, it is a limit. The minimum speed is not a speed at all; zero is the absence of speed. As such, it is a limit case. Both are endpoints of a series, but limits are themselves part of the series, whereas limit cases stand outside it.

Applied to photography, the limit case is the photographic event that the image endlessly replicates but can never reproduce. What does this mean? The snapshot replicates the social event that it records, which is simultaneously the context of origin of the picture and the limit case of photography. The context of origin is the setting of the event recorded, both enframed by the image and inscribed in memory by its maker/subject. Because the event recorded is always temporally distant, as poet Susan Stewart observes, the souvenir points "to an increasingly abstract, and hence an increasingly 'lost' set of referents."[8] A part that references its whole as does object to experience, it is incomplete without the narrative supplement of its possessor. The photograph as souvenir "is a logical extension of the pressed flower," Stewart writes, "the preservation of an instant in time through the reduction of physical dimensions and a corresponding increase in significance supplied by means of narrative."[9]

As distinct from its context of origin, or social event, the limit case is its photographic event, the union of subject and object at the instant of its making. The social event may be replicated as image, but the photographic event, which is past, may not. For its maker/subject, use makes the souvenir phenomenally transparent. Indeed, its experience as transparent is exclusive to that use. "There they are!" I say, pointing to a decades-old snapshot I took of my grandparents, both of whom have long since passed. A thing activated by language, my snapshot brings forth the past-presence of the event recorded, and my transhistorical presence (present in the present and present in the past) as maker then and observer now. Photography is a medium of experience, and it is a medium of time. The temporal operations of the photograph are no less important than its mimetic and narrative operations, and those operations are variable from one setting of encounter, or use, to another.

We may make visible the affective relations of the souvenir by considering queer theorist Sara Ahmed's concept of an affective economy of signs. "[E]motions work as a form of capital," she writes, arguing that emotional value attaches to things, and does so differently from one setting of use to another.[10] The memorial token arouses affect for its recipient, for example, but does so differently for one outside the network of exchange that attaches emotional value to it, the family or community. Because "affect does not reside positively in the sign or commodity but is produced only as an effect of its circulation," therefore, the more things circulate within specific networks, moving along a specified path, "the more affective they become, and the more they appear to 'contain' affect," which we experience as intensity.[11] The more things circulate, the more affect they appear to contain, and the more we experience them through the intensity of our emotional attachments.

The photograph is not an ordinary sign, however. Because of the emotional intensity I attach to it as the limit case, I may say of my snapshot of my grandparents, "There they are!" Its affect is to affirm the ontological status of its subjects, solidifying my emotional attachment to them. Unlike the word, which Ahmed describes emotion as "passing by," the photograph is causally rigid in relation to its referent.[12] This was Barthes's essential discovery: "[I]nescapably," he wrote, "I passed beyond the unreality of the thing represented, I entered crazily into the spectacle, into the image, taking into my arms what is dead, what is going to die."[13] Value attaches to photographs differently from signs that emotion passes through. Within an economy of signs, the souvenir is not just a currency of knowing, but also one of being. We experience its temporality not as past or present, but as past *and* present; a simultaneity. It is this that I have described earlier as the phenomenal transparency of the souvenir, which is exclusive to it.

When the souvenir outlasts its original use, it enters into a setting of encounter with a user who is not its maker/subject, becoming an object of exchange. I use metaphor to organize and make visible the operations of the photograph as it moves from one setting of encounter to another. The operations of the photograph as souvenir may be formulated as: (a) the reference to the event recorded, and (b) the narrative supplement of its possessor (the maker/subject). The narrative supplement is what I bring to the photograph that is already inscribed in memory as maker/subject. Because the souvenir typifies an exclusive relationship of maker/subject to thing, other metaphors of use must be formulated for different types of exchange. I shall add three such metaphors to that of the souvenir. These are not the only possible settings of encounter with the photograph, of course, but several that help track its mobility beyond its context of origin. When the photograph outlasts its original use, but maintains its relation to a specified path, it does so as heirloom. Diverted from that path in a commodity context, it will be encountered as antique. In addition to these, I shall introduce a fourth metaphor, the photograph as relic. It is through this fourth metaphor that I shall interrogate the attraction of discarded photographs.

In fact, as sociologist Pierre Bourdieu observed, the souvenir is always potentially mobile. Bourdieu described photographs as joining "the circuit of gifts and counter-gifts" that typifies social events such as weddings and funerals.[14] Gift exchange is inherently integrative, a means of articulating family and community bonds across temporal and spatial distances. Because it is often embedded in kinship rituals, gift exchange is usually recognized not as an economic system, but as a social system in which things of value circulate without any explicit expectation of future returns. Rather than considering its exchange-value within one such setting or another, my objective is to track the photograph as it circulates between them, becoming an independent thing and acquiring a new identity at each step of the way.

Having outlasted its original use, the photograph now exemplifies what anthropologist Arjun Appadurai terms the "commodity situation" of exchanged things. As they circulate, Appadurai writes, things undergo a reordering of their use and valuation. The commodity situation encompasses the constancy of that reordering. Appadurai argues that the commodity is not a particular kind of thing, but a stage in the social lives of some things. He defines exchange-value as that which endows a thing with mobility, such that "its exchangeability (past, present, or future) for some other thing is its socially relevant feature."[15] The commodity situation encompasses a trajectory that is sometimes characterized by economic relations, but always characterized by social and affective relations.

We may observe the photograph as an object of exchange, as described by Bourdieu, in the circulation of photographic mourning jewelry. In the nineteenth century, this practice conjoined two more ancient customs: the making of memorial portraits, often in the form of painted miniatures, and the exchange of tokens of the recently dead. In Colonial America, guests at a funeral often received such tokens from the family of the deceased. According to historian David E. Stannard, different objects were typical of different places. In New York, for example, silver spoons were customary as gifts, while in Massachusetts, gloves, scarves, and rings were more common.[16] These were marked with birth and death dates, and sometimes with symbols such as skeletons or death's-heads. After the invention of the daguerreotype, jewelers quickly adapted photography to the mourning apparatus.[17] Early photographic mourning jewelry was made by duplicating a preexisting painted portrait. In the late nineteenth century, the ritual of hiring a limner to paint a posthumous portrait was supplanted by a lifetime visit to the photographic studio.

During that period, too, the glove or ring was succeeded by a wide variety of photographic accessories. Photographic pins and buttons were popular during the daguerreotype and tintype eras and could be manufactured in large numbers after the invention of celluloid. Lockets and pendants, made for more private viewing, were enclosed in a mourner's pocket or dangled from a necklace and held near the body of the bereaved. These intimate objects were often accompanied by a plaited lock of hair, transforming them into reliquaries. Such portraits were viewed, and sometimes made, in observance of the anniversary of a death. In posthumously made mourning photographs, visual signifiers of absence, such as the empty chair or the funeral garland, were easily recognizable.[18] In relation to the late nineteenth century's culture of mourning, it was not uncommon for members of a community to amass large personal collections of memorial jewelry. Such collections are exemplary as the setting of encounter for our second metaphor, the photograph as heirloom.

The commodity phase of a photograph's social life is initiated by its movement from private use to gift exchange. In its use as heirloom, the maker/subject of the souvenir is succeeded by the recipient of the gift. This change in use also initiates a variation in temporality. Whereas the souvenir asserts presence, the souvenir transformed to heirloom asserts pastness. No longer capable of performing its original use, it becomes meaningful in relation to the pastness of that use. In its new setting, the photograph now asserts the perpetual finality of the preserved thing. Passed on to my daughter, thereby moving along a specified path, my snapshot of my grandparents will retain a meaningful relatedness to a past use that its preservation substantiates. One step removed from its context of origin, however, it will also be experienced as proportionally distanced from the limit case. I may pass on my pictures, but not their original use, and not the subtle beyond of each that its viewing evokes for me. Exchange opens the photograph to a secondary action, the displacement of its narrative operations. The photograph, undergoing this transaction, acquires a new identity. Its operations may be formulated as: (a) the reference to the event recorded, and (b) the narrative supplement of its possessor (the recipient). The heirloom establishes a metonymical relatedness by discontinuity, substituting the name for the thing. Passed on to my daughter as heirloom, my snapshot's identity will be "Dad's grandparents."

To the characteristics of a general commodity situation, Appadurai adds the concept of paths and diversions. Within any regulated system of exchange, he writes, "[t]he diversion of commodities from specified paths is always a sign of creativity or crisis, whether aesthetic or economic."[19] In relation to the photograph, the souvenir, as an exclusive relationship of maker/subject to thing, is a setting of use but not necessarily one of exchange. Gift exchange initiates a specified path, and the path of the heirloom is from maker/subject to recipient, a variation in the photograph's use that distances it from the limit case, its photographic event. The heirloom becomes newly meaningful in relation to a past use, of which it affirms both an end and an enduring relatedness. It is not only the image that performs its maker/subject's agency, however. The recipient must also be a desirous target of that agency. Thus, the recipient of the heirloom becomes not just a carrier of images, but also a carrier of the dead through images.

In memorial settings such as the personal collection, the heirloom enacts the maker/subject's agency in relation to a past use. Something of the maker/subject's particularity sticks to it. When, at last, the discarded photograph surfaces at the flea market or the photographic fair, it does so as a commodity. As gift exchange initiates a shift from the maker/subject to the recipient, so commoditization initiates a shift to the finder/possessor. At the flea market, encountered in bins of like pictures, the discarded photograph becomes recoverable when the finder/possessor attaches her values to it. If it is exemplary either pictorially or of its class, then my desire for it as an object is aroused. As finder/possessor, my desire exceeds the narrative operations of its context of origin, and the thing takes on the values I attribute to it. That attribution becomes its new identity.

In the antique, as I refer to the photograph diverted from a specified path, whatever attachments had accrued to it through its circulation are severed from it. The thing without recourse to the name is no longer capable of saying what it shows. The operations of the antique may be formulated as: (a) the reference to the event recorded, and (b) the narrative displacement of its possessor (the finder/possessor). The antique retains the metonymical reference of part to whole but abstracted from any capacity for meaningful presence. It is an index that points to itself, becoming a courier of the values attached to it. The narrative displacement of the finder/possessor is a substitution in the sense described by Susan Stewart as arousing "the social disease of nostalgia."[20] It does so by wrenching things metaphorically into the present. The antique photograph becomes, for example, a wall decoration, arousing nostalgia through the allure of its sepia tone. Severed from its particularity, but persisting as a temporally disordered trace, it asserts an aura of pastness in the present.

Our fourth metaphor, the photograph as relic, is the antithesis of the Bourdieuan souvenir. Within the framework described by Bourdieu, the photograph ritualizes existing social roles by capturing behavior that is socially approved and regulated; the souvenir validates the photograph as an object of exchange. In this setting, the photograph that outlives its maker/subject continues to perform a normative task, fulfilling the function of funeral rites. Psychology arrives at a similar conception of the photograph as a transitional object in the work of mourning. In her admittedly brief formulation of the relic, Stewart has something different in mind. "If the function of the souvenir proper is to create a continuous and personal narrative of the past," she writes, "the function of such souvenirs of death is to disrupt and disclaim that continuity." A surviving trace of the corpse, Stewart's relic signals "the end of sacred narrative and the interjection of the curse." Curiously, her conception is related not to the miraculous properties of sanctified body parts revered by medieval Christians, but to the "malicious magic of voodoo."[21] From the perspective of psychology, Stewart's description is closer to the operations of the fetish. While the photograph may be useful as a transitional object in the work of mourning, other uses characterize the fetish by extending its psychical burden. For her, the displacement of death constitutes an averse or deviant use when pictures of the deceased are carried on the body of the bereaved as a means of holding on to that which has been cut away and belong to the order of fetishes. Put differently, a fetish is the sign of an inappropriate or unhealthy attachment, a thing from which emotional attachment has not been permitted to pass through. For our purposes, what distinguishes the fetish is its resistance to the normative use of the heirloom. In protracting the work of mourning, the bereaved isolates from a community that demands reintegration. As the photograph becomes a site of anxiety for its possessor, so the possessor becomes a site of anxiety for their community.

Stewart's formulation is inconsistent with the relic's work. She refers to the concept of voodoo death, or death by suggestion, performed by a priest using a doll, or fetish, endowed with magical properties. The doll is not malicious, however, any more than the photograph is deviant. What makes either of them fearsome is an antisocial usage. The medieval relic, by contrast, was socially beneficent, and encountered not as index but as person. To become usable as relics, ostensibly ordinary objects were subject to a testing of their efficacy. The medieval relic was required to prove its status by working wonders. The relics of saints performed miracles worthy of those saints and were recognizable to their observers as such. The cult of the relic was thus dependent upon its work, tales of which were authenticated as text by hagiography, and by its enclosure in the reliquary, a symbolic counterpart of the text. A physically detached fragment of the saint whose agency it enacts, the relic operates not by signification but by doing, which becomes a sign in its own right.[22]

Why is a metaphor of the relic necessary? As metaphor, the antique organizes things in relation to commoditization and helps make visible how those things have been mediated and interpreted from one commodity setting to another. It cannot illuminate the affective relations of discarded photographs circulating freely. Consider Barthes's account of his discovery of the Winter Garden Photograph in *Camera Lucida* (1981). Found in a box or drawer, the encounter occurred in that space described earlier as between life and death. Leafing through his mother's personal collection, he described "gradually moving back in time with her."[23] Having figuratively experienced her birth through the reversal of their roles during her illness, Barthes then experienced her birth in pictures through the reversal of time in her photographs. "This movement of the Photograph (of the order of photographs) I have experienced in reality," he wrote.[24] His experience was opposite that of the antiquarian, who displaces the narrative of the photograph by wrenching it metaphorically into the present. Rather, Barthes described "going through" and again "sorting" his mother's photographs in search of an essence.[25] When he found it, the discovery disrupted time, the photograph becoming a souvenir of death for him. "There she is!" he cried out.[26] A new limit case was established, uniting the subject and the viewer of the photograph at the instant of its temporal and narrative disruption.

The Winter Garden Photograph was a found photograph, but the metaphor that best organizes its use is the heirloom. Retaining its relatedness to a specified path, the heirloom becomes newly meaningful in relation to a past use, which is its essence. Essence as such is the unique meaningfulness of the beholder, which the metonymic substitution of the name for the thing brings forth as presence. Literary theorist Hans Ulrich Gumbrecht suggests that, in certain circumstances, "language being open toward the world of things," can produce presence-effects.[27] That was certainly true of Barthes's encounter. The Winter Garden Photograph produced an accord that could only be expressed through "a series of adjectives."[28] Collecting in itself "all the possible predicates from which my mother's being was constituted," it brought forth "a sentiment as certain as remembrance," but one that was not remembrance because its object was real.[29] "There she is!" is the ekstasis of the encounter with the photograph as relic. A "strictly revulsive movement which reverses the course of the thing," he named it "the photographic ecstasy."[30]

Visual culture scholar Shawn Michelle Smith observes that Barthes's approach to the photograph—passing "into the spectacle, into the image, taking into my arms what is dead, what is going to die"—constitutes a new modality of encounter with photographs.[31] "Entering into a photograph," she writes, "one might embrace its subject, allowing one's self to be touched, without demanding reference or representation. One might identify without consuming or subsuming the other."[32] The potentiality of photographic ecstasy, as she has noted elsewhere, was predicated on Barthes retaining "an affective intentionality."[33] "Affect was what I didn't want to reduce," he declared.[34] The metonymy of the relic, making past things present, is the wellspring of photographic ecstasy. It is for this reason, finally, that a metaphor of the relic is necessary. In addition to the antiquarian, we require a reliquarian, who affirms affective intentionality and the potential of photographic ecstasy.

The antiquarian, without recourse to the photograph's context of origin, displaces its story. Whether at the flea market or in the museum, that displacement is its transformation into material culture, the substitution of the name with an identity. Our fourth metaphor does not insist that the discarded photograph is always a relic, but that, in certain circumstances, it produces affective relations as one. By encountering such photographs as targets and sources of agency, we open ourselves as targets and sources of desire. The operations of the photograph as relic may be formulated as: (a) the reference to the event recorded, and (b) a narrative reawakening by its possessor (the beholder). I have noted that, in its movement from souvenir to heirloom to antique, as the photograph grows distant from its limit case, its photographic event, it becomes mute in relation to its context of origin, its social event. The antiquarian, having no recourse to the context of origin, displaces its story, creating a narrative disorder proportional to the temporal one. The reliquarian, reinscribing the photograph with the desire of being, awakens its story, which is now a ghost story. It is that desire that brings forth from the mute object a sentiment as certain as remembrance, albeit an impossible memory.

I have argued that the operations of the photograph are variable according to its settings of use. This is also to say that photographs are performative. Observing them as such, we bring into focus both the essential maker/subject as distinct from his or her reiterative gestures and the essential qualities of images in relation to ourselves, as embodied observers. It is in this transaction that some photographs speak to me. Turning now to examples, the photographs I shall consider, some from Barbara Von Eckardt's *Junk Drawer* project, date roughly from the 1850s to the 1950s. Those hundred years were a transitional period in the self-representation of the portrait subject that occurred in parallel to the larger historical shift in photography, from the studio era to that of the snapshot. In each of the following examples, the expression of identity by the sitter breaks through the conventionality of the portrait. Not every portrait exceeds the banality of convention, of course; these are simply among the ones that, in doing so, have spoken to me. By considering their surplus of identity, mirroring their subjects' affective postures with my own, I open myself to an impossible memory, a new limit case.

A snapshot from one of Von Eckardt's junk drawers (PLATE 0.16) may be classified as a vernacular family photograph. Its message (home, family, plenty) is self-evident. Now consider its circulation as an object of exchange. Beginning with its context of origin, this snapshot has (a) served as souvenir for its maker/subjects, for whom it was already mobile through (b) its enclosure in a frame, likely viewed standing with other framed images. Perhaps it was then (c) passed from hand to hand as heirloom. It was eventually (d) disposed of. Diverted from its specified path, the snapshot embarked upon the commodity phase of its career. It was then (e) found or bought by a dealer, acquiring a new identity as a thing of potential economic value. It was then (f) purchased by Von Eckardt, acquiring a further new identity as exemplary of the junk drawer. The snapshot (g) resides physically with Von Eckardt, one among other like objects authenticating her *Junk Drawer* collection. It also (h) resides digitally on the hard drive of my computer, the setting of my encounter with it. Finally, (i) serving as an illustration for this text, it exemplifies the metaphor of the photograph as antique.

What attracted Von Eckardt to this picture? How has it spoken to her? In this essay, I am investigating as objective an experience with photographs that is purely subjective, but not at all uncommon. That is the experience of photographic presence, the intrusion of the past into the present through photographs. Just as the attraction to discarded photographs is necessarily subjective, so the language to communicate the experience of photographic presence is necessarily descriptive. In describing my subjectivity, I am embodying content. I become the medium of the photographs I describe, enacting their conveyance of affect. It is not the photograph that opens to its beholder, but the beholder who opens to it. Likewise, the voice of the photograph is not a voice at all, but an openness of the beholder. Encountered with affective intentionality, the voice and my response to it are inseparable. Launching an associative chain of images, my affective response is a mutual attachment. Animating the beheld, the story that chain tells becomes my story.

What struck me on first viewing Von Eckardt's photograph was the peculiarity of its space. A couple stands for their photograph on a brick and stone slab stair. Behind them, four figures stand behind a screen door watching. The proximity of the camera to the central figures has had a foreshortening effect, making the figures behind them appear oddly small. Its eye-level placement with a second set of stairs behind the couple has had a flattening effect, making the enclosed space above them, and the figures in it, seem to float. These are typical flaws of snapshot photography that give the picture its visual charm. What moves me in the photograph, however, is the performance of its story by its participants. Whether it records a wedding or an anniversary, an arrival or a departure, each figure in it, including the unseen maker, is enacting that event's commemoration. Each is a maker/subject of the image. Each will bring to its later viewing the "There they are!" of the souvenir, which is inscribed both in the image and in memory through their enactments.

However these photographs have come to us, we have a role to play. The public stories of private lives and values were created and deliberately preserved by their makers for future generations of unknown viewers. They have found us and would speak to us if we could listen. From another of Von Eckardt's junk drawers comes a group of images that she has titled "Twelve Small Wedding Photos" (PLATE 0.35). Here, as in the previous example, the subjects are all enacting the commemoration of an event, and that event is plainly a wedding. The photographs are snapshots made by an amateur photographer, likely a guest with a handheld camera. By their grouping on the page here, the snapshots are reminiscent of a family album; more than just wedding photos, they are legible affirmations of family ties. As a memento that records its subjects in relation to their social group, the wedding photograph is a souvenir in the sense described by Bourdieu. It ritualizes existing social roles by capturing behavior that is socially approved and regulated, which it also validates as an object of exchange. While this is related to the concept of an affective economy of images, Bourdieu did not anticipate the disposal of photographs and their circulation beyond the social milieu. The discarded photograph has no socially approved function, therefore the encounter with it requires of the viewer an affective intentionality beyond what can be accommodated within the Bourdieuan framework.

I have suggested that we must think of photographs as no less importantly mimetic than temporal. Photography is a medium of time, and time invokes the voice of the maker/subject, the oratory of the photograph. On the one hand, historical pictures seem to speak more readily because the affective interplay of subjects in and with images was more commonly practiced in the past than it is by makers now. Early photographic processes may be accurately described as having fixed the very light reflected from the subject onto the glass or metal plate. The invention of the negative/positive process introduced a distance to the encounter, as the paper print is one step removed from its source. The digital camera adds further distance, for it cannot be viewed without a display and all the hardware and software therein. Yet, as *Camera Lucida* insisted, it is only "in relation to what we romantically call love and death" that the voice of the relic may be encountered.[35] The discarded photograph does not become anonymous as much as it becomes unloved. The found photograph asks that we love what we cannot name. On the other hand, my next examples are temporally closer to the prototypes that they index, and that proximity is powerfully affective for me.

I shall now consider examples from my own collection of discarded photographs, describing the affective encounter with them. FIGURE 3.1 is a quarter-plate tintype. On its surface, the dotted pattern of an overlying brass mat, now missing, is visible. To the right of the subject stands the photographer's white reflecting wall, which the mat would have covered. Made before the adoption of artificial lighting, the shutters of a studio skylight would have been used to direct sunlight onto the subject, and the movable partition to reflect light onto her face. This technique created a diffuse, even effect, softening any unusual shadows that might have been created by the skylight alone. In our privileged view of the photograph, as unmatted, we find evidence not only of its maker, but also of the care with which it was preserved by its subject. Roughly cut to 3½ × 4½ inches, too large to hold or carry comfortably, its size and markings suggest that it was once framed and viewed hanging against a wall.

The subject sits on a chair, the back of which is just visible behind her. She reclines gently to the left side of the photograph, leaning against an upholstered prop. She is wearing a detailed taffeta dress, belted at the waist and open at the neck, where it is secured by a leaf-shaped brooch. Around her neck hangs a simple string necklace with a heart-shaped clasp. On her knee rests a handbag, and on her head a floral-patterned tiara. Her perfect curls have been draped across her shoulders, exposing her neck and echoing the flow of her dress. The dress fills the bottom third of the picture. The photographer has colored her brooch and belt buckle and applied a dot of gold to her ear. Her eyes have been painted blue with such subtlety that the detail was almost unnoticeable for me until I was drawn to it by her gaze. Then I observed what the camera has revealed, which a painter of the period would likely have hidden: the pale skin of her face is spotted with youthful freckles.

FIGURES 3.1 and 3.2 are both portraits of women using nearly identical conventions. In both photographs, the figure is centrally posed, and her face is sharply focused and well illuminated. FIGURE 3.1 emphasizes possession, both the sitter's physical and material possessions, whose importance to the portrait the photographer has indicated through pose and with his markings, and the sitter's self possession as subject, which becomes an offering through the directness of her gaze. Moreover, the sitter is holding something. One of her hands falls loosely against the upholstered prop. On the other, just above the wrist, she wears a chain bracelet. This hand, placed near the center of the photograph, rests against her bag and is slightly open. She is holding something but not revealing it.

FIGURE 3.2 emphasizes dispossession. In this example, the light directed onto its subject's face is sufficient to reveal a white lace collar decorated at the neck with a wide grosgrain ribbon. Beneath her shoulders, the sitter's figure disappears into darkness. All that is visible in the lower two-thirds of the photograph is the hand in her lap. This woman is also holding something, but it is effaced by darkness. With no further evidence of its maker,

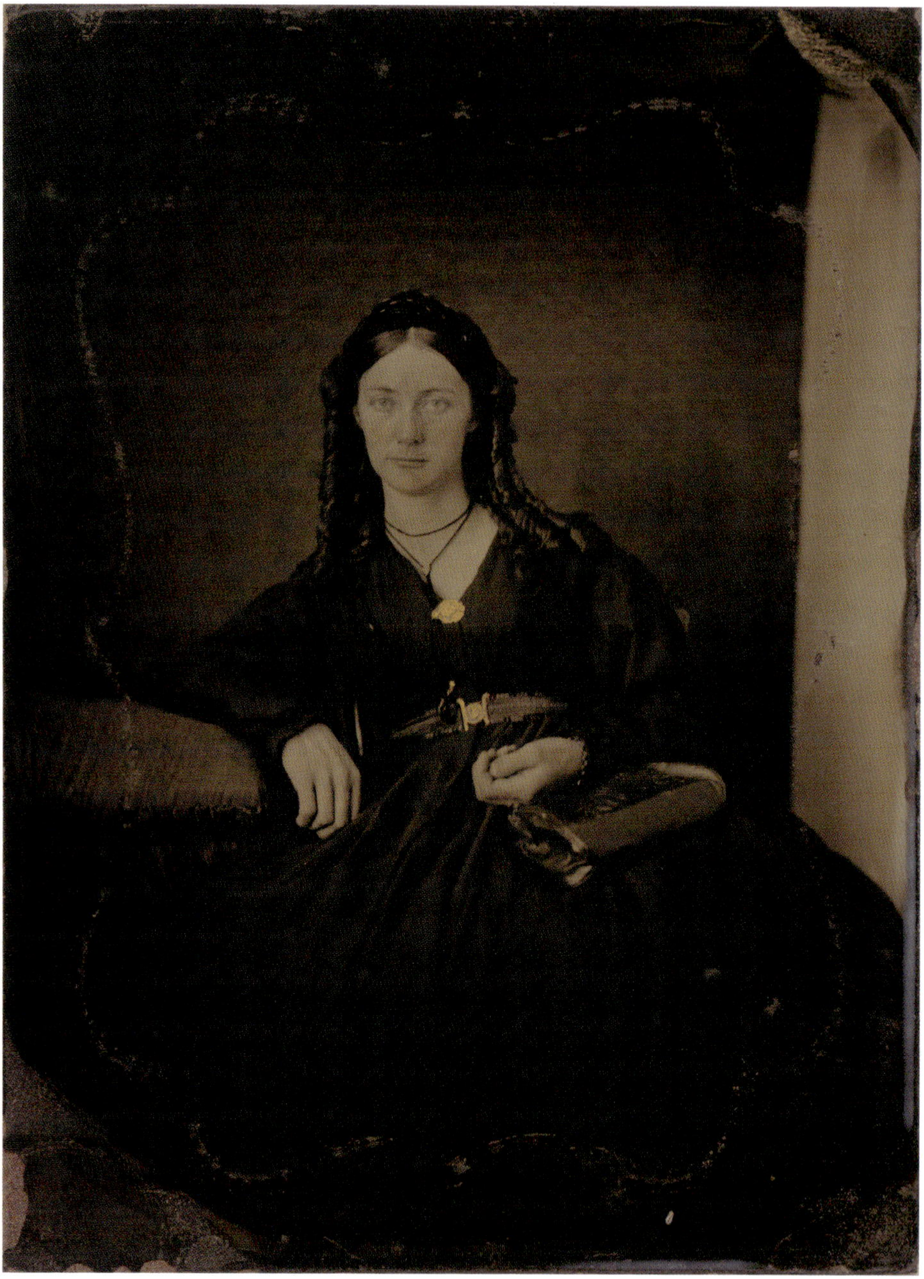

FIGURE 3.1. Portrait of a woman, n.d., tintype photograph.

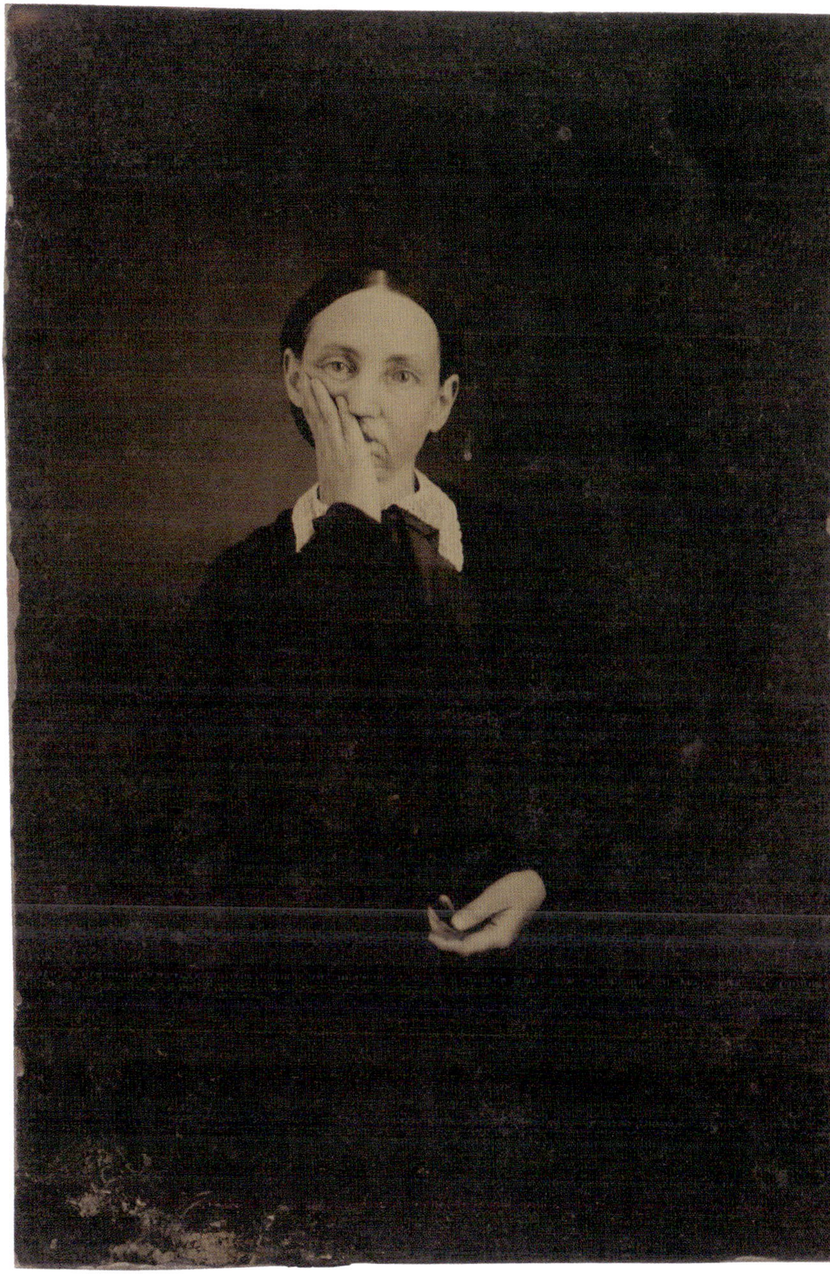

FIGURE 3.2. Portrait of a woman, n.d., tintype photograph.

it is impossible to know if the dramatic chiaroscuro of FIGURE 3.2, cloaking the sitter, was deliberate. Intentional or not, the implied withdrawal into shadows is highly affective.

In both examples, the photographers have used the same conventions of pose and lighting, yet each tells a different story, and my affective response to each is different. Turning to the subject, it is through the face, and the hands, that possession and dispossession are articulated so uniquely, so individually, by each. The nineteenth-century subject, whose body was completely enshrouded by her clothing, learned to communicate by other means. She was an expert of affective posture, the full embodiment of communication. The instrumentality of the body, which in nineteenth-century painting was largely denied to its subject by the idealizing gaze, is unfailingly revealed in the photograph. That is its pathos, to which I, as its beholder, unfailingly respond. Both photographs are, I believe, commemorative but of what is not clear. The commemorative nature of each is indicated by what its subject is holding, which is both given and withdrawn from the photograph. In FIGURE 3.1, what is held is proffered, but not revealed. In FIGURE 3.2, what is held is revealed, but effaced by darkness.

Once again, when we encounter the photographs with affective intentionality, we bring into focus the essential subject as distinct from her reiterative gestures, which, in each of these examples, is the conventionality of the pose. We also encounter the photographs in relation to ourselves, acknowledging and interrogating our affective response. I respond to FIGURE 3.1 with the affective posture of love, receiving its subject's offering of her self-possession. I respond to FIGURE 3.2 with the affective posture of loss, the effaced thing of the photograph finally leading me to its singular difference. In FIGURE 3.2, the effacement by darkness of the held thing is echoed by the self-effacing gesture of the sitter. Pushing against her face with her hand, she disfigures herself, wrinkling her chin, stretching her lips, and unsettling her gaze. In both portraits, the subject faces the beholder (me). Whereas I become the referent of the offering in FIGURE 3.1, fixing me, the gaze of the subject of FIGURE 3.2 passes through me, unsettling me. Just as the held thing is effaced, so the gaze is withdrawn, an enactment of loss. But that is not all that is given here. Embracing them as beloved things, and mirroring their affective postures with my own, I have received their contagious presence.[36] Animating the beheld, their stories becoming my own, the photographs have become souvenirs of death for me.

In FIGURE 3.3, two standing women and a seated man pose for their portrait. The backdrop, though flat, has been painted to create an illusion of depth. Inside the painted space there is a curtained window to the left and a sunlit table with a vase containing flowers on top of it. To the right, a carved column rises from floor to ceiling. The peculiar decorative elements of the column are a smiling lion and an ornamental leaf, which sits like a hat on the lion's head. The group, perhaps a family, poses at the center of this compressed, illusionary space. The man sits on a fine chair

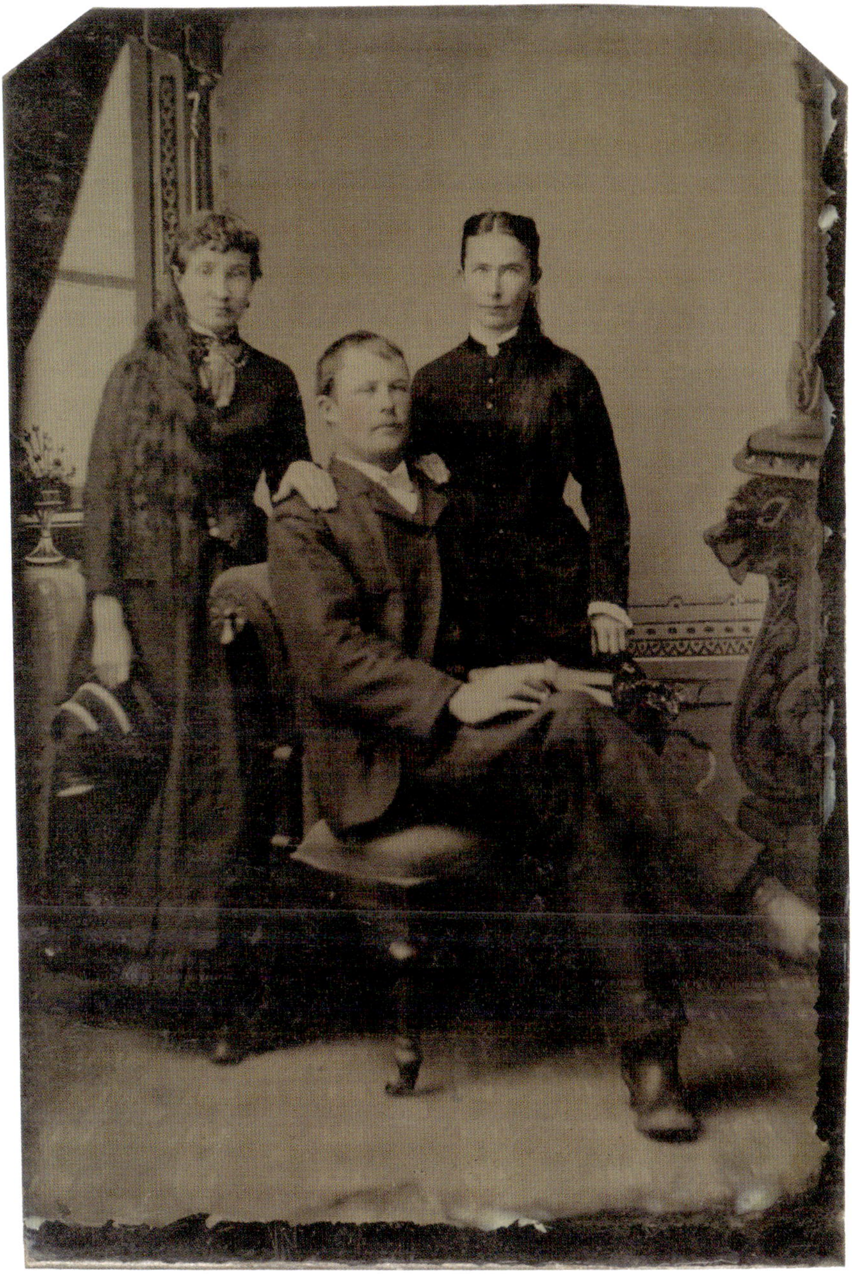

FIGURE 3.3. Portrait of a man and two women, ca. 1860s, tintype photograph.

with carved wooden legs and an upholstered seat and back. He holds a book open in his lap, using the finger of one hand to hold his place. In contrast to his companions, who face forward, the man sits diagonally, shown in profile. The women stand behind him, each with one hand on one of his shoulders and the other hand holding a hat to her side. The woman on the left wears a beaded necklace with a cross, and the woman on the right a brooch.

The family photograph is, generally speaking, a thing made by two or more people, at least one of whom is present in the image and the photographer, usually not present in the image. Thus, an absent presence is implied by the photograph, as a condition both of making and of viewing. In the nineteenth century, the absent presence was often deployed as an element of photography's narrative structure. I believe that is the case with this photograph. The man's physical centrality assures me that he is also at the center of the social configuration encoded by it. He is, however, a generic figure. He is unaesthetic, pure convention. The three people are positioned so close, yet each seem to be in their own separate world. It was, in part, this distance in the picture that initially attracted me to it. What strikes me now is the contrast in what each person is exposing to the camera, performing for the beholder. The man yields nothing, but the women have let down their hair, a remarkable gesture of self-revelation at the time when the picture was made. It is the hair, and then the look of each woman, one's eyes averted and the other facing the camera (she faces me), that attracts me now.

Not all six hands of the sitters are visible in the picture, but no rings are present on those that can be seen, as might be the case if the absent referent was a husband. Instead, noting again the contrast in their expressions, I conjecture that the standing women are enacting remembrance, and the seated man is, in fact, enacting the absent father. That would explain the contrast between the women and man, for whereas the women are performing private recollection, the man is performing a public pose. His posture denotes his status rather than his individuality. While the women hold onto the man, as benefactor, he holds onto the book, symbolizing all that is external to the picture. He holds onto power—the power of words, by which his inheritance has been legally and spiritually transferred, and the power of history, which ensures that transfer to the son. The man is enacting his worthiness, which the women's touching gesture affirms.

I experienced a strong sensation of attraction the first time I held this image. I responded to a coded gesture, the women's let-down hair, whose affect was amplified by another element, their hats, simultaneously concealing and revealing. Responding to its encodings, I also intuited the subtle beyond of the photograph, that which is beyond the frame where each sitter has differently posited his or her attention. Someone is speaking, but their message is unspeakable. Here, the desire of the subject is to be remembered as remembering.[37] For that desire to be fulfilled, however, their enactment must be observed. The observer of the photograph has a role to play. Where the unsteady gaze of the woman on the left enacts bereavement, and the man enacts the absent father, I am the referent of the woman on the right. The mirrored gaze establishes a relatedness by discontinuity, drawing me at first into the picture and then beyond its frame, beyond the event, beyond the ritual; there it whispers its secret. It whispers the death of the father (of their father, of my father, and of myself as father). It whispers the unspeakable of this particular photograph, the return of the dead father in the son.

Like with the previous example, I experienced a strong sensation of attraction the first time I saw PLATE 0.36, a junk drawer photograph that Von Eckardt labels "Snapshot of Conversation in the Garden." It is indeed a snapshot, but I was drawn to it by its reversals of the conventions of snapshot photography. Snapshot photographs made outdoors, at night, are highly unusual. The absent presence in this one is a photographer with a flash apparatus, whose relation to the picture's subjects is as unclear as its story is ambiguous. This ambiguity and the murky darkness of the image are reversals of the lightness and levity typical of snapshot photography. In PLATE 0.35, for example, the indoor pictures were also illuminated using a flash, which can be seen reflecting from the glasses of some sitters and the shiny walls or objects in some rooms. The rooms themselves were lit, however, so the effect of the flash is to discreetly fill in the shadows.

The harsh illumination of the flash in this snapshot, however, is reminiscent of crime scene photography. The image that comes immediately to mind for me is Weegee's *Their First Murder* (1941), a night shot using a strong flash to illuminate the smiling faces of children at a crime scene. Here, the smiling child is inscrutable. The story that the snapshot's subjects are enacting is so private that it is unknowable, except to the three who participated in its making. Yet I am drawn to it, over and over again. Drawn by the reverie of the child in costume, by the mystery of her right hand held above the table. Drawn by the shape of whatever is on the table beneath her hand, blasted to unrecognizability by the flash. Drawn to the posture of the woman who leans in to face the child, so large that her knees barely fit under the child's table. Drawn to the woman's hands, both clenched into fists at the table's edge. Drawn to the white fence and gate delimiting the chiaroscuro background, the trees beyond and the outlines of a home. Drawn to its blackened windows.

Returning to my own collection, two final examples of discarded photographs were found together in an album: FIGURE 3.4, picturing a tombstone, was tucked behind FIGURE 3.5, a portrait of a woman. The latter is a sixth-plate tintype. Its subject sits at the center of a plain domestic space. The painted backdrop shows a patterned wall behind her, with a corner and a window to the right. Its illusion is of light coming through the window, brightening the sitter's face. She sits in a chair with a small, carved wooden back and an upholstered arm, against which she holds herself steady. She wears a black dress decorated with large black buttons, a white lace jabot at the neck, and black lace at the sleeve. A headband sits on her head,

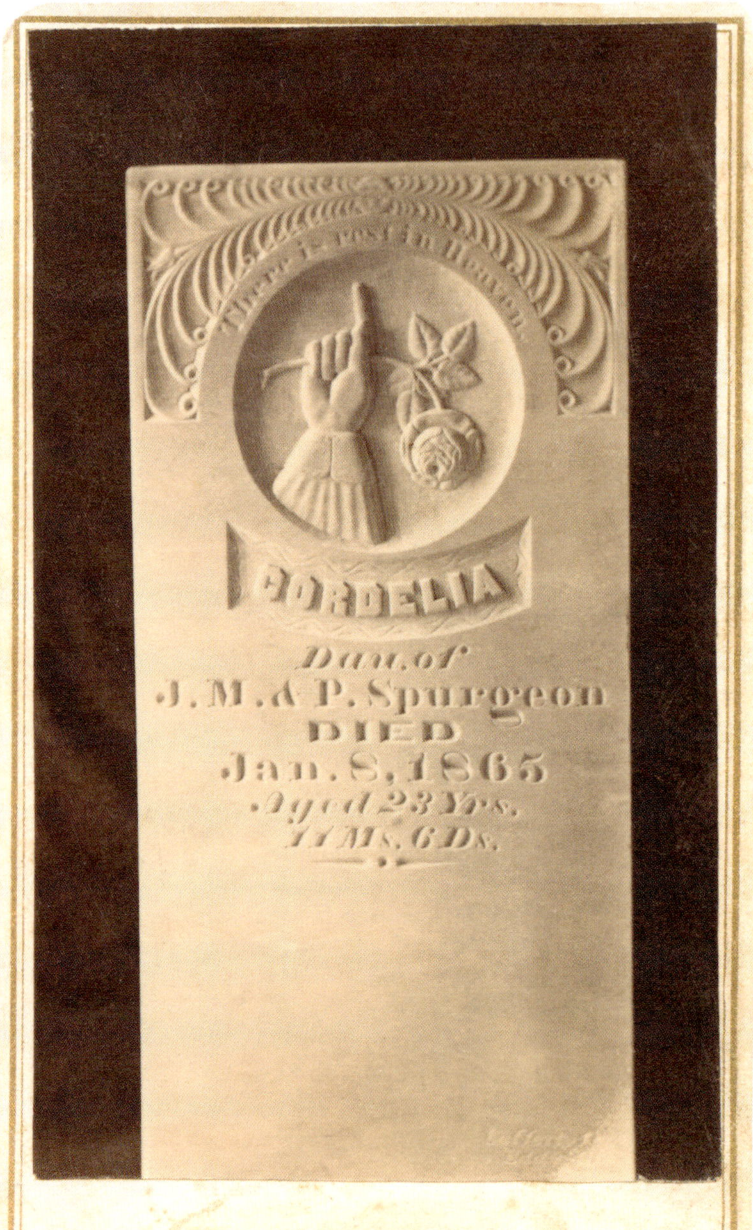

FIGURE 3.4. Tombstone of Cordelia, 1865, carte-de-visite.

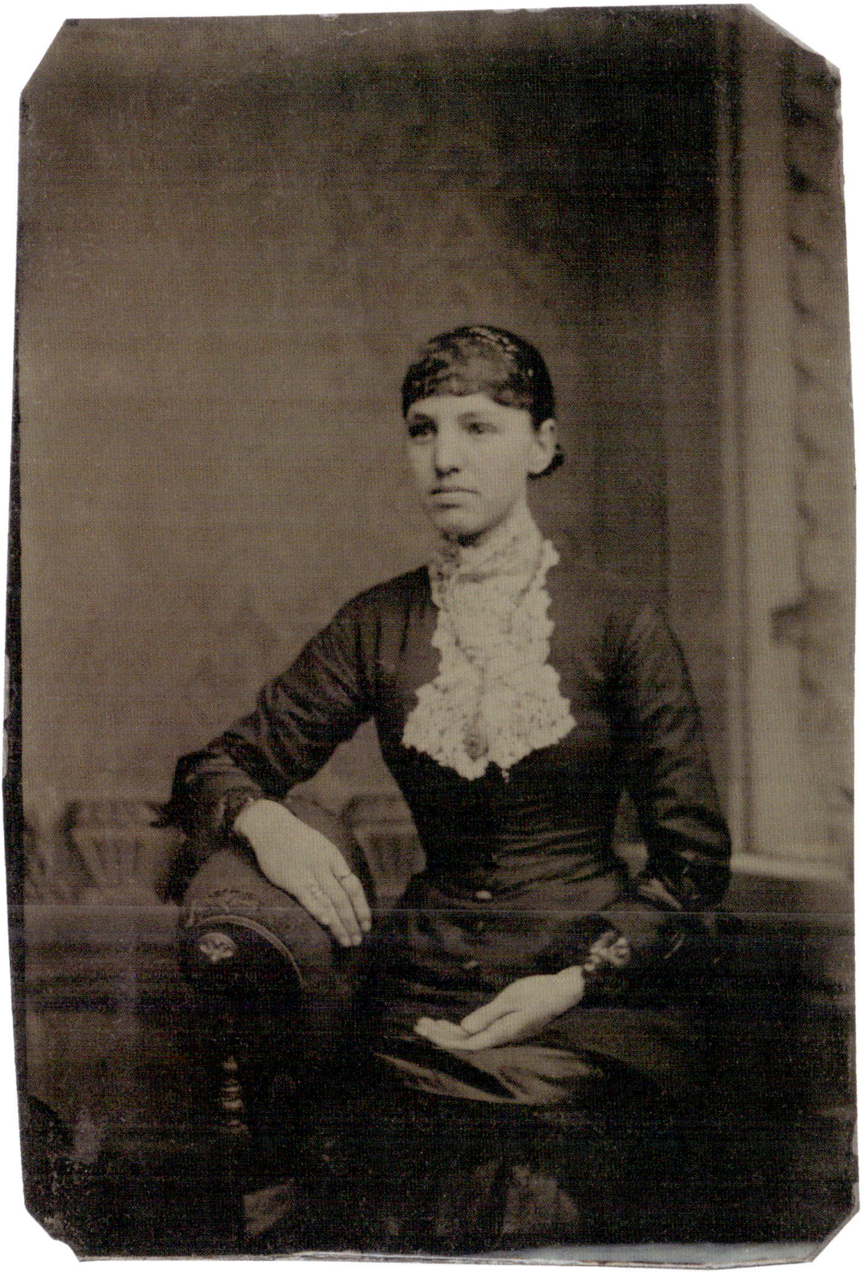

FIGURE 3.5. Portrait of a woman, ca. 1860s, tintype photograph.

and around her neck she wears a necklace. A locket, extended by a chain from the necklace, rests upon her heart. Perhaps the locket contains an image or a lock of hair. On the hand that rests against the chair arm, three rings are visible, one on her index finger and two on the ring finger. The other hand lies open in her lap.

We have seen this pose before in FIGURES 3.1 and 3.2. From its pairing in the album, I infer that FIGURE 3.4, a carte-de-visite, is a posthumous portrait of the woman in FIGURE 3.5, a commemorative image made after the death of its subject. Here, the living figure of a deceased subject has been displaced by a symbolic figure, that of her tombstone. The decorative element at the top of the stone is evergreen, betokening the eternal, toward which the hand below, holding a plucked rose, points. The rose symbolizes the transience and beauty of all living things, which must come to pass. The circle in which the hand and rose are carved contains the legend "There is Rest in Heaven." The photograph was made in a real or makeshift studio. The tombstone is not pictured in its final resting place but propped against a black cloth backdrop. Its inscription reads, "Cordelia Dau. of J.M. & P. Spurgeon. DIED Jan. 8, 1865 Aged 23 Yrs. 11 Ms. 6 Ds." The back of the card, often used by photographers to advertise their services or by families to inscribe information about the sitter, is blank. Its message, as a posthumous portrait, is complete. The carved hand points toward heaven: There she is!

Returning to FIGURE 3.5, on further observation, another detail emerges. On her right arm, the sitter, whom I now presume to be Cordelia, wears a black bow just below the elbow, a sign of mourning or death. The bow embodies the psychic veil separating the living from the dead. The portrait captures her on both sides of that veil, a living subject portrayed both as dead and as undying. It portrays her as she wishes to be remembered, as a living being, and as she hopes death will allow, as not forgetting. Indeed, Cordelia looks beyond the frame, enacting remembrance. Her three rings and the locket are each memorial symbols, and they are talismans of memory. She has thus embedded in the portrait not only her enactments, but also signs of memories that she hopes to recall after death, and herself as she wishes to be remembered. These signs are proffered to the beholder. The social transaction of remembrance was not executed just by the making of a memorial portrait, but by its viewing and annual revisitation as part of the mourning ritual. The beholder of the portrait, known or unknown to its sitter, has a role to play in that ritual.

Looking one last time at the portrait of Cordelia, let us finally return to the detail of the open hand. As in FIGURES 3.1 and 3.2, the open hand is a convention of the pose. In FIGURE 3.1, what was held was something offered. In FIGURE 3.2, what was held was something withdrawn, effaced by darkness. Cordelia's hand lies open, but empty. Holding nothing, she releases everything. At once lifelike and corpse-like, the open hand receives death, and it proffers life. The hand is open to death, in other words, but it is also open to the beholder to receive and care for her image.

As the locket, a sign of remembrance, rests upon Cordelia's heart, so, in that touching gesture, the beholder's heart is opened. I respond to Cordelia's open hand with my own, receiving her image as my own. "In the names of the dead," historian Eelco Runia writes, "we glimpse the numinosity of history."[38] The metonymy of naming, launching desire beyond what the photograph permits us to see, makes past things present. Uttering Cordelia's name, which is given here as an act of grace, I enter crazily into the spectacle. I receive her contagious presence, opening to an impossible memory, a new limit case.

Monuments and photographs are some of the settings where, against all logic, we permit the modest, shared hallucination of the past intruding into the present. Facing them, touching them, caring for them, we utter the names of the dead, bringing forth presence.[39] Conjoining sensory perception with ritual utterance, performative things presentify, as Gumbrecht describes the experience, moving us momentarily outside the order of time.[40] Images beget images, and images in the world beget images in the mind. In memory, as in the world, they accrue affect. Responding to them as real, the beholder brings forth presence through an interplay of internal and external imagery, a perceptual conveyance that is entangled with the emotions, with feeling. The past, Runia writes, is present in the present, and sometimes intrudes upon it. That intrusion is always surprising because, when it occurs, it changes everything.[41] What surprises, in the well-differentiated mind, is the sudden experience of non-differentiation from the familiar object of scrutiny.

At last, I must finish as Barthes did with the query: mad or tame? The encounter with images is not either mad or tame, but both mad and tame; a maddening simultaneity. We may substitute one image with another, or one setting of encounters with another, but we may never halt the mad begetting of images by images. Non-differentiation remains an essential feature of our experience of them. We may get to know an image; we may indeed grow to love an image. We may imprint images upon a medium, but only images are capable of imprinting themselves upon human consciousness and, in so doing, of engraving themselves upon human history. Images are species, not quite animate yet inexplicably active.[42] As active things they become us, and as dead things we become them.[43] That is our bond with images, the paradoxical union in which we glimpse, flickeringly, the numinosity of history—the past hurtling impossibly into the present. In that mad union with images, we are reunited with ourselves.

1. This essay draws on research done following the author's receipt of the 2012 Shpilman International Prize for Excellence in Photography. The closeness of that research to Dr. Von Eckardt's project felt like an auspicious invitation to return to it. As originally conceived, the prize was initiated by the Shpilman Institute for Photography, in Tel Aviv, with the Israel Museum, in Jerusalem, to support research projects in photography that integrate theoretical issues with practical ones. I use this opportunity to thank: Dr. Monika Faber (Nominator); Dr. Nissan N. Perez (Prize Committee

Chair); Prof. Dana Arieli-Horowitz, Prof. Hanan Laskin, the late Prof. Dr. Bodo von Dewitz, and Anne Wilkes Tucker (Prize Committee); and Noriko Fuku, Sander L. Gilman, Horst Hendriks-Jansen, Alison Nordström, Mark Sloan, and Nancy M. West (gentle readers). This essay is for my daughter, Acadia Jacob, with love and thanks.

2. Curator Joel Smith, citing photography historian Geoffrey Batchen, observed that "in the acute self-consciousness of this, the early digital era, the analog photograph has 'taken on a memorial role, not of the subjects it depicts but of its own operation as a system of representation" (Smith, "Roll Over: The Snapshot's Museum Afterlife," *Afterimage* 29, no. 2 [2001]: 8).

3. I am indebted to Régis Debray's mediology, a theory of looking that encompasses three eras of the image, with attendant optical technologies and image-related ideologies, "Three mediological cesuras of civilization—writing, printing, and audiovisuality—separate the time of the image into three distinct continents: the idol, art, and the visual" (Debray, "Remarks on the Spectacle," *New Left Review* 1/214 [1995]: 134–41 [135]).

4. In relation to this, the family photograph is indeed exemplary, for what we mean when we speak of found photographs is usually family pictures that have been set into motion by death. In that way, it is as persons that they induce our sympathy and our superstition, yet the found photograph has no socially approved function. It has no ordinary use, as do the family photographs from which they originate; therefore, I consider both the mental and the social operations of images, distinguishing perception from use in a variety of settings.

5. Roland Barthes, *Camera Lucida: Reflections on Photography,* trans. Richard Howard (Macmillan, 1981), 93.

6. Carol Mavor, "Collecting Loss," *Cultural Studies* 11, no. 1 (1997): 111–37 (121).

7. Barry Miller, *The Fullness of Being: A New Paradigm for Existence* (University of Notre Dame Press, 2002), 137.

8. Susan Stewart, *On Longing: Narratives of the Miniature, the Gigantic, the Souvenir, the Collection* (Duke University Press, 1993), 138.

9. Stewart, *On Longing,* 138.

10. Sara Ahmed, "Affective Economies," *Social Text* 22, no. 2 (2004): 117–39 (120).

11. Ahmed, "Affective Economies," 120.

12. Ahmed, "Affective Economies," 124.

13. Barthes, *Camera Lucida,* 116–17.

14. Pierre Bourdieu and Shaun Whiteside, *Photography: A Middle-Brow Art* (Stanford University Press, 1990), 20.

15. Arjun Appadurai, ed., *The Social Life of Things: Commodities in Cultural Perspective* (Cambridge University Press, 1988), 13.

16. David E. Stannard, "Custom and Change," in *A Time to Mourn: Expressions of Grief in Nineteenth Century America,* eds. Martha V. Pike and Janice Gray Armstrong (Museums at Stony Brook, 1980), 16.

17. For a history of objects viewed intimately that also considers the transition from miniature portraiture to cased photography, see Hanneke Grootenboer, *On Treasuring the Gaze: Intimate Vision in Late Eighteenth-Century Eye Miniatures* (University of Chicago Press, 2012). On photographic jewelry, see Larry J. West and Patricia A. Abbott, *Antique Photographic Jewelry: Tokens of Affection and Regard* (Larry West, 2005). On mourning jewelry, see Sarah Nehama, *In Death Lamented: The Tradition of Anglo-American Mourning Jewelry* (Massachusetts Historical Society, 2012).

18. On posthumous portraiture, see Phoebe Lloyd, "Posthumous Mourning Portraiture," in *A Time to Mourn,* 71–90. Also, Stacy C. Hollander, *Securing the Shadow: Posthumous Portraiture in America* (American Folk Art Museum, 2016).

19. Appadurai, *Social Life of Things,* 26.

20. Stewart, *On Longing,* 23.

21. Stewart, *On Longing,* 140.

22. "As a physical object, divorced from a specific milieu," historian Patrick Geary wrote, "a relic is entirely without significance. Unlike other objects, the bare relic—a bone or a bit of dust—carries no fixed code or sign of its meaning as it moves from one community to another or from one period to a subsequent one" (Geary, *Furta Sacra: Thefts of Relics in the Central Middle Ages* [Princeton University Press, 1990], 5).
23. Barthes, *Camera Lucida*, 109.
24. Barthes, *Camera Lucida*, 71.
25. Barthes, *Camera Lucida*, 63.
26. Barthes, *Camera Lucida*, 109.
27. Hans Ulrich Gumbrecht, "Presence Achieved in Language (with Special Attention Given to the Presence of the Past)," *History and Theory* 45, no. 3 (2006): 317–27 (322).
28. Barthes, *Camera Lucida*, 70.
29. Barthes, *Camera Lucida*, 70.
30. Barthes, *Camera Lucida*, 119.
31. Shawn Michelle Smith, *At the Edge of Sight* (Duke University Press, 2013), 116–17.
32. Smith, *At the Edge of Sight*, 37.
33. Smith, *At the Edge of Sight*, 30.
34. Barthes, *Camera Lucida*, 21.
35. Barthes, *Camera Lucida*, 73.
36. Drawing the connection between intromission and the transmission of images, art historian Michael Camille wrote that "medieval accounts of perception described the mechanism of sight as the actual impress of objects upon the soul through rays that both emanated from the eye and returned to it. This made visual contagion a very real possibility" (Camille, *The Gothic Idol: Ideology and Image Making in Medieval Art* [Cambridge University Press, 1989], 23–24). For medieval observers the image was a highly actual presence to be taken in and absorbed.
37. I am indebted to Geoffrey Batchen, who argued in *Forget Me Not: Photography and Remembrance* (Princeton Architectural Press, 2004) that people who have themselves photographed looking at a photograph want to be remembered as remembering. I have added to this the notion that people who have themselves photographed performing remembrance share the same motivation.
38. Eelco Runia, "Spots of Time," *History and Theory* 45, no. 3 (2006): 305–16 (310).
39. As Runia suggests ("Spots of Time," 309), think of the Vietnam Veterans' Memorial in Washington, D.C., and of strangers reaching out to touch the names embedded as memories in its image.
40. Gumbrecht, "Presence Achieved in Language," 325.
41. Eelco Runia, "Presence," *History and Theory* 45, no. 1 (2006): 1–29 (6).
42. From ancient times until at least the thirteenth century, the term *species* referred to the free-floating image that imprints itself upon the beholder. "Species," historian Jean-Claude Schmidtt wrote, "circulated and penetrated the eye, which, far from being passive, exercised its *virtus* over the external world" (Schmidtt, *Ghosts in the Middle Ages: The Living and the Dead in Medieval Society*, trans. Teresa Lavender Fagan [University of Chicago Press, 1998], 23). "What do pictures want?" art historian W.J.T. Mitchell asked (Mitchell, *What Do Pictures Want? The Lives and Loves of Images* [University of Chicago Press, 2005]). They want to exercise their *virtus*.
43. Maurice Blanchot in "The Two Versions of the Imaginary" employed a language of presence to describe what is given and what is withdrawn from the corpse. The cadaverous presence, he wrote, appears at the moment of death as "that which has been disdainfully withdrawn from us," and, in its withdrawal, "begins to resemble himself." Thus, he concludes, "The cadaver is its own image" (Blanchot, *The Space of Literature*, trans. Ann Smock [University of Nebraska Press, 1982], 257–58).

THINKING ABOUT JUNK

CHAPTER 4

FROM "JUNK" TO "JUNKED"

MARGARET OLIN

INTRODUCTION: WHAT IS JUNK?

Faced with Barbara Von Eckardt's depictions of objects taken from boxes of miscellaneous items she bought on eBay, the label "junk drawer" feels misleading. These pristine images of objects carefully spaced and composed thematically or formally read more comfortably as "collections" than as "junk." Or perhaps the title itself is meant as a commentary. These objects started as junk and likely looked like junk when Von Eckardt opened the boxes containing them. Yet she has, through her treatment, redeemed them. We could consider them objects that used to be junk but that have now been "unjunked." Indeed, I am not sure there is such a thing as "junk." Rather, I suspect that "junk" makes more sense as a verb than as a noun. This interesting word seems to apply to many kinds of objects. Even leaving aside vernacular applications of the word—"junk" is used to denote, for example, heroin—"junk" covers anything that has been or should be (in someone's opinion) discarded. Any poorly made object is "junk." Costume jewelry—jewelry made with fake, rather than authentic, precious stones—is sometimes called "junk jewelry." In the *Oxford English Dictionary*'s definition of junk, "old or discarded articles that are considered useless or of little value," the most important phrase is probably "are considered." Significantly, the definition is passive; it doesn't reveal who does the considering.

This anonymity of the arbitrator is important. The existence of junk shops suggests that an item considered junk by one segment of society might be something for which another segment will pay money. This example shows also that although the meaning of "junk" is unclear, there surely is a rough hierarchy of objects that are called by that name. This hierarchy might have consequences for the objects in question. At one end are objects that are not decorative and lack any immediately obvious utility. Yet, people nevertheless keep them on hand, for one reason or another, sometimes in a "junk drawer." From there, the definition of junk escalates to objects that, because they are considered junk, should or must be discarded, and further, to objects that are junk because they have already been discarded, and so on. The objects kept in a junk drawer are at the beginning levels of "junk," on one of the first steps toward disposal, while there is still time to arrest the trajectory.

I have had the experience of rescuing an object from a junk drawer. "Junk drawer" was a new expression for me when I first heard it. I had always regarded junk as those useless objects that one clears out of one's closets to take to the trash. An organizer helping my family with my mother's rather cluttered home after her death, however, used the term in an email. She told me that she had found something in the kitchen "junk drawer" that she thought might be an heirloom. "Junk drawer" seemed like an oxymoron. Why save something in a drawer if you regard it as junk? Doesn't it belong in the circular file? The object that the organizer found had not been placed there as junk. It was the record of the meetings of an intimate, much beloved gourmet club, complete with menus, recipes, and the names of special guests. No doubt my mother placed it in the drawer to save it, not to dispose of it. It may have been stored there because it was not easy to classify. It was not exactly a cookbook, which would have belonged on a bookshelf, nor was it a diary or journal; yet, it was certainly worth keeping, and the fact that it pertained to food and happened to fit in the kitchen junk drawer destined it to be stored there. Of course, the family kept it; I have no idea what other junk may have been in the drawer. Its other contents were probably actually junked or perhaps placed on eBay in boxes like those that Von Eckardt ordered for her photographic project. Surely, as suggested by the *Oxford English Dictionary* definition, or even more explicitly by the motto of an annual community yard sale in my old neighborhood, "Our junk, your treasure," junk (like beauty) is in the eye of the beholder. In that sense, the buyers of the junk drawers on eBay are surely on a form of treasure hunt.

Moving from the eye to the camera, what is the difference between the photograph of junk and the junk itself? What does it mean to photograph the junk in an eBay junk drawer, then to sort and photograph these objects individually, beautifully, and respectfully, rather than to find them strewn throughout the house or shoved into a drawer or, as in the eBay sources of Von Eckardt's *Junk Drawer* project, into a box? As I have argued elsewhere, photography is itself a means of transmuting attention into form.[1] Taking the phrase "junk is in the eye of the beholder" literally, I argue here that the "photography of junk" should be understood as a term that pertains to modes of seeing and modes of attention that can ultimately lead to action. These modes follow the same path, or perhaps sometimes proceed along, the path of junk itself, as it moves from the noun for what is worth saving to the finality of the verb. In the following brief contributions, I try to follow the steps of photographic attentiveness to junk.

PREHISTORY OF JUNK PHOTOGRAPHY: COLLECTIONS

Artists have long been interested in collections of objects, although not always in "junk." Still lifes can be considered a type of collection, and before photography, seventeenth-century Dutch painters of still lifes sought to display their skill by including close observations of seemingly trivial objects, such as breadcrumbs on jumbled tables arranged with exotic delights like precious, imported fruits set out on sumptuous silver trays or in glass bowls. While the accoutrements and their surroundings identify their unseen owners as wealthy and privileged, the crumbs identify them as human nevertheless, and assure the reality of the scene, however magnificent.

Photographers' interest in still life began with photography itself. William Henry Fox Talbot, the inventor of the early photographic technique the "calotype," showcased his new invention in 1844 with *The Pencil of Nature*, a portfolio of images published in six periodic fascicles available by subscription.[2] The selections included landscape and cityscape paintings, as well as still lifes reminiscent of those painted by the Dutch, which were often imitated by painters of Talbot's own period. But he also photographed actual collections, such as a shelf of books and cabinets of china and glass objects (FIGURE 4.1). The objects were not what we normally consider junk, except according to the criteria that they were not actually used. His explanation of the images suggests the mundane utility the photographs might have for creating inventories. Talbot's text also discusses technical considerations when representing objects through photography. The images themselves, however, transmit the beauty of the medium's transfiguration of its subject.

PHOTOGRAPHY AND THE TRANSFIGURATION OF JUNK INTO ART

As the transfiguring effect of photography became an end in itself, it eventually extended to objects more likely to be described as "junk." While collections continued to attract the attention of photographers, the excitement generated by the new medium also encouraged people to apply it over a wider and increasingly humble range. Stylistic characteristics of photographed images also changed. The transformational photography of junk acquired a history. Occasionally, the purpose was straightforwardly aesthetic: to create beauty through visually unexpected means. In photography, this kind of attention, when extended to trivial items or junk, generally depicted each piece individually. Perhaps a form of "junk photography" began in 1930, when photographer Edward Weston transfigured the humble green pepper by lighting it and photographing it like a precious sculpture in "Pepper No. 30." The pepper, although not junk or even junk food, was not an exotic import in twentieth-century California; it was also no subject for a Dutch still life. Yet, its isolation against a black background identifies its owner as a member of a different kind of elite, those capable of transforming the humble into the mighty. The home of an impoverished tenant farmer, too, could be classifiable as "junk," yet in a photograph by Walker Evans, *Home of Bud Fields, Alabama Sharecropper, Hale County, Alabama* (1936), it acquired an austere, modernist beauty (FIGURE 4.2). The humble character of the object became a potent element of photographic transfiguration.

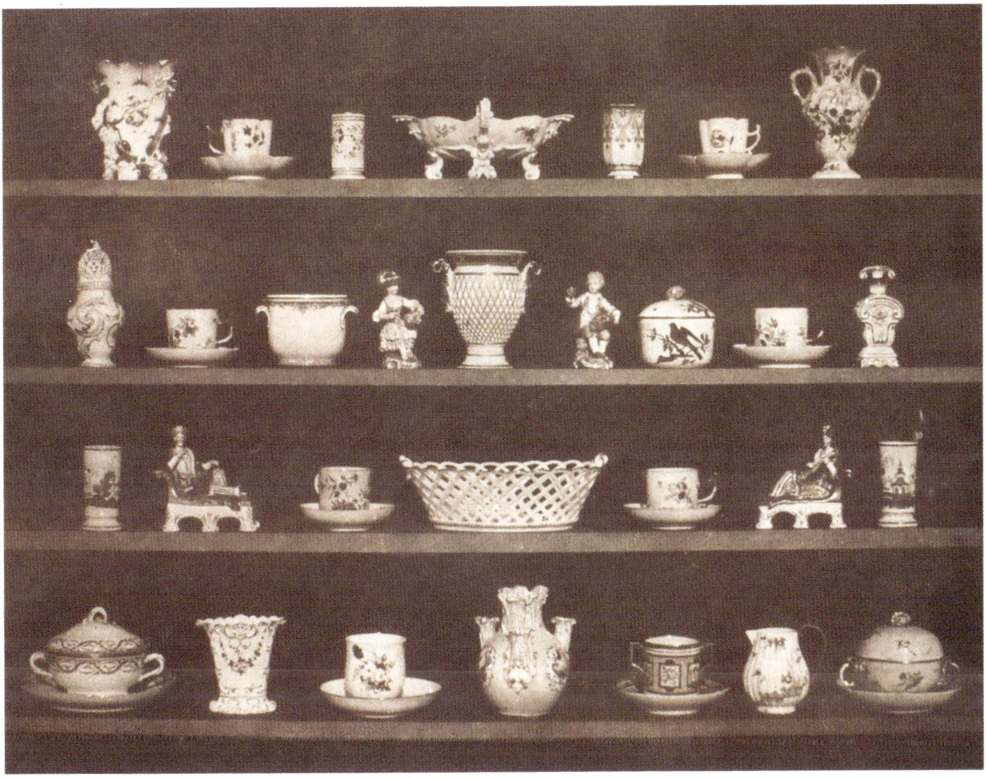

FIGURE 4.1. William Henry Fox Talbot, *Articles of China*, ca. 1843–44, salted paper print from paper negative.

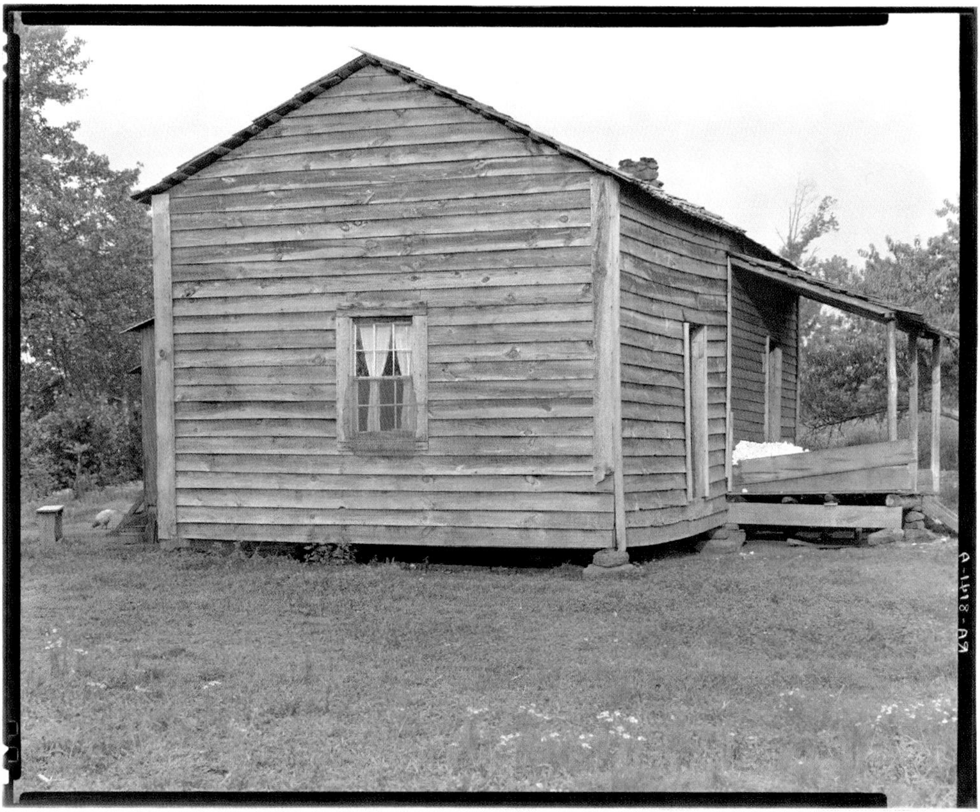

FIGURE 4.2. Walker Evans, *Home of Bud Fields, Alabama Sharecropper, Hale County, Alabama*, 1936, digital file from black-and-white film negative.

PHOTOGRAPHY MAY TURN JUNK INTO A GAME

None of what we have discussed so far fits the category of "junk" as it occurs in the phrase "junk drawer." However, photographers have long redeemed mundane, everyday junk by photographing it as part of a game. In some cases, photographed junk can be the basis of a scavenger hunt. Children learn from miscellany, sometimes including junk. They may first learn their ABCs through colorful block books that include a photograph of a familiar object along with its first letter. The *I Spy* book series, which began in 1992 with the publication of *I Spy: A Book of Picture Riddles* by Jean Marzollo, with photography by Walter Wick, serves to hone children's linguistic abilities and, as importantly, their observational skills.[3] The double-page spreads show everyday objects artfully, but with great care, jumbled in a non-hierarchical arrangement (FIGURE 4.3), and Marzollo's riddles encourage children of the targeted age (preschool through kindergarten) to identify some of the more difficult-to-spot objects by means of rhyming clues.[4] Like many children's books, the *I Spy* books exult in cheerful primary colors and emit a delight in the household objects that make up the world of the small child. Many of the objects pictured are toys, but some spreads include the sort of discarded items, such as safety pins, keys, screws, and golf tees that one finds in a junk drawer. If unattended, little children sometimes overturn these drawers onto the floor to play with. The layouts of the books recall the look of the floor during such explorations. Naturally, I speak from experience. Not only do the photographs transform the mundane objects that they portray into treasure, but they also transfigure into art the sight of a kitchen floor after a chaotic rampage, or of a playroom floor after an intense play session.

THE DARK SIDE OF THE PHOTOGRAPHY OF JUNK

The eye of the beholder, in this case of the *Junk Drawer* project, is Von Eckardt's eye, working in tandem with her scanner to develop a mode of attention that does not reproduce junk, but rather uses the objects to think about the lives of people through the things they owned and kept in drawers with other miscellany, to which they may or may not ever have devoted any conscious thought. Her photographs may encourage the viewer to question the term "junk" itself, but they have a darker side: because of the objects' origin as unwanted items in the estates of the deceased, they evoke the thought of death and encourage the viewer to contemplate it.

Already, the photographs of Box 1 raise the issue of the limits of the term "junk." There is a wedding photograph (PLATE 0.04), a baby photograph (PLATE 0.03), baby shoes (PLATE 0.03), and a family portrait that trace and commemorate the birth and growth of a family. In Box 5, there is a New Testament (PLATE 0.19) inscribed inside the front cover from an uncle to his nephew. Surely these are mementos and not discardable junk. However, the presence of knick-knacks along with them—an ashtray and

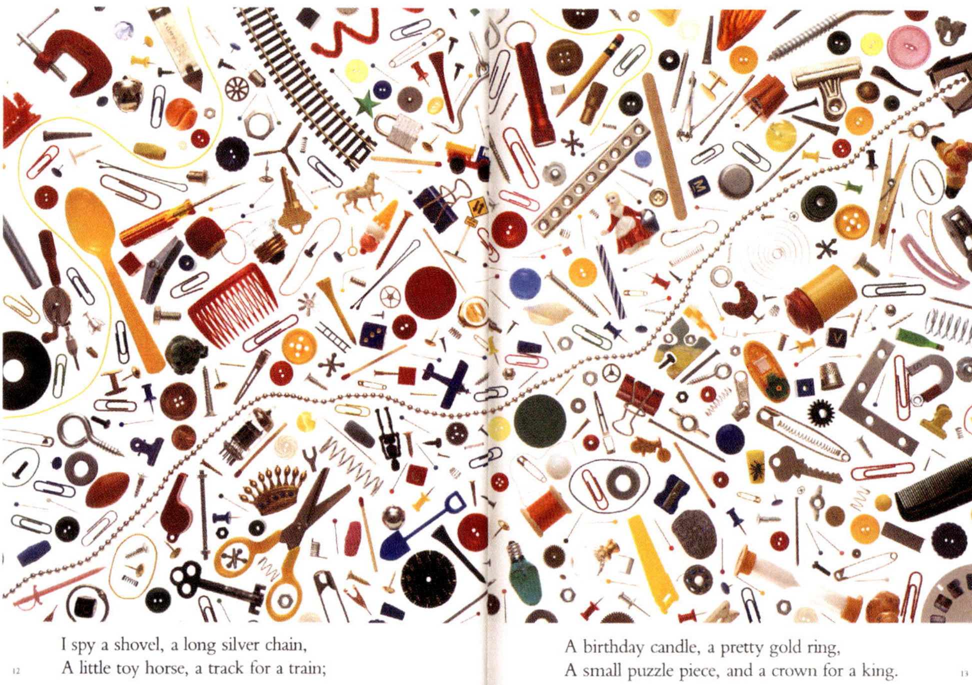

FIGURE 4.3. Two-page spread from Jean Marzollo with photographs by Walter Wick, *I Spy: A Book of Picture Riddles* (New York: Scholastic, 1992).

other items connected with smoking (PLATE 0.01)—suggests that the contents are indeed junk. Indeed, it suggests that, after death, one's mementoes become junk. Yet, to photograph the objects seems to retrieve for them a meaning that they had before they were junk. It seems almost to resurrect the owners of the junk.

The relation of the contents of junk drawers to the concept of death is complicated when we note that some of the photographed objects are themselves photographs. Photography itself has long carried the connotation of death, an association that intensified after the publication of Roland Barthes's *Camera Lucida* (1980), which memorializes Barthes's mother in the form of a theoretical essay that understands photography as carrying with it the trace of death.[5] A photograph, Barthes argues, bears the mark of something that has been, but whose moment has ended without any guarantee that it continues to exist.[6] Even the way in which the objects are photographed by Von Eckardt suggests the end of life. Rather than spontaneously scattering objects across a surface in the manner of *I Spy*, arranging them meticulously on shelves like the china in Talbot's photographs, or photographing them isolated at eye-level, like Weston's pepper or Evans's tenant farmer's shed, Von Eckardt chooses to use a scanner, which gives her objects the look of having been photographed from above. The arrangement resembles that of objects in vitrines in museums. These objects are often regarded as dead objects, isolated and deprived of their functions. A growing literature regards museum artifacts as looted from the dead or dispossessed, rather like boxes of items from junk drawers.[7]

PHOTOGRAPHY AS A NAMING RITUAL

If there is a dark side to the photographs of Von Eckardt, it is the evocation of an extra layer of anguish that characterizes another widespread mode of the photographic transformation of junk. It is self-explanatory that not everyone has a collection of china to inventory. But it should also be remembered that not everyone has a junk drawer, or a place to store objects that are unused and often forgotten. Possession of a junk drawer assumes excess space to keep these things. The reason that we can fantasize that the junk drawer contains a treasure is that it stems from having a stable household with enough resources to possess a treasure or two.

The United States is home to many whose dwellings permit no such things as junk drawers or, for that matter, treasures. Their possessions are limited to what they can carry on their person. Our next example of junk pertains to one classification of such people: migrants. In the last several years, the attention paid to migration in news reports, and in the outbursts of politicians, has inspired photographers to try to draw attention to their plight. Aid organizations also use photographs to raise sympathy, and funds, for their work. Many of the resulting photographs portray migrants or refugees themselves, often in abject poses.[8] Photographs taken from a higher angle, whose subjects literally look up beseechingly at the camera, make migrants look helpless and pitiful. While it is easy to accept that the subjects of the photographs are probably deserving of assistance, the photographs themselves are unlikely to deliver to the settled middle-class viewer the gut-punching stimulus to imagine what life is like for migrants, not to mention what it would be like to share their plight.

Such photographs have often been criticized for portraying their subjects as victims. Photographs of migrants tend, in fact, to be tautological. They tell you little or nothing about the migrant in question, but they seem to offer up the person who is photographed, along with the photograph itself, to a sacrificial naming ritual that helps to create and perpetuate categories like "migrant" and "refugee." The word "migrant," accordingly, has come to mean in practice someone who is photographed as a migrant. One such iconic migrant photograph is now seen as the very image of the iconic photograph in general, as testified by its presence on the cover of a book on the subject (FIGURE 4.4).[9] *Migrant Mother*, by Dorothea Lange, has few of the drawbacks mentioned above. It shows its subject at eye-level, and rather than beseech the viewer, she looks away. Yet, the subjects of even such classic photographs risk losing all individuality as they turn into a visual definition for the term "migrant." Their personal histories, hopes, and plans, even the existence of family not visible in the picture, as with a presumed husband in the case of *Migrant Mother*, disappear. In short, everything that might help the viewer identify with rather than pity them, is missing.[10] These absences, along with the form of the pictures themselves, help iconic photographs define the subjects of which they are iconic representations, often in problematic ways.

THE REDEMPTIVE PHOTOGRAPHY OF MIGRANT JUNK

In the photographs, supplicant migrants represented as beseeching the viewer are portrayed by the camera as pitiful victims, sometimes further humanized by the inclusion of props. In practice, this often means that a migrant child is photographed with their doll. The doll helps the photograph to speak to the middle-class viewer whose child also has a doll. Just as a cake crumb humanizes the wealthy owner of a luxury item portrayed in a painted still life, a doll has the power to humanize the impoverished migrant. Recent alternative projects, like those I discuss below, go further. Like Von Eckardt, the photographers of these projects substitute objects for the faces of the migrants themselves. These objects, which usually qualify as junk, are things that migrants have kept by them or that the photographers, or border guards, have found in their wake or confiscated from them. The photographers then photograph the objects meticulously and artfully with the idea of letting them stand in for, or humanize, the migrants themselves. These photographic projects often suggest that

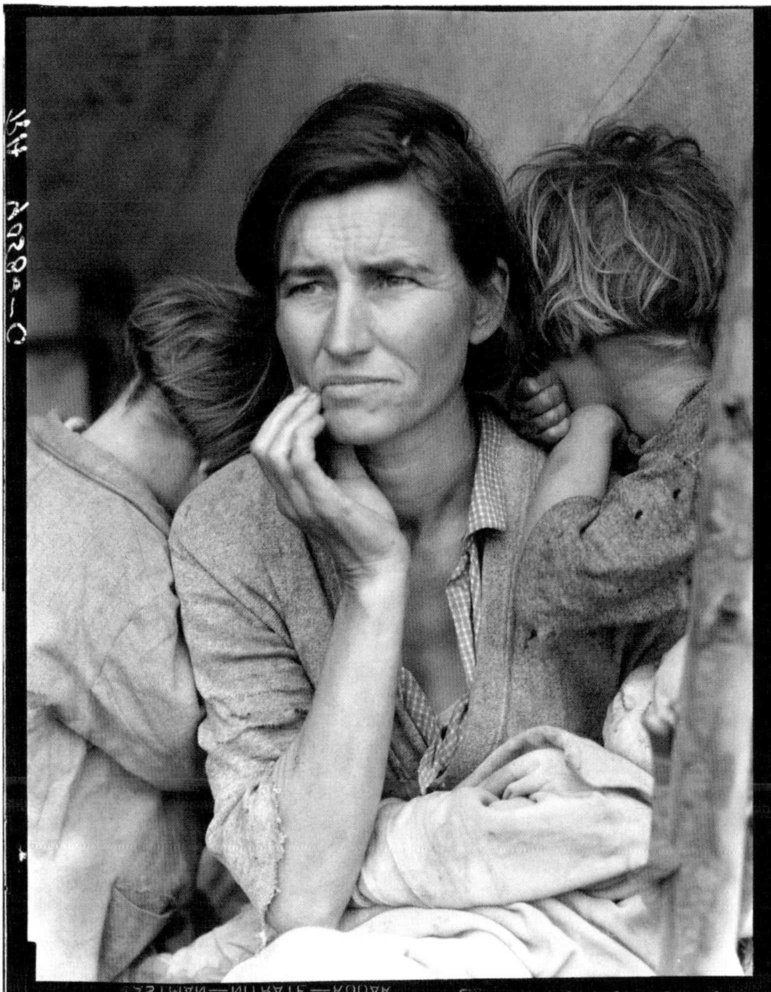

FIGURE 4.4. Dorothea Lange, *Migrant Mother*, 1936, digital file from black-and-white film negative.

possessions can speak at least as eloquently of their owners as the owners themselves can, perhaps even more so. They can also speak to the experiences, and sometimes the fate, of their owners.

The debris collected and photographed by Gideon Mendel from the Calais Jungle refugee camp consists mainly of objects that were ruined in the destruction of the camp between February and October 2016.[11] The Jungle's inhabitants, many of whom were North African, were typically hoping to continue their migration to the United Kingdom. The photographed items consist of fragments of blankets, scorched pages from children's books, rows and rows of toothbrushes or gas canisters, damaged dolls, soccer balls, and cooking utensils. Some objects are laid out in groups, others photographed by themselves. The often-crushed objects read as crushed lives, but the photographs lack the confrontation entailed in photographing the people to whom these objects belonged. In the book of photographs from the camp, verbal accounts from the refugees themselves, some of them poetic, some of them sensational, accompany the images. While the photographs substitute for portraits of abjection and despair, some of the texts go a long way toward undoing the powerful understatement of the carefully arranged and ordered debris.

Indeed, many similar collections of objects left behind by—or carried with—migrants on their way to a hoped-for better existence are accompanied by texts that do the work of bringing the owners of these possessions to poignant, often tragic, life. Tom Kiefer, in *Pertenencias/Belongings*, part of his ongoing project *Sueña Americana/The American Dream*, photographs shoes, toothbrushes, and other possessions of migrants that are similar to those captured by Mendel, although these objects, confiscated by American border guards or left in backpacks abandoned when border guards loaded their owners onto buses, are not in a state of ruin. According to his website, Kiefer, a graphic artist, moved from Los Angeles to Ajo, Arizona, to "concentrate his efforts in studying and photographing the urban and rural landscape and the cultural infrastructure of the United States."[12] In 2003, he began to work part-time as a janitor at a nearby U.S. Customs and Border Protection processing facility. A few years later, when given permission to collect the food that migrants and asylum seekers carried with them while traveling to the United States, he also found personal belongings seized and discarded by officials: "The migrants' belongings, necessary for hygiene, comfort, and survival, were deemed 'non-essential' or 'potentially lethal.'"[13] Kiefer began to collect these objects and photograph them.

"Non-essential" objects are, in our reading, junk. The decision that coin purses, Bibles, rings, brushes, and other items carried by refugees fit this definition must surely originate in the eyes of the officials of U.S. Customs and Border Protection, since no one carries junk with them for a long and arduous journey across the desert. The photographs are intended to force the viewer to confront the cruelty shown to migrants by exhibiting the kinds, and quantities, of objects that have been confiscated.

In the photograph *Oral Hygiene* (2015), the photographer arranges a large mass of toothbrushes and toothpaste tubes for the purpose of showing how many items of hygiene get confiscated. Nearly everyone who undertakes a long journey needs a toothbrush. *Shoe Assembly* (2016) gains some of its power through its unavoidable association with the piles of shoes, not only poignant but also horrifying, that one finds in museums and memorials to the Holocaust (FIGURE 4.5).

A bible, however, can make its point even if it is photographed alone. FIGURE 4.6 shows that border authorities regard a bible as nonessential, at least if it is one of the few items carried by a migrant. Indeed, the collection includes photographs of the pages of a bible, and of several inside covers of bibles, with inscriptions that emphasize their personal value. Through Kiefer's images, a viewer is implicitly encouraged to imagine what they might have taken on a migrant voyage, and to use the objects to facilitate empathy with the migrants: "I ask the viewer to consider these photographs as untold and unknown stories, markers of human journeys cut short."[14] Thus, the interpretation of a bible is very different here from that of the inscribed New Testament in Box 1 of Von Eckardt's *Junk Drawer* (PLATE 0.19).

A few such projects do include photographs of the owners of the objects, as well. In 2015, *Time* magazine commissioned thirteen diptychs about refugees and their possessions by James Mollison.[15] The project is not specifically about junk, although some of the images look like the sort of items one would expect to find in a junk drawer. Each diptych consists of a photograph of a refugee next to an object they had succeeded in keeping with them in their migration, and a statement concerning the object. Some items have sentimental value; others, like a phone charger, are practical and often indispensable. One photograph is blank. The accompanying photograph is of "Mohammad," who explains in the text that he did not bring anything with him except the clothes on his back.

The items of "junk" in these photographs I have been discussing were not junk to begin with, and their owners did not use them up or store them in drawers of miscellanea. Many of them were objects transformed into junk by border police, who took them from their owners and threw them away. They created this junk because they saw these objects, and the people who owned them, as junk. Photographers like Von Eckardt, Mendel, Mollison, and Kiefer have sought to reframe this "junk" through photographs that do not see the objects as such, but as the precious remnants of a life that has been cut off, in Von Eckardt's case by death, and in the case of the others by flight, abandonment, and migration. The photographers have sought to reclaim not only the objects, but also their owners.

In all cases, the treatment of the objects as remnants, whether of treasure or of ordinary life, is what makes junk poignant, interesting, or tragic. But the immaculate way in which the junk is laid out and displayed in these photographic projects, even if it is not actually displayed that way in a drawer, and certainly not in the ruins of a camp or the trash can

FIGURE 4.5. Tom Kiefer, *Shoe Assembly*, 2003, from the series *El Sueño Americano / The American Dream*, ongoing.

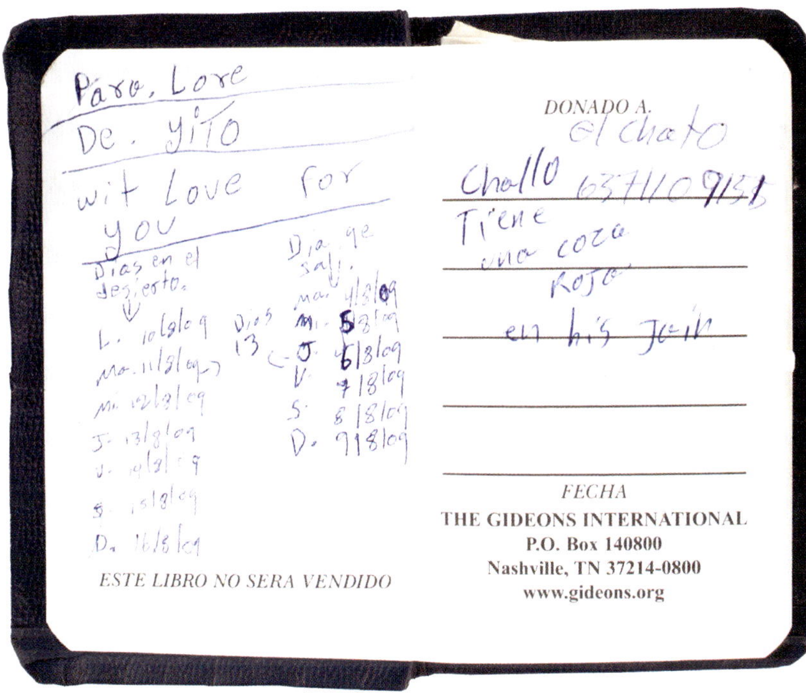

FIGURE 4.6. Tom Kiefer, *Inside Cover*, photograph of inside cover of a New Testament with record of a migrant's travel to and entry into the U.S. via the Mexico/Arizona border, 2003, from the series *El Sueño Americano / The American Dream*, ongoing.

of a border patrol station, suggests that it is not junk, but rather saved treasure. The familiarity of the objects makes their owners seem familiar as well, like one of "us," whoever "we" may be. When junk is photographed as though it were precious, the meeting between the concept of junk and the homage paid to it by a photographer can impart the feeling of the uncanny, as do Von Eckardt's photographs (see Bergstein's chapter "The Abject and the Uncanny in *Junk Drawer*"). This is a beautiful, redemptive light in which to regard photography.

PHOTOGRAPHIC CREATION OF "JUNK"

But photography can be as cruel as a border guard. Given that junk is a function of the kind of attention granted to it, and photography is a visual form of attention, it follows that photography can be cruel, even if unintentionally so. It can be cruel by being inattentive, inconsiderate, and thoughtless. Does it perhaps follow that junk, like the term "migrant," can be a function of the manner in which something is photographed? If so, then photography cannot only redeem junk, it can create junk, too. Objects can be transformed into junk, sometimes violently, by the attention, or inattention, of the lens. Not only small things can become junk, but also large ones, including buildings, and even villages, can. A photographer can help transform an entire place, and by extension, the people living in it, into "junk." We have seen the beauty that a humble shed can acquire through the lens of a Walker Evans, but its beauty can return to the status of junk in an instant. And when it does, the result can be dangerous, sometimes lethal.

How can we tell a village from a junkyard? In the Occupied Palestinian Territories, those territories in "Area C" where, in accordance with the Oslo Accords, Israel is in control, Palestinian villages are often slated for destruction to make room for new Israeli settlements or the expansion of existing ones.[16] One of the villages repeatedly slated for demolition and the expulsion of its inhabitants is Al-Khan al-Ahmar, in the Occupied West Bank next to the sprawling settlement of Ma'ale Adumin and its outpost Kfar Adumim. The village predates the settlement; most of its inhabitants arrived in 1952 after they were expelled from the Negev. In September 2018, the Israeli High Court ruled that since the fact of private Palestinian ownership of the land was no longer relevant, there were no further legal obstacles in the way of destroying the village, and the Israeli government gave the residents a week to evacuate. The decision had been made to raze the village and move its inhabitants to a place between a garbage dump and a sewage treatment plant outside of the Palestinian town of Abu Dis. The newspaper *Haaretz* ran an article on September 23 about the evacuation that inadvertently touched on the issue of junk. The main illustration in the article was captioned: "A Palestinian woman sits with her children in the Bedouin village of Khan al-Ahmar, West Bank, September 13, 2018" (FIGURE 4.7).

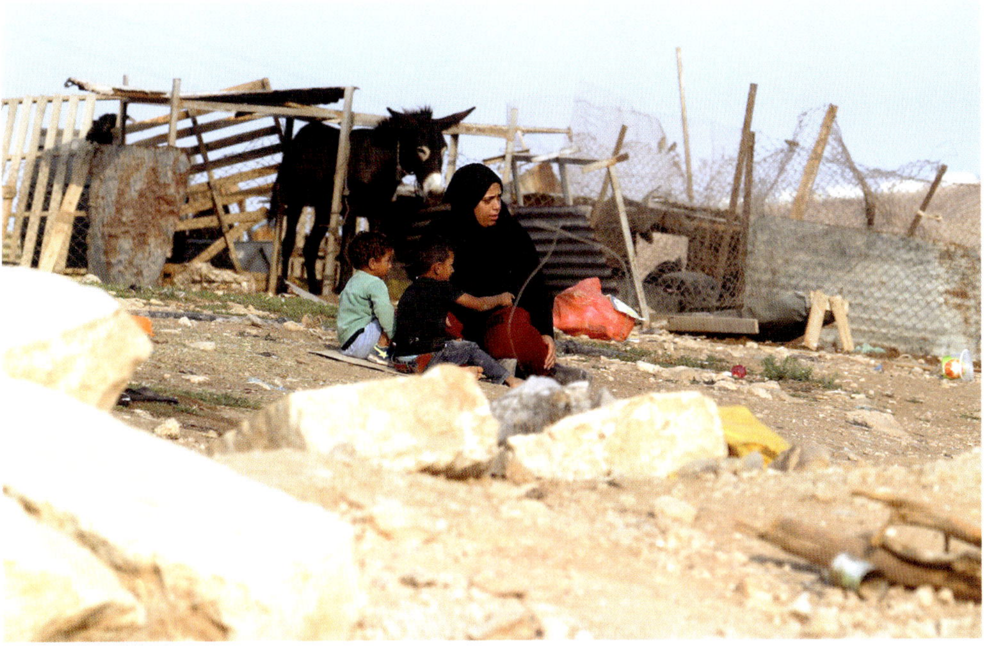

FIGURE 4.7. Ahmad Gharabli, "A Palestinian Woman Sits with Her Children in the Bedouin Village of Khan Al-Ahmar, West Bank, September 13, 2018," photograph from *Haaretz*, September 23, 2018.

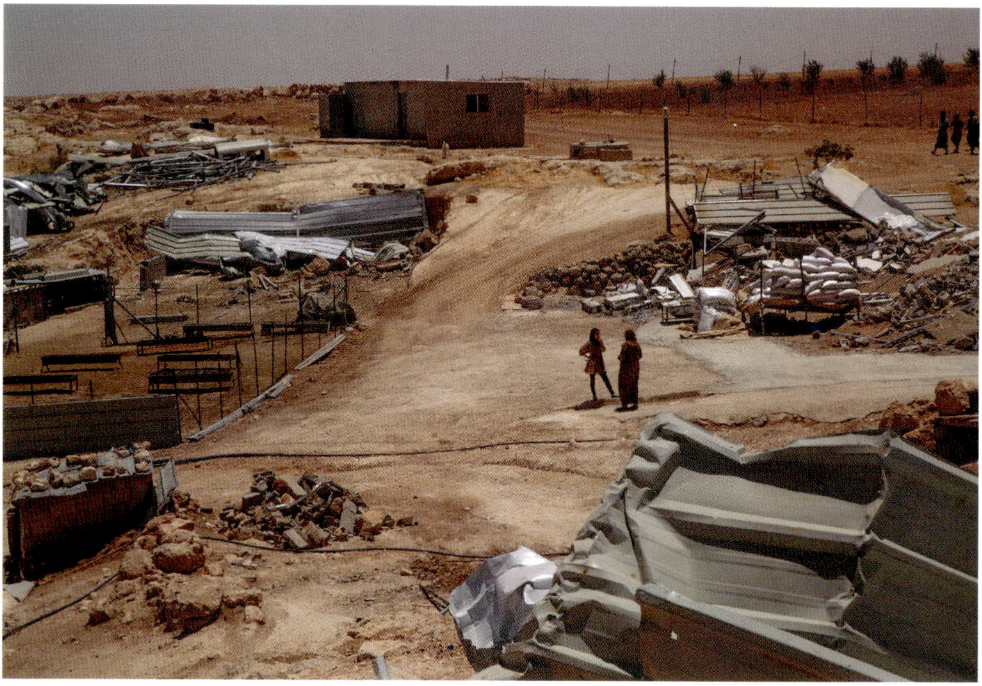

FIGURE 4.8. Margaret Olin, *Demolitions in Al-Mirkez, Occupied Palestine*, 2022, photograph.

The question of junk arises in the comments section, where a reader asked the question: "Where's the village? The photo looks like a junk-yard."[17] A village is a place where people have homes, where their lives are centered. People who live in a junkyard are generally considered squatters, not villagers. Assuming that the photograph suggests the latter interpretation, how does it do so? The photograph does not turn the woman into a victim because of the camera angle or her appearance. The photographer has bent or kneeled to photograph the woman and her children at eye-level; neither she nor the children are looking beseechingly—or at all—at the camera. It is the appearance of her surroundings that has the potential to transform her. The photograph situates her in the center, seated on the ground with two children on what seems to be a piece of cardboard next to a ramshackle animal pen with a donkey looking out of it, and construction debris lying about. The reader might assume that her family lives on this patch of ground, that they have no actual home. A photograph like this one, which suggests that the subject already lives in a junkyard, makes the idea of forcibly evacuating the woman, even to a city dump, look somewhat less unjust than it might otherwise. Indeed, arguments in favor of the resettlement of Palestinians from this area often ignore the fact that they have lived in the same village for decades and turn on the idea that they are really migrants, not residents. Bedouins, it is often said, are transients and, consequently, to move them away from their "temporary" homes and give them a permanent one—wherever that home might be—would be to give them a settled existence and improve their lives.

IRREDEEMABLE PHOTOGRAPHY

There is junk that cannot be redeemed by photography. When an entire neighborhood or village is destroyed, the distinction between junk and treasure is as crucial as that between existence and destruction, life and death. Such sights are the ultimate destination of junk (see FIGURE 4.8). They also show that junk is not a fait accompli. Few things start out at the bottom end of the junk hierarchy I described at the beginning of this chapter; there is a possibility of redemption anywhere along the way. But this is the last stop on a continuum where the trajectory of junk is similar to the trajectory of life to death and sometimes can even mirror the transition of its owner from life to death. This passage from treasure to junk can be sped up by bulldozers. But sometimes photography itself can help incite the bulldozers.

I have already made the point that a junk drawer is a luxury item particular to people who have enough space to keep things that they never use. But it is also the luxury of people who have enough time to accumulate things, who are not leaving on forced transports or fleeing on foot, who do not have to make hurried, crucial decisions about which possessions to drag out of their homes ahead of the bulldozer or which to carry with them and which to abandon to the elements, to vandals, or to looters.

Or to photographers. The photographers and their projects reveal their differing views and assumptions about life, from the sanguine notion that everyone has a junk drawer to the idea that junk is the outcome of state-run terror, wielded against people deemed inessential. Even if photography cannot redeem the objects in these village-size junk piles, perhaps photographs of unredeemable junk can encourage those who have some influence to try to prevent photography and, better, the viewers of photographs, from giving the impetus to create more such junk. Barring that, perhaps the ability to read the process of attention that creates photographs can somehow help prevent the inversion of the slogan "Your junk, our treasure" into the cruel slogan, "Your treasure, our junk."

1. Margaret Olin, "Attentiveness and Visual Imagination in Looking and Photographing: A Gay Liberation Rally in Chicago 1970," in *Photography and Imagination*, ed. Amos Morris-Reich and Margaret Olin (Routledge, 2020), 118–32.
2. William Henry Fox Talbot, *The Pencil of Nature* (Longman, Brown, Green and Longmans, 1844).
3. Jean Marzollo, with photographs by Walter Wick, *I Spy: A Book of Picture Riddles* (Scholastic, 1992).
4. Wick was given the commission for the first (and subsequent) *I Spy* books on the basis of a similar photograph of the nuts and bolts lying around in his studio, which he used to promote his work. Clancy Morgan, "Meet the Photographer Behind the 'I Spy' Books that Captured Millions of Readers' Imaginations," *Business Insider*, July 30, 2019, https://www.businessinsider.com/i-spy-walter-wick-photographer-can-you-see-books-2019-7.
5. Roland Barthes, *Camera Lucida: Reflections on Photography*, trans. Richard Howard (Macmillan, 1981).
6. Margaret Olin, *Touching Photographs* (University of Chicago Press, 2012), 50–69.
7. See Ariella Aïsha Azoulay, *Potential History: Unlearning Imperialism* (Verso, 2019).
8. Several recent studies of the use of photography in relation to refugees offer interpretations similar to those elaborated here about exploitative aspects of migrant portraiture. See, for example, Jannis Hamilakis, "The Redistribution of the Sensible: Photography and Contemporary Migration," in *Pearls, Politics and Pistachios: Essays in Anthropology and Memories on the Occasion of Susan Pollock's 65th Birthday*, ed. Herausgeber*innenkollektiv (ex oriente, 2021), which contains further bibliographical references.
9. Robert Hariman, *No Caption Needed: Iconic Photographs, Public Culture, and Liberal Democracy* (University of Chicago Press, 2007).
10. Hariman, *No Caption Needed*, 53–67. Some recent literature on *Migrant Mother* seeks to bring to light the person in the picture and details the process of creating the picture. See Sally Stein, *Migrant Mother, Migrant Gender: Reconsidering Dorothea Lange's Iconic Portrait of Maternity* (MACK Books, 2020).
11. Gideon Mendel, *Dzhangal* (GOST Books, 2017).
12. Tom Kiefer, *El Sueño Americano/The American Dream* (2018), accessed September 2022, https://www.tomkiefer.com/el-sueno-americano.
13. Kiefer, *El Sueño Americano*.
14. Kiefer, *El Sueño Americano*.
15. Megan Gibson, "See the Objects Refugees Carry on Their Journey to Europe," *Time*, October 6, 2015; James Mollison, "What Refugees Carry With Them: Series of 13 Diptychs of Objects that Refugees Carry on Their Journey to Europe," accessed September 2022, https://www.jamesmollison.com/what-refugees-carry-with-them.

16. In theory, Israel's control is temporary, until such time as final peace accords are signed, which, however, seems unlikely to happen in the near future.
17. Yotan Berger, "Israel Gives Residents of West Bank Bedouin Village Week to Evacuate," *Haaretz*, Sept. 23, 2018, https://www.haaretz.com/israel-news/2018-09-23/ty-article/.premium/israel-gives-residents-of-west-bank-bedouin-village-week-to-evacuate/0000017f-f67c-d318-afff-f77fca720000, accessed April 23, 2024. The comment "CounterPoint by Joel Stein" has since been deleted. The uncredited photographer of the photograph to which the comment pertains is Ahmad Gharabli (AFP). The Hebrew version of the article does not use this illustration.

CHAPTER 5

FROM "JUNK" TO "JUNQUE"

SANDER L. GILMAN

JUNK AND SOCIAL CATEGORIES

I am the grandson of a "junk man" who plied the streets of Buffalo, New York, in a horse-drawn cart (and later a revoltingly home-painted green truck), taking "stuff" away that people no longer wished to possess, evaluating it, and then selling it for his living. My emotion at his "stuff," often baled up in the garage of my childhood home, was not disgust but curiosity. "Junk" and all its variables seem to be connected to the concept of "valuelessness." According to the *Oxford English Dictionary,* "junk" began as a nautical term for old, discarded, useless hawsers, and evidently, only in the age of Victoria did it become a more general term for the marginally valuable. Yet even the hawsers seemed to have value. Remember the prisoners in Victorian "gaols," such as Reading, where Oscar Wilde was incarcerated in 1895, learning to becoming a rehabilitated citizen, earning his keep by "pickin' oakum" with bloody fingers: "We tore the tarry rope to shreds / With blunt and bleeding nails."[1] The "tarry rope" was indeed those useless hawsers, now—it was said—providing value by reforming the prisoners through meaningful work earning profit for the "gaol" through "recycling," a term coined in the 1920s for just such a process.

Yet, the City of New York banned people like my grandfather from the streets in 1845, stating that, "No person shall draw or drive . . . any handcart . . . for the purpose of collecting junk, rags, old rope, old iron, [etc.]."[2] This was not merely an aesthetic choice, but was freighted with anti-immigrant and anti-Black feeling, as the junkmen, even in 1845, were social outsiders. By my—Eastern European and Jewish immigrant—grandfather's day in Buffalo, "the mass media's common portrayal of Jewish sellers as dishonest and greedy applied double to junk dealers, who were viewed as a public sanitation hazard, and even a moral menace."[3] Indeed, in American slang, the pejorative term for Jew, "sheeny," at the time became the equivalent of the junk collector, as in 1928 in Detroit: "'The Sheeny Man,' . . . We all seem to know him as something different the Junk Man, Rag and Bone Man, The Alley Man. I knew him by the name he would call out after a short toot on his dull old bugle 'The Sheeny Man!'" As Jenna Weissman Joselit has noted, thinking of turn-of-the-century New York City:

> A significant number of people at the margins of society made a living out of salvaging trash and turning it into something else: rags into paper, metal bits into steel. It didn't take much at first—just a sack—to get started as a junkman, a ragpicker, a scrapper, or an "old clo" man. The capital investment was nil.

> The requisite physical investment, though, was something else again, calling for a sturdy constitution, a strong nose capable of tolerating odiferous smells, and a thick skin with which to withstand the social disdain that came with the job. Many were Jewish immigrants.[4]

Junkmen equaled junk people, junk demarcating a border that defined the acceptable from the unacceptable, the clean from the dirty, the healthy from the diseased. Indeed, "scrap handling [was seen] as dirty work, work that was not just physically dirty, but morally degraded. That perception reflected revulsion at the kinds of people who did the work as well as the work itself, conflating the unsanitary status of the work with xenophobic stereotypes of the immigrants willing to do the work.... The popular image of the junk dealer at the turn of the century was a hook-nosed, scheming Jewish immigrant bent on cheating honest American businessmen." Indeed, by the 1920s, Southern Italians and Jewish immigrants, at least Yiddish-speaking Jews, came to define the junk dealer.[5] Among the latter, in the 1930s, was my grandfather.

Harold Frederic, the London correspondent for the *New York Times*, ventured to Marseille during the cholera outbreak of 1884 and reported to his British readers that "The shops have a poverty-stricken air about them. Many of them are devoted to the sale of rags, and the sweepings of a city, bones, junk—a collection of pestilence-breading filth."[6] The East End of London was little different. As many as two thousand Jewish ragmen prowled the streets of London in the late nineteenth century, certainly not a majority of the ragmen, but their very presence labeled the trade as unhygienic and unacceptable.[7]

Sigmund Freud, in 1875 and then again in 1908, visited his merchant half-brothers in Manchester, where the British Jewish community was second in size only to that of Victorian London. As an acculturated, Western Jew, he would have seen such Yiddish-speaking ragpickers, newly arrived from Imperial Russia, as "unclean and disturbing," as a medical commission of the British Emigration Service wrote in 1889. The committee continued: "the Russians, more particularly the Russian-Polish Jews, are extraordinarily filthy.... We were taken into a cabin recently occupied by this class of emigrant, and found the deck covered with soil. They refuse to avail themselves of the closets provided for the passengers. They seem totally indifferent to the filth and stench they create, and in this respect have either lost, or never possessed, any sense of shame."[8] Such rag-and-bone men would have been nothing new for Freud, as the Viennese "Tändler" (rag-bag men) were also primarily Eastern European Jews. The perceptions of many like him who needed trash (and worse) removed was that those on the margins dealing with "cast-offs" were little better than the stuff that they hauled away.

Freud's father, a merchant from the Eastern reaches of the Austro-Hungarian Empire, moved to Vienna in 1860, and by 1881, had a doctor in the family when Freud graduated medical school. His leap from the social periphery to being a middle-class professional was fraught both for him and his father. Freud remarks to his fiancée Martha Bernays in a letter dated August 5, 1885, on the poorest of the poor, "a man as poor as only a Jew can be. Or rather, his father was as poor as that; I am not sure whether he was a peddler or . . . a dealer in second hand clothes." Freud continues that he is, "a typical little Jew with sly features, a boundless vivaciousness and the gift of the gab," studied medicine, and made it eventually into the middle class as a professor of medicine, a status his father only accomplished in middle age.[9] Perhaps imagining such junkmen as those he saw in his youth led Freud in his essay on "Character and Anal Erotism" in 1908 to comment obliquely, in English, on his memories of Manchester: "Cleanliness, orderliness and trustworthiness give exactly the impression of a reaction-formation against an interest in what is unclean and disturbing and should not be part of the body ('Dirt is matter in the wrong place.')"[10] If "cleanliness, orderliness and trustworthiness" is a definition of bourgeoisie virtues under Victoria and Franz Joseph, including those of the deserving poor, then the antitheses are the collectors of junk. For Freud's use of the English phrase "Dirt is matter in the wrong place" may well have had its origin, unbeknownst to him, in Lord Palmerston's high Victorian notions of the boundary between the useful and the useless, between urban sewage and rural fertilizer, between the immigrant's "crap" and the orderly running of the state, symbolized by the new hygienic standard of the new "Crappers." The Crappers—"WCs" (water closets), named, it is said, after one of their developers Thomas Crapper (*nomen est omen*)—flushed away the "crap," the filth, and the stench that, as the British Emigration Service medical commission recorded, soiled the decks of the ships bringing Russian Jews to Great Britain.[11]

Such Mancunian (read: Jewish) junkmen were seen not only as the collectors of the refuse that even the poorest no longer wanted, but also as—perhaps—the primary purveyors of stolen goods, always disturbing the social disorder, yet always having a place in it.[12] Thus, they were not quite without value but only possessed a value out of the norm. Today we might speak of the ethics of my grandfather's activity as giving value via recycling, upcycling, or even laundering, a clearly negative term taken from the act of cleaning. Indeed, marginal value means defining what value truly is.

Claude Lévi-Strauss wrote in *La Pensée sauvage* (1962) of the bricoleur, the person who creatively assembles the fragments of the world into the new, the innovative, always keeping the fragments' functionality in the now in mind, ignoring their origin and their original purpose.[13] For my grandfather, each object he collected fit into his world as a source of income derived from that which, with respect to its original function, no longer had any value or any purpose for its prior possessor. He was not an engineer, not a scientist, pace Lévi-Strauss's alternative to the bricoleur, but someone who indeed gave junk new value, in David Graeber's sense as the "false coin of our dreams."[14] Value, of course, is an affective quality added to objects.[15] But value is a fuzzy category that spans from Adam

Smith's claim of the ascribed utility of an object to David Ricardo's and Marx's (and Graeber's) notion of the determination of value through the labor used in its production to a version of Walter Benjamin's intrinsic notion of "aura," an object having aesthetic value because of its perceived uniqueness.[16] Is Benjamin's idea of an "aura" in his "The Work of Art in the Age of Its Technical Reproducibility" (1936) actually an antithesis of Freud's disgust, or is it merely a means of evaluating the difference between an aesthetically valuable object and its copy, a copy that may have market value as such but does not have intrinsic value?

What defines then our emotional reaction to "junk" or "crap" or "garbage" or "trash" or "litter" or "refuse" or "debris" or "rubble" or "castoffs" or "scrap" or "tchotchkes"? And how do all of these then give shape to our quotidian life, in Freud's sense? *Crap* is the title of a recent study by the American intellectual historian Wendy A. Woloson in which she defines it as consisting of "consumer goods that are typically low priced, poorly made, composed of inferior materials, lacking in meaningful purpose, and not meant to last. Such crap has insinuated itself into just about every aspect of daily life, filling countless kitchen 'junk' drawers and clotting garages and basements across the nation. So ubiquitous, crap is nearly invisible, like white noise."[17] What interests me here is to think about such "junk drawers" as a category of affective experience, not solely of intellectual organization, which is why disgust is an underlying theme of Woloson's work. As she explains, her book was written from the "angry" standpoint of a cancer survivor whose world was "awash in a sea of medical-related crap."[18] What interests me here is what makes junk emotionally visible, what affective forces define its value. How do we overcome our senses of disgust with junk in the process of giving or denying it value?

For we seem not to be repulsed by our junk in the same way that we are carefully taught to be repulsed by our feces or even by weeds, or are we? Do we sublimate our disgust at the discards of our society in rather different ways than we do our disgust at our own dejecta? We write of our "body politic," but its material castoffs are emotionally evaluated on a very different scale than those bodily products that each of us constantly (and normally) generates. "Crap," according to Woloson, is cheaply but not necessarily poorly made objects created as a result of generating a desire for them as products through modern advertising. And advertising is, of course, how twentieth-century society was able to generate such desire for objects that may or may not have a value in our quotidian lives but have value in our affective lives. In other words, crap is a product of conspicuous consumption rather than true need, which would give an object intrinsic value. Thus, junk may have been valuable in an exchange market at one time and is now marginal to it.

Some junk may acquire an "aura" in Benjamin's sense and is valuable both aesthetically and monetarily. Think of the extraordinary monetary and cultural value placed on the clichéd "most famous painting in the world," Thomas Gainsborough's *Blue Boy*, in 1922 when the National Gallery in London sold it to Henry Huntington for $620,000.[19] Today its cultural value is much less, replaced as the most sought-after image in popular advertising, perhaps, by the *Mona Lisa* (not Andy Warhol's silkscreen "Colored Mona Lisa" [1962] but today once again Walter Pater's idealized *Mona Lisa*, at least for the tourists crowding her gallery at the Louvre, soon to be replaced by an ever-larger space for this one tiny painting). No biscuit companies today can sell "crap" cookies by just mechanically embossing the *Blue Boy* on the lid. Yet "kitsch" too can have both monetary and cultural value, as well as an "aura." But it also can become junk, as with the empty and cheaply made *Blue Boy* biscuit tins of 1900, used and then trashed, which today, as kitsch, have in turn become prized collectors' objects. As most are discarded, most become junk, and thus disappear from the marketplace; yet they have more value over time as they become rarer. Remember Andy Warhol's collection of 175 commercial, kitschy cookie jars in the shapes of cute pandas, Humpty Dumpty, sheep, and piglets that were highly valued objects in the auction of his effects in 1988, bringing in almost a quarter of a million dollars, and that individually still bring high value as objects because of their association with Warhol. Their value is not as cookie jars but as rare examples of Warhol's aesthetic, turning kitsch into art.

WHEN DOES JUNK BECOME JUNQUE

By the 1990s, "junk" had indeed morphed into "junque."[20] Woloson notes that "the objects people had been bringing into their homes for decades—souvenir spoons, china figures, printed ephemera, bottles—were now going out. They were sold to the antique dealers, pawned at the pawnshop, traded at the junk market."[21] Flea markets sell the sort of stuff my grandfather probably would have collected alongside much that he would not have, as it did not have a ready market in the 1960s. Indeed, "as the flea market has increased in size, more so-called 'junk' has entered the market, producing a Gresham's Law effect of sorts: higher quality material has moved elsewhere. However, a wide range of regional, cultural, occupational, social class, educational, lifestyle, and age segments is present at the market."[22] As a result, as the commentator in the *York County [Maine] Coast Star* commented on April 29, 2004: "The junkman has gone the way of the iceman and the milk man because today we have yard sales to take care of our family flotsam and jetsam."[23] The disjecta membra of society begins to have value because of the shift of its audience, for whom Thorsten Veblen's notions of value are tied not only to class and race but also to the very notion of collecting itself.

Cultural historian Henry Louis "Skip" Gates, Jr., early on began to collect racist "Sambo art" at flea markets when he was my younger colleague at Cornell University in the 1980s, much as I had collected "antisemitica" when I was a student in West Berlin in the 1960s.[24] And this transvaluation of such objects, now collected as evocations of racism in the past, gives racist images a new monetary and cultural value in a race-sensitive society. The shock value they inspire for the present provides a frisson, which is clearly marketable. These objects have collective memories tied to them; they achieve value specifically because they evoke a bygone context, providing the present collector with more than merely objects to possess. A black cast-iron jockey, the function of which was to tie up your horse to, becomes the evocation of a distant past, an object in which the lost function no longer matters. Yet the newest moment in history provides a different frisson for such objects, not collected because they purposely distance the past, but because they evoke it. It's hard to say when it started, but sometime over the last decade, or maybe year, or was it possibly only the last month?—the public has been treated to a remarkable number of glimpses into people who should know better flirting with the trappings of Nazism. Praising Adolph Hitler. Making casual suggestions about sending people to the gas chambers. Throwing what at a minimum sure *looked* like a Sieg Heil salute and then laughing at anyone who cared. Parading a mock-up of the gates of Auschwitz in a Catholic Thanksgiving Day parade. The sale of Nazi memorabilia, ever-present after WWII, but usually underground, now has a new audience, for whom Nazi material kitsch becomes a means of "owning the libs" and thus has added political value.

Collecting, in the end, for Benjamin, soon to suicide at the Spanish town of Portbou, having abandoned all hope of escaping the clutches of the real Nazis, as for the rest of us, represents "a relationship to objects that does not emphasize their functional, utilitarian value—that is their usefulness—but studies and loves them as the scene, the stage, of their fate."[25] It is of the present moment, as the objects collected of the imagined past resolve the "dialectical tension between order and disorder."[26] But, and this is central to the notion of junk, "the phenomenon of collecting loses its meaning as it loses its personal owner."[27] Objects, as they pass from hand to hand, may regain their "aura," lose it again, and still have the capacity to be transmuted. This is not a false consciousness but a collective rethinking of value. As Kevin McLaughlin has noted, "the collector, for Benjamin, knows that what he collects are such empty forms—mere pieces or patches that can be invested with meaning or value only because they are decontextualized.... The collector may try to 'decipher' or 'get behind' the objects he collects (in the way we might try to 'decipher' or 'get behind' commodities to uncover the social relations that hide in their 'hieroglyphic' character). But regarding what they once were, the collected objects are empty."[28] Empty, but valued nevertheless.

When "junk" morphs into "junque," it is suddenly:

> ... an emic descriptor connoting a distinction achieved through disrepair or neglect. Although the bulk of the merchandise is categorized as "antiques" or "collectibles," the kinds of goods assigned to these categories are legion. Furniture, linens, glassware, crafts, plates, stamps, baseball cards, tools, signs, books and magazines, clothing, archaeological artifacts, music cassettes, antique weaponry, jewelry, statuary, tramp art, war memorabilia, military patches, beer cans, toys, knock-off perfumes, engraving service, rust-proofing chemicals,

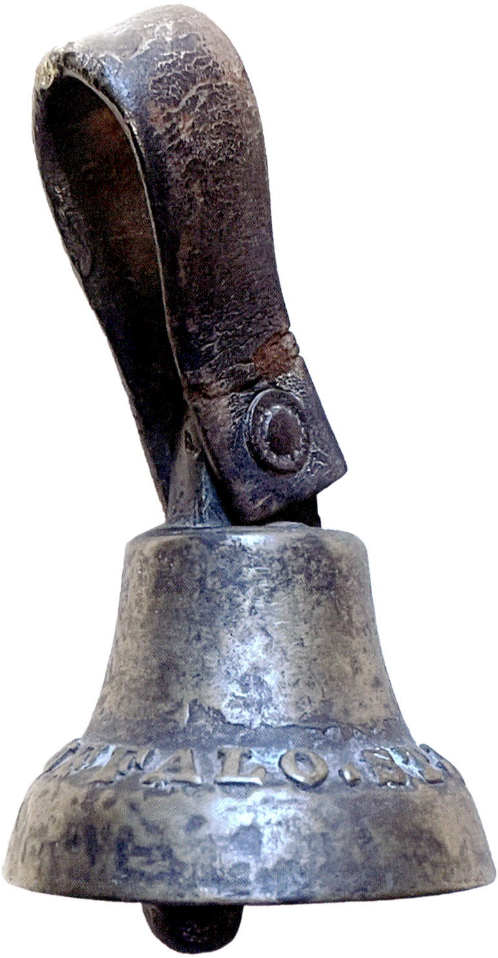

FIGURE 5.1. Sander Gilman, "Buffalo St. RR Co." bell, 1919, digital photograph.

hardware, and appliances are just a few of the categories of items available. Many consumers and dealers liken the market to a museum because of the sheer variety of items available and the sense of history experienced.[29]

Yet the portmanteau "junque" is evocative not only of "jun-k" but also of "anti-que." When does the antique become valuable? When someone gives it value? But "junque" is not antiques. It is the stuff of affective life, not the products of self-proclaimed high culture. It is playfulness as embodied in "camp," tongue-in-cheek and private, until the American Visionary Art Museum in Baltimore, home of outsider art, or the more prestigious Museum of Modern Art, decides that it has (aesthetic) value and thus gives it (monetary) value. The transformation of *Blue Boy* biscuit tins into collector's items into the stuff presented in galleries where perhaps the original painting itself once hung is not beyond imagining.

Be certain that this will come, if it is not already here in our NOW. This is Benjamin's fantasy museum in his *One-Way Street* (1928), as his "dream house" where "the home becomes a temporary lodging. The objects it holds are pared down. Much has become the stuff of memory alone. Things return in dreams or nightmares but may no longer resemble themselves, are not what they once were. Or they are filled with the junk of everyday existence, the stuff gathered simply to fill a space in the absence of a life, or at least one worth living."[30] And here junk can be transformed into art (think Joseph Cornell, as Levitt and Ost discuss in their essay) or into "junque" or indeed into "crap." Indeed, Jennifer Le Zotte has claimed that "Dadaists and surrealists were among the first to recognize secondhand commerce, especially flea markets, as a 'model for a kind of culture refuse dump that dissolves the relationship between art, history, and junk.'"[31] Art ("aura") and junk ("crap") are intertwined in the liminal space at the boundaries and history and, indeed, in my own imagining, sitting in my childhood garage wondering at the objects collected by my grandfather that tomorrow would be transformed by him into cash. My curiosity at "junk" turned them into objects of aesthetic value, like the one object I still possess from that time: a small bell, with a leather handle, inscribed "Buffalo St. RR Co.," redolent of the horse-drawn streetcars that had vanished long before my youth (FIGURE 5.1).

1. Oscar Wilde, *Poems* (Doubleday, Page and Co., 1923), 260.
2. By-laws & Ordinances N.Y. lxxiii (1845), 526, as cited by the *Oxford English Dictionary*, "junk n. 5.1."
3. Jennifer Le Zotte, *From Goodwill to Grunge: A History of Secondhand Styles and Alternative Economies* (University of North Carolina Press, 2017), 28.
4. Jenna Weissman Joselit, "The Jewish Woman Who Invented Recycling," *Tablet Magazine*, Oct. 18, 2019, https://www.tabletmag.com/sections/community/articles/jewish-woman-who-invented-recycling. Accessed September 12, 2024.
5. Carl Zimring, "Dirty Work: How Hygiene and Xenophobia Marginalized the American Waste Trades, 1870–1930,"*Environmental History* 9 (2004): 80–101 (80, 84, 88).
6. Harold Frederic, "Two Plague-Ridden Towns," *The Pall Mall Gazette*, Aug. 6, 1884, 11.

7. Adam Mendelsohn, "The Rag Race: Jewish Secondhand Clothing Dealers in England and America," in *Capitalism by Gaslight: Illuminating the Economy of Nineteenth-Century America*, ed. Brian P. Luskey and Wendy A. Woloson (de Gruyter, 2015), 76–92 (79).
8. "Report of the Lancet Special Commission on the British Emigration Service," *The Lancet* 133, no. 3410 (1889): 40–41 (41).
9. Sigmund Freud, "Letters of Sigmund Freud 1873–1939," in *The Standard Edition of the Complete Psychological Works of Sigmund Freud*, ed. James Strachey, vol. 51 (The Hogarth Press, 1963), 51, 163. For the context see Tony Kushner, *The Jewish Pedlar: An Untold Criminal History* (Manchester University Press, 2025), 149–50.
10. Sigmund Freud, "Character and Anal Erotism," in *The Standard Edition of the Complete Psychological Works of Sigmund Freud*, ed. James Strachey, vol. 9 (The Hogarth Press, 1959): 167–76 (171–72). For the context see Tony Kushner, *The Jewish Pedlar: An Untold Criminal History* (Manchester University Press, 2025), 149–50.
11. Richard Fardon, "Citations Out of Place," *Anthropology Today* 29, no. 1 (2013): 25–26.
12. Wendy A. Woloson, *In Hock: Pawning in America from Independence through the Great Depression* (University of Chicago Press, 2010), 128–29.
13. Claude Lévi-Strauss, *La Pensée sauvage* (Plon, 1962).
14. David Graeber, *Toward an Anthropological Theory of Value: The False Coin of Our Dreams* (Palgrave, 2002).
15. There are several scholars who explore the relationship between value and affect, including many postmodern theorists, who have considered the economic relation as a social value "from below," such as Antonio Negri and Michael Hardt, "Value and Affect," *boundary 2* 26, No. 2 (1999); 77–88.
16. Walter Benjamin, "The Work of Art in the Age of Mechanical Reproduction," in *Illumination*, ed. Hannah Arendt, trans. Harry Zohn (Schocken Books, 1968), 217–52; on "aura," see 221ff.
17. Wendy A. Woloson, *Crap: A History of Cheap Stuff in America* (University of Chicago Press, 2020), 1.
18. Wendy A. Woloson, "Selling Hope." *Boston Review*, Feb. 14, 2022, https://bostonreview.net/articles/selling-hope/, accessed July 12, 2023.
19. Tessa Salomon, "Why Thomas Gainsborough's Iconic 'Blue Boy' Was Once the Most Famous Painting in the World," *ARTnews* (Feb. 4, 2022), https://www.artnews.com/feature/blue-boy-painting-thomas-grainsborough-what-is-it-why-is-it-important-1234617832/. Accessed February 25, 2025.
20. John F. Sherry, Jr., "A Sociocultural Analysis of a Midwestern American Flea Market," *Journal of Consumer Research* 17 (1990): 13–30.
21. Woloson, *Crap*, 253.
22. Sherry, "Sociocultural Analysis," 24.
23. "Junkman," as cited in the *Oxford English Dictionary*, "junkman, n. 2"; *York County [Maine] Coast Star*, April 29, 2004.
24. See Henry Louis Gates, Jr., *Stony the Road: Reconstruction, White Supremacy, and the Rise of Jim Crow* (Penguin, 2019).
25. Benjamin, "Unpacking my Library: A Talk about Book Collecting," in *Illumination*, 59–67 (60).
26. Benjamin, "Unpacking my Library," 60.
27. Benjamin, "Unpacking my Library," 67.
28. Kevin McLaughlin, *Imitation and Exchange in Nineteenth-Century Literature* (Stanford University Press, 1995), 82.
29. Sherry, "Sociocultural Analysis," 24.
30. Esther Leslie, "Homes for Ghosts: Walter Benjamin and Kurt Schwitters in the Cities," *Societies* 3 (2013): 414–26 (421).
31. Jennifer Le Zotte, *From Goodwill to Grunge*, 58.

CHAPTER 6

ORDINARY AND EXTRAORDINARY OBJECTS AND THEIR AFTERLIVES

LAURA LEVITT AND RUTH OST[1]

TREASURE TROVES: THRIFT SHOPS, CONSIGNMENT STORES, AND JUNK DRAWERS

Ruth and I (Laura) come to this collection of essays to consider our shared and our distinct responses to Barbara Von Eckardt's *Junk Drawer* project. Part of what Laura wants to address here are those similar but quite different objects that compel her writing, objects brushed by violence, displacement, and loss. For her, having a sense of their backstories, even if we cannot know those stories with certainty, drives her writing, especially about Holocaust objects and evidence held in police storage facilities. Like those depicted in Von Eckardt's photographs, these are ordinary everyday objects that have become, in poet Maggie Nelson's words, "number pieces of [criminal] evidence."[2]

For Ruth, Von Eckardt's junk drawer holds out other possibilities. The objects become the stuff of art, part of a box that takes its inspiration from artist Joseph Cornell's constructions, or an Albert Barnes-inspired wall ensemble.[3] We are reminded of a recent story about a treasure trove packaged up for Ruth by a shop owner in Michigan who, after observing Ruth in her shop, gave her a big bag of trinkets. These constructions include not only photographs but also small handmade items, tiny individual mittens, customized miniature holiday stockings, pillows, and postcards.[4] The objects in that collection, once sorted, have become many other things, just as the contents of eBay junk drawers became the inspiration for the images created by Von Eckardt. In the broader scheme of things, Ruth finds many uses for such acquisitions like this Michigan trove—as thematic gifts, whether in a curated space within the confines of Temple University's Honors Program or in her own home, or eventually in the homes of friends and family as birthday, graduation, or condolence presents. Most, if not all, of Ruth's creations are conceived as gifts for specific people: a series of pillows made from the favorite shirts and ties of a lost husband and father; or handmade napkins to go with a set of dinner dishes as a wedding present, boxed and beribboned with a necklace in the colors of the napkins, ready for a dinner party.

Von Eckardt's project has forced us to consider what propels our shared but different work with objects. In what follows, we explore how and when, and also where, these efforts intersect. We also want to explore how our engagement with displaced ordinary objects, the stuff lost and found in any number of junk drawers, is in conversation with Von Eckardt's efforts. We take up Von Eckardt's invitation to think with her about her project and build on her invitation to bring other frameworks, other disciplinary and affective registers, to this work. Unlike her, we come to this project from the humanities, and from the visual and material arts. That said, we appreciate her desire to open up her project to a range of voices and perspectives.

We do not share the voyeuristic pleasure she finds in some of these collections; instead, we reflect on what is left behind, and the limitations built into these collections' stories. As we found ourselves looking through the junk drawer lots available on eBay in mid-June 2022, we were struck by how curated these collections already are before they make it to the Internet marketplace. There is already an aesthetic that shapes what these offerings look like in their preview photographs. Seeing any number of these next to each other makes the case. Presented for optimal curb appeal, they play with themes—a color, a collection of silverware, an array of buttons. For us, this suggests an even more difficult task to get back to any semblance of those to whom these objects once belonged. The "drawers" have to be at least two steps removed from their sites of origin. These are the lots that no one in the family wanted, and perhaps didn't sell at the family yard sale or at auction. They are then the property of a reseller who winnows down the collection, choosing what to keep and what to toss. Then, there is the process of photographing the collections for eBay. In this case, Von Eckardt's photographs offer an additional mediation—one that builds on her own sense of loss, which she brings to the photographs through not only her curation but also a visual wash, a sepia filter that lends a mournful air to the project, making the objects feel more distant in time.

Von Eckardt argues that there is a testimonial aspect to her images. We appreciate this insight, but we also question, given the layers of curation described above, how it is possible to get back to those to whom these possessions once belonged. The mediation of so many hands limits these efforts. Given all of this, we join Von Eckardt and the other contributors to this volume in the work of revisiting and reanimating these kinds of collected objects and ask how they might become meaningful to others in new ways. We mourn the sadness of their lost stories and the fact that these often-intimate possessions have become commodified as "junk." Appreciating this state of affairs, we are interested in how to breathe new life into these objects and collections through art and story, through creative and critical engagement in the present. We are interested in the afterlives of these objects and are committed to their recirculation.

In what follows, we each explain how, given our shared commitments to reviving these kinds of objects, we work in tandem. We produce afterlives acknowledging the uncertainty that haunts these objects.

ASSEMBLED GIFTS: INTIMACY AND THE OBJECTS THAT ARE LEFT BEHIND (RUTH)

ARTISTIC RESONANCES: FORMAL CONNECTIONS

The only essential is this: *the gift must always move.*

—Lewis Hyde, *The Gift*[5]

Thinking with junk drawers and what to make of their contents, whether random or curated, takes me to reflecting on objects. How do the treasures, the valuables, the castoffs, many brushed by grief, matter and to whom? How can objects, handled anew, carry creative afterlives?

When my father died, I asked my mother if I could have the small black worn leather-bound box (4 × 7 × 1½ inches) he carried with him sometimes when he visited the sick and afflicted. The local minister in a small town for almost thirty years, he was pretty much on call 24/7, my mother often at his side. His box housed four tiny glasses, as well as a shiny aluminum container for bread and a small bottle for grape juice kitted out for Holy Communion. When I was little, I especially liked helping with the preparation for the ritual, cutting the bread into tiny cubes, filling the bottle. Ours was not a wafer or wine tradition, nor a frequent Communion tradition for that matter, but if a family couldn't make it to church to partake on Communion Sundays, they hoped he would go to them. He did.

I have housed that box for almost five decades and over many moves. At the moment, on a bookshelf in my living room, it keeps company with a small empty micrometer box from my mother's work during World War II, a wood-covered book of dried flowers from the Holy Land, a tiny book of my own making, splayed open with favorite quotes, pictures, and feathers, and, for now, a carved figure of an old Swedish woodsman, sternly in charge.

Though the box is in plain sight, no one has asked about it, let alone asked to open it—not that I would mind. It stays closed for now, yet it comforts me knowing what's there, what's inside; it is a reminder of how the box contains and carries connection, and what can happen in the liminal spaces that rituals and engagements with religion and art afford. It signifies possibilities of making and remaking relationships. It is, as it turns out, about communion.

Is that enough of an afterlife for an object, this new story about a worn black leather-covered box, the contents, the company, and this telling?

In *The Gift: How the Creative Spirit Transforms the World* (2019), Lewis Hyde writes, "*the gift must always move.*"[6] Thinking with Von Eckardt's finds, how her junk drawer curation could be understood as the gift moving, took me to making fresh connections and noticing relationships between artist Joseph Cornell's assemblages and art collector Albert Barnes's wall ensembles, stopping along the way with poet Charles Simic and artists Betye Saar and Miriam Schapiro.

Cornell builds boxes and fills them with what he finds in his travels on foot. He juxtaposes, layers, and alters what he has retrieved, placing those items in his collections to create unexpected relationships among small objects and scraps of things—the compelling detritus he has found, scavenged, or rescued, rooting around in used bookstores, thrift shops, and other stray places.

In "Where Chance Meets Necessity," poet Charles Simic characterizes Cornell's way of working:

> Somewhere in the city of New York there are four or five still-unknown objects that belong together. Once together they'll make a work of art. That's Cornell's premise, his metaphysics, and his religion, which I wish to understand.
>
> He sets out from his home on Utopia Parkway without knowing what he is looking for or what he will find. Today it could be something as ordinary and interesting as an old thimble. Years may pass before it has company. In the meantime, Cornell walks and looks. The city has an infinite number of interesting objects in an infinite number of unlikely places.[7]

I carry Simic's words with me as I find myself in the Art Institute in Chicago. I know they have a lot of Cornell pieces, forty-two to be exact. I have come to see them. No sense of direction, I ask a guard, "Where are the Cornell boxes?" One has to weave around corners and enter a space that feels like entering one of Cornell's assemblages. The shelved boxes are small, eccentric, and inviting worlds, full of surprises. Cutouts of birds, old photographs, pages of text, seeds, and goblets share space in these *Wunderkammers*, sites of mystery, domains of imagination, curated vertical junk drawers. I want to own one. I want to make one.

In Cornell's work, what is left behind comes forward—take notice. The chance to make something new of what might turn up, even in a junk drawer, is the necessity.

I see how Simic is drawn to the work: this looking, always being on the alert, finding objects of interest in unlikely places but in the shape of stray words, scraps of sound, shards of thought, could this be what poets do making a poem? Is this what Simic wants to understand? Is this, too, the work of scholars, hoping to make something of that old thimble? Maria Stepanova in *In Memory of Memory* (2018) writes:

> Cornell perfected his complex system of internal rhyme to the point where he could couple anything together with little or no effort. In this lay his sense of secret delight.
>
> His objects learned a new obedience—each item considers for a moment, then lies down in its place and makes itself useful: all the objects become a family. Every object has the chance to bask in the gold light of "being seen"; the wood shavings, the colored sand, and the cork balls exhibit a majesty and poise more befitting to ballerinas and poets. It seems as if the fact of future oblivion and decline was enough to make any object invaluable to Cornell. Every new work was constructed like Noah's Ark, with the intention of preservation at its heart.[8]

Stepanova's pairing of Noah and Cornell highlights the creative urgency of rescuing and making something to salvage and to protect what or who one values. For me, it raises the question not so much about preservation, but about what's next, whether for the animals on the Ark, the finds in Cornell's assemblages, or, for that matter, Von Eckardt's carefully orchestrated photographs of the objects from the junk drawers. What happens when "being seen"? How is that different from being remembered? Art veers away from obituary.

Pairing Cornell and Barnes in the context of this essay might seem unlikely, but junk drawers open to odd encounters. Both were collectors: Cornell mostly scavenged; Barnes shopped lavishly. Cornell built boxes for his assemblages; Barnes built a building for his ensembles: The Barnes Foundation.

By his death in 1951, Barnes had acquired 181 Renoirs, sixty-nine Cézannes, fifty-nine Matisses, forty-six Picassos, sixteen Modiglianis and seven Van Goghs, not to mention the Soutines, Chardins, Courbets, Pippins, Glackenses, De Chiricos, and more. The list is long, but contains no Cornell and no photographs. This lineup of astonishing holdings, though, is not what the collection—from a Barnesian point of view—is about any more than Cornell's is about a found thimble. It is about learning how to look at and experience art. Barnes's "ensembles" in the Barnes Foundation become his art—chairs, andirons, hinges, candlesticks, pitchers, and chests cohabit with paintings, drawings, and sculptures, sharing the four walls and a modicum of floor space in every room. One can imagine his acquiring a new painting (or a dozen), pacing the rooms, trying to decide what to move, what visual point to make with this acquisition, what to hang or locate nearby, what to remove to make room. The viewer is in the Barnes box, keeping company with the ordinary and extraordinary.

What difference does it make to put that chair beside that painting? That piece of hardware by that painting? These ensembles generate questions, certainly puzzlement along with pleasure. These rooms through which to wander make room for engagement, for wondering about the odd juxtapositions, as unlikely a pair as Cornell and Barnes.

The issue of what to keep and what to let go is very much part of the Barnes legacy. The collection was, in effect, fossilized when Barnes died, his will insisting that nothing be changed, going as far as including diagrams of the walls of each room, indicating the precise location of each piece of his collection.[9] But, and without rehearsing the history of the litigation that made way for the move from the original building to one that looks exactly like a box (if a beautiful one) on the Benjamin Franklin Parkway in Philadelphia, it is interesting to note that Tod Williams and Billie Tsien, architects of the "new" Barnes, curated a *Wunderkammer* project for the Venice Biennale in 2012, echoing the kind of thinking that links Cornell and Barnes: "[an] installation explores the interwoven phenomena of inspiration, collection, and meaning in everyday objects."[10] Looking at the thirty-five boxes from thirty-five artists in that exhibition, even online, takes me back to the forty-two Cornells and the fascination for cabinets of curiosities, even large-scale ones like the Barnes Foundation.

Betye Saar's assemblages, inspired by Cornell, belong in conversation with junk drawers. In *Omen*, "we see her early reuse of everyday objects in an old kitchen utensil drawer that became the foundation for this assemblage."[11] What Saar makes of her finds is at the intersection of the personal and political, understood both broadly and deeply, as she explains in an interview with Sara Cochran.

> SC: So when the objects are incorporated into your work, they take on a completely new life?
>
> Betye: I feel that. I think that they're telling my story. I might not know what that story is, but they're together and they work together.
>
> My creative process is a sort of ritual. And that ritual is first in the hunting and gathering because that's great fun to go to flea markets and thrift stores, and just finding the materials, and find out what objects and images speak to me, like they almost become and say, "Take me home. I'll be a piece of art for you." And so the hunting and gathering is the beginning.[12]

More about gathering, coining the term "femmage," Miriam Schapiro makes use of lace, handkerchiefs, aprons, fabric, paint, layering, items like those I work with. I appreciate her decorative exuberance, her celebration of women's work and the quotidian. Early on in Schapiro's career "she had been traveling and lecturing through the country and meeting the many women who were part of her new audience. She asked them for souvenirs—a handkerchief, a bit of lace, an apron, a tea towel—some object from their past that they would be willing to have 'recycled' in her paintings.... she created an imposing handkerchief femmage ... her dealer, André Emmerich ... could not understand why she would want to include in her artist's statement expressions of gratitude to over forty women."[13]

I understand her practice all too well. I too find a need to express my gratitude.

Von Eckardt takes eBay junk drawers and changes the function of the objects within them, like these artists, transforming the objects into something new, offering what I think of as communion, if lowercase.

LOST AND FOUND: MY BOXES, MY SHELVES, MY SUITCASES

> What is contained must be released.
>
> —Helène Aylon, *Whatever Is Contained Must be Released*[14]

This junk drawer project is so compelling because it forces me to think about my own everyday practice. What do I notice in thrift shops, pick up, consider buying, maybe come back for, relieved if it is still there? What can't I resist looking at? What can't I part with? What do I do with the stuff I accumulate? What do I release? And once I have made these decisions, what do I do with the pieces I decide to keep?

I make things. Like Cornell, Saar, and Schapiro, I gather feathers, fabric, buttons, ribbons, paper, old books, photographs of people I know, and ones of people I don't know. I travel with a glue stick and stamps just in case when I am on the road I need to make something of what I have just found and send it to someone. Like Barnes, I think in ensembles, whether I'm making them from paper or fabric—or both—or they are a 3-D vignette, like the shelf where I keep that Communion kit.

But mainly I make things of stuff contained in my suitcases and boxes. I counted fourteen such containers (not including the roller bags reserved for travel), many of which Laura has found in her thrift expeditions and passed on to me. The artist Helène Aylon entitled her autobiography *Whatever Is Contained Must Be Released* (2012)—this could be my mantra. I make postcards, layered with text, fabric, whatever, that is glued or sewn down by hand or machine. I make pillows with small pockets into which I tuck papers with text, or coins, or a small object. Sometimes I make an assemblage for myself and sometimes for others. When I was at Temple University, and during my entire teaching career, I populated spaces and walls as if I lived in my office or classroom. In fact, I had a suitcase Laura gifted me in my office, full of cards, like a portable shop. Anyone was free to take one or supply one.

It's the juxtaposing, layering, and arranging, the surprise that I like, the play of making something but almost always with someone in mind. If I were to inventory the people I send things to, it would be a playlist of those I trust with these gestures. I don't consider these as works of art. They are about relationships, these things I make. They usually head in the direction of someone specific, though once in a while the stuff, as Saar notes, insists on being together even before I have someone in mind for it. Like Barnes, I am conscious of how each piece implicates the next.

What is now something of an obsession, making things and giving them away, began in earnest years ago not long after my grandmother died. A close friend recently turned sixty and I wanted to send her something that I made. I stitched her a pillow and accounted for the making in an accompanying letter:

> This birthday wish begins with my grandmother's pink chenille bathrobe, the only glamorous thing she ever owned. As a kid, I thought it was beautiful. It was my inheritance.
>
> I had that robe for years before I decided to turn it into gifts for my aunts Margaret, Helen, Ruth, Thelma, and little Trid [my mother]. One year I made them tiny bags; another I made them tiny pink chenille Christmas stockings. When I was thinking about you and your 60th, I thought, I need to make something for you. Looking through my suitcases, I saw that pink chenille, and . . . well, you define glamorous! But truly, you are in my family, so how could you not have a share of my treasure?

What is brushed with grief is also brushed with comfort. It comforts me to make things out of that robe (I still have some left).[15] For me, making things from what is left over addresses a longing, if only for patching sadness. Carefully making, mending the tatter, reusing the mended object, I find myself in the company of Hyde: "the gift must always move."[16] It is not just that it moves; its movement is compelled by its re-creation, not unlike the gifts I have made from that robe.

So, in the end, I did make a "Cornell" box. I have made a few by now, some more like the work of Saar or Schapiro. As I reflect on Von Eckardt's work, I wonder if it is time to play with my father's Communion kit. I was thinking I might stand it up and display it open, Cornell-like. Then maybe I would add a piece of talismanic jewelry for Saar and fringe it with my grandmother's crocheted lace for Schapiro. Then I'd have to rearrange the shelf, which would be straight-up Barnesian. That Swedish carved woodsman might have to go, but then I would photograph it for Von Eckardt. And then mail that photograph to Laura.

THE OBJECTS THAT REMAIN: URGENT TALES TOLD THROUGH ONCE ORDINARY OBJECTS (LAURA)

ARTISTIC RESONANCE: FORMAL CONNECTIONS

The objects that I have written about most recently, material objects held in police storage and in Holocaust collections, come with a kind of urgency that demands attention. Trauma, violence, and loss animate these once ordinary objects. I find myself thinking about images I know, photographic projects that focus on seemingly everyday objects, projects that share formal connections to Von Eckardt's work. The difference is that my frame of reference is traumatic and brutal. I am reminded of Ziyah Gafić's haunting images of everyday objects found at mass gravesites in Bosnia that are horrible evidence of genocide. I am also reminded of the images of objects shed or otherwise left behind at the Southern border of the United States, photographed and curated by Tom Kiefer (FIGURES 4.5, 4.6).

As described in the introduction to his 2014 TED Talk, "Everyday Objects, Tragic Histories," "Ziyah Gafić photographs everyday objects—watches, shoes, glasses. But these images are deceptively simple; the items in them have been exhumed from the mass graves of the Bosnian War. Gafić, a TED Fellow and Sarajevo native, is photographing every item from these graves in order to create a living archive of the identities of those lost."[17] His project has continued but this description makes explicit the urgency of Gafić's work and the ways that once ordinary objects take on the weight of tragic histories through their proximity to those who have died. Driving Gafić's project is his hope that the objects he photographs might help identify some of those who perished. This is, in part, why the project is entitled *The Quest for Identity*. His wager is that perhaps a unique item might become a trigger of memory for a family member or friend.

Maybe the owner of a particular wristwatch, pendant, or pair of eyeglasses might be identified. These are traces, remnants of once vibrant lives that gesture toward an effort to remember those to whom those remnants once belonged. He suggests that this process of looking at these photographs might be less horrible than trying to bring family members and loved ones to a morgue.

After obtaining permission to photograph these now forensic materials at the site where they have been stored, he places individual bags of the remains on stainless steel tables to photograph them. He chose the tables, as he explains, because: "It's the same background as where they assemble the bodies. That was a creative choice but it was in front of me. My assistant would get the bag [of items]. Each bag contains a number of items and has keywords and a code. [My assistant] would write down the code. The idea was to keep all the contents in one bag in one frame.... The camera is almost fixed like a copy stand. The arrangement is a choice. That is me, my voice in the pictures."[18]

His are disturbingly beautiful images, their presentation and curation very much in his own hands. He says he had Walker Evans's photographs of tools as beautiful objects in mind even as he created a kind of archival aesthetic making sure that the photographs were uniform, with the same background and that "almost fixed" stand.[19] Gafić wants *The Quest for Identity* to serve as a more accessible archive. And after having learned about a scandal around the Hague tribunal where after the legal proceedings some related items were destroyed, Gafić believes his project is that much more important. Despite destroyed or lost material evidence, his accurate images remain.[20]

Like Gafić's project, Tom Kiefer's *El Sueño Americano/The American Dream* also presents images of once ordinary objects, the remains of lives very much in peril. These collected compositions of repeating ordinary objects—toothbrushes, tubes of toothpaste, backpacks—all carefully curated in neat rows one after another, speak to the experiences of those enduring another crisis at the Mexico-United States border. This time, the logic is that of like objects, rows of versions of the same item arranged on brightly colored surfaces: an array of CDs with a case symmetrically placed at the center of the composition, many over-the-counter medications still in their blister packs neatly arranged as if on display for purchase—not unlike junk drawer lots on eBay.[21] These brightly lit images filled with the vivid colors of ongoing life stand in sharp contrast to the backstories of these confiscated and abandoned objects.

Writing in 2018, religious studies scholar Rachel Lindsey explained how Kiefer began his project with the intention of capturing "the things that make America, America." As she states, "Like others before him, Kiefer's aesthetic of America explores national identity through banality of place and transfiguration of the familiar."[22] Working as a part-time janitor at the Ajo Station of U.S. Customs and Border Protection, Kiefer came to collect many of the possessions that had been confiscated from those detained at the border. The collecting began with foodstuffs that were first distributed to food pantries by the authorities, and when those practices ended, Kiefer took on the task as a volunteer. He then began collecting other items: "keys, clothing, water bottles, ID cards, wallets, toothbrushes, combs, medicine, toys, and other articles migrants had deemed essential to their journey and the start of their new lives."[23] There were also devotional items, among the many possessions confiscated by U.S. authorities. In conversation with Lindsey, Kiefer explained that although he has been able to donate some of these items to a local thrift store, there are other things that have just been too intimate to let go: "You 'don't donate a wallet or a rosary or a Bible,' at least not those still pulsating with the lives of the people from whom they were taken."[24] The ethical task of this project is in the everyday, the quotidian and familiar common items made strange by their confiscation and loss at the border. In this way, the work sacralizes the objects in an effort to humanize those caught in this vicious system.

In many ways, I struggle to consider how to move between these kinds of objects and those captured from the discarded objects sold in the junk drawers photographed by Von Eckardt. The stakes are so different. Even as the objects strangely resonate with each other, what draws me to Gafić's and Kiefer's projects is their moral urgency. Although all of these works take as their focus once, and still, ordinary objects, for me the question is what kinds of stories these objects, and these images, show us. Why do they matter and to whom? Do they or do they not have urgent stories to tell? Might they? My dilemma as I consider Von Eckardt's photographs is how to talk about these everyday objects that I experience as having no clear connections to any particular story or, more pointedly, to any known traumatic legacies I have written about, but still to ask what they might portend. How might they take on new meaning in the eyes of different viewers?

To be clear, there are formal connections between Gafić's and Von Eckardt's projects as they each carefully stage and photograph ordinary objects. Both works, in their own way, recuperate images as repressed narratives of memory. I think there is also a connection to Kiefer's *El Sueño Americano/The American Dream* that has helped me clarify the stakes of the work I do. At the same time, however, I think the distinction between the works stands. There are, as Von Eckardt explains, real limitations on what we can know about the drawers she has purchased and their wares. This means that what we can say and what we can bring to her work has real constraints. But what Ruth and I have come to appreciate is that such constraints cultivate other quite different kinds of interpretation or engagement. They present many perhaps more imaginative possibilities for what these collections might mean, even if these efforts carry less urgency than those yielded by Kiefer and Gafić's projects.

The desires that propel Von Eckardt's drawer project are about the familiar and its ephemeral character. What are the scattered pieces of an ordinary life? What do we leave behind and what do such things tell us about ourselves and others? How might we honor the quotidian? And, even in contrast to these two other photographic works, this project also suggests something about the work of photography in the aestheticization of such ephemeral objects. The projects all ask us to consider the work of curating, editing, and stylizing that mark various stages of their construction. And, most especially in the case of these drawers, the work reminds us of the way the collections arrived at eBay, were sold via eBay, and were then curated by Von Eckardt, who came to them from their commercial configuration, and then reconfigured them in her own compositions.

TALISMANIC EVIDENCE, THE STUFF OF EVERYDAY LIFE

Given all of this, the *Junk Drawer* project has pushed me to consider, in a different way, how its images might be viewed and understood. To do this, I turn to a series of resonances between this project and not only my own work, *The Objects that Remain* (2020), but also some of the literary texts that inform that work.[25] I offer a reading that allows me to get at what the *Junk Drawer* project might portend, and how its images might bring new images into view that could allow other viewers to tell their stories.

The Objects that Remain opens with the words of Maggie Nelson from *Jane: A Murder* (2005), a book of narrative poems about the life and death of her aunt. Like Nelson, I have a lot to say about ordinary objects that become something else entirely, like "numbered pieces of evidence, talismans"[26]: possessions taken from my own home the night that I was raped in Atlanta in November of 1989; the evidence held in police storage from the night Nelson's aunt Jane Mixer was murdered in Michigan in 1969; a broad array of artifacts held in the United States Holocaust Memorial Museum in Washington, D.C. Let me share the full quote from Nelson that serves as the epigraph for my book: "A sudden death is one way—a terrible way, I suppose—of freezing the details of a life. While writing *Jane* I became amazed by the way one act of violence had transformed an array of everyday items—a raincoat, a pair of pantyhose, a paperback book, a wool jumper—into numbered pieces of evidence, into talismans that threatened at every turn to take on allegorical proportions."[27] These words were my way into an extended meditation on all of those objects that remain or, like my own, have been lost, such as in police storage, and those that remain in both private and public collections.

What was so electrifying about paying attention to those pantyhose or that wool jumper? They were my way into telling my own story of violation anew. Hearing about this other woman's clothing from the night of her murder took me back to the night I was raped. What had the police taken from my apartment? What remains? Reading *Jane: A Murder* and Nelson's memoir *The Red Parts* (2007) about the belated trial, I found an opening into my own experience. Her words taught me how writing about the objects left behind evokes the landscape of memory. The stories of others, their attention to specific possessions at the scene of the crime, could help me tell my story. They help us touch the pain that might not otherwise be accessible. This was certainly true in my case. Nelson's example allowed me to write about my sweatpants taken from my Atlanta apartment. In this way, my book was an invitation to others to share, to do what Nelson did for me. Reading my story might open up a space for others who have suffered to tell their stories. In this way, like my previous work on Holocaust memory, I was enacting what becomes possible as different losses occur. The stories need not be the same, but placing them in close proximity, drawing both connections and distinctions, can make them less lonely. These are the kinds of connections I think it may be possible for viewers of Von Eckardt's *Junk Drawer* project to make between their stories and some of the drawers' discarded objects.

However, those everyday objects depicted in Von Eckardt's photographs may or may not serve this purpose here. Nelson and I share a concern about how objects brushed by violence become something else, both evidentiary and talismanic. But, in this case, although the stakes might appear lower, the objects depicted can also become something else. I would like to suggest that the *Junk Drawer* project can be an occasion for making different kinds of connections that might constitute an important afterlife for at least a few of the objects. These connections need not be the radical transformation that some objects undergo because of their encounter with violence, loss, and displacement; rather, they can hold the key to other memories.

Let me say this a bit differently: instead of making the project all about urgent legacies as Gafić and Kiefer do, I want to suggest that something in a photograph can capture our attention. It may not be overt or self-evident, it may be that the connection is intimate and otherwise unfamiliar to most viewers. The object in question may come to carry unique meaning for a specific viewer. This is what Barthes calls the "punctum," that something that pricks us, that calls out to us in ways that demand our attention.[28] For some viewers it may be the mangled leg of a small child's once beloved doll, a candy wrapper, or another tiny trinket that opens up a memory. As memory prompts, such objects take us to another time and another place. These memories might be simply nostalgic, but the feelings they elicit may also be something else—they may carry the weight of geopolitical change, the loss of a regime, a migration, or the loss of a beloved parent.

This is precisely what artist and literary scholar Svetlana Boym writes about so eloquently as "diasporic intimacy" in *The Future of Nostalgia* (2001). Boym sets up her account of this phenomenon by writing about Berlin in ways that echo a kind of potentiality that I want to keep open in my account of Von Eckardt's photographs. Boym writes: "Berlin is a place of immigrant alienation but also offers these immigrants occasional joys and 'profane illuminations.' The simple graffito OTTO on a Berlin pipe strikes Nabokov as an image of strange harmony that 'fits so well to this snow that lies quietly here and to this pipe with its two holes and mysterious profundity.' Immigrant Berlin is composed of transient epiphanies, instantaneous friendships and illicit dreams."[29] Like Nabokov, a viewer of these photographs might be compelled by any one of the objects depicted. That single object might be a way back into a lost childhood, or some other time or place.

But what I am thinking of most is this, and it sets up my larger claim: Boym writes about not only Nabokov but also another exiled Croatian writer, Dubravka Ugrešić. Boym explains how Nabokov and Ugrešić are both drawn to the Berlin Zoo. Many years after Nabokov wrote about the zoo, Boym writes that the Croatian novelist's favorite exhibit is "Roland, a dead walrus. The things found in the stomach of Roland, who died in 1961, are exhibited in the zoo." Boym goes on to explain that "they seem like scattered immigrant souvenirs: 'a pink cigarette lighter, a metal brooch in a shape of a poodle ... a child's plastic water pistol ... a baby's dummy, a bunch of keys, a padlock, a little plastic bag containing needles and threads.'"[30] Boym then further explains,

> Berlin for Ugrešić is a city-museum, and she—like her fellow exiles—are museum exhibits. Collecting becomes a substitute for the loss of collective memory. The writer, however, doesn't merely collect souvenirs from her vanished Yugoslavia, but rather trades in memorabilia with the other fellow exiles, sharing with them displacement and estrangement more than the place of origin. This is not a trade in dead souls, but a therapeutic exercise, a mental homeopathy. The immigrant found objects do not comprise a single narrative, but rather preserve a fragmentary and arbitrary character mirroring her own fragmented biography.[31]

The shards of the lives they have lost offer a kind of comfort and connection. Perhaps for some viewers, there may be objects held in some of Von Eckardt's drawers that touch such a nerve. I believe that might be a real possibility but, for me, the seeming proximity between her photographs, the ordinary objects they recollect, and those objects that move me is why I am here. In this case, I do not find myself moved. The magic is not there, the alchemy that for me is always about a kind of urgency, about loss so profound that such small things can become so large with resonance and meaning, is not what I personally experience in my viewing of these images, but I also know that I do not necessarily speak for others.

What I have shared from Boym's reading of Ugrešić is what matters to me. I want to honor this possibility of how small things can touch us deeply and help us feel what we may not be able to touch more directly. And right now, I experience this possibility as a form of grief—not knowing yet what small gesture, what image or memory of my own father, Irv, will allow me to feel his absence, to touch my grief, and to be able to cry. I keep trying to anticipate what this might be. The Bryn Mawr pool finally opened when I began writing about these matters just one month after my father's death in early February of 2022. I anticipated returning there after a few months' absence and, for the first time since my father's death, feeling something. I hoped that my return to a familiar ritual might trigger my tears, as my regular practice had been to call him on the way out of the gym. I did this most days during the fall of 2021. With my hair still wet, I would tell him that I was on the Bryn Mawr campus. I knew that he loved to imagine me there. When long ago we went on a father-daughter trip to visit colleges, he fell in love with Smith and hoped that I, like him, might obtain my degree at a women's college. He had attended and finally gotten his own degree care of the GI bill, at Russell Sage, making him one of the first men to earn a degree at that onetime women's college. I tried in March of 2022 to imagine that being at Bryn Mawr again might make me cry, but I only had a pang of sadness as my muscle memory made me reach for the phone to call him. What if I had seen an old paintbrush or a Delaware campaign button in one of the junk drawers—would such images have made me cry? These are the kinds of objects my father collected.

Of course, I am curious about what the junk drawer collections mean to the artist and why she was so drawn to them. That would be helpful to know, but I also feel like this nexus of connections is worth writing about even if we but hold out the possibility that something in any one of these photographs might occasion a recollection (I keep wanting to write "recollect" every time I have used it here, but I think you already suspected this).

A PHOTOGRAPH: BABY SHOES WITH PORTRAIT, TOWARD A CONCLUSION (LAURA AND RUTH)

Of the images in Von Eckardt's collection, the one that spoke most powerfully to the two of us comes from Box 1 (see PLATE 0.03) and features a baby photograph and a pair of white baby booties. The tiny pale white shoes are in the foreground. They appear to be made of soft felt and are carefully decorated with a series of tiny sewn flowers on their vamp. These are hardly visible at first sight, but examining the image online allows viewers to zoom in and see the details. The shoes are untied. They appear to have been recently worn, their shiny laces loosely figured. The soles of the shoes are scalloped, perhaps a kind of treading used to keep the wearer from slipping. Behind these booties is an aging baby portrait. It is not at all clear that these objects belong exactly together. The shoes, on closer examination, appear to be of a later period than the portrait, and are perhaps even contemporary. Here, the sepia tint on the image blurs these distinctions. Nevertheless, the portrait in its aging matte frame is figured at a right angle. The matte is worn. There are visible marks on it. The baby is pictured propped up on a drape-covered chair, eyes wide open and focused on someone or something in front of them, to their left. The baby's large hands are on their lap, a ring on their left ring finger. Is the baby dressed for a ritual? Their hands stand out in sharp contrast to the folds of the long white gown and its many lacy layers. The baby's hands are still, but their feet are restless. They are visible but blurred, clearly in motion. This is despite the baby's otherwise calm composure. The baby's feet are naked under the elaborate gown. We wonder if Von Eckardt meant to supply the baby with these shoes after all this time, to cover those feet in some imagined future.

As the baby looks off to the left, we see only one of their ears, the left one. The baby's gender is not clear, and their expression is calm with an air of expectancy. What are they looking at? A toy? Perhaps a pair of shoes? We do not know, but what we do know is that the photograph and booties found their way into Box 1, a junk drawer that was sold on eBay and then bought by Von Eckardt, and then they were finally photographed as a pair. We were attracted to the shoes and their relationship to the photograph. The objects initially looked like a set but on closer view we realize how distant they seem to be from each other. The image makes us think of other losses: What happened to that baby? Who was this tiny person? Where are their shoes? Did the baby kick them off? Who did this baby become? Did they live a long life? And whose shoes are the ones pictured? Where did they come from and why didn't anyone claim them or this photograph? Who preserved those worn shoes and this old portrait, and why were they discarded? Given that we have no answers to these questions, we consider other things.

The image reminds us of the ephemeral, how we hold on to and ultimately let go of so many of the objects that make up our ordinary, everyday lives. Where are our baby shoes—even those that were bronzed in the early 1960s and made into a set of bookends or an ashtray? And what happened to all those family photographs that got shed when we packed up our parents' homes? For us, this image is an occasion for further reflection, and the musings here constitute, in a sense, the afterlives of these quite specific anonymous objects.

(RUTH)

Years ago, I heard Ron Padgett give a reading of his poem, "Nothing in that drawer." "Nothing in that drawer," the line repeated fourteen times, read like an incantation. Even as a fan of minimalism, the poem troubled me. It has stayed with me, showing up as if on call, as good poems do.[32]

I think of opening drawers, frantically hoping to find what has to be there: empty, empty, and, again, empty. This sense of loss, the opening of drawer after drawer where we hoped to find something, some trace of whatever the drawer contained—grief is like that, over and over the reminder of that loss: there had been something in that drawer that is now gone. But those drawers had to be emptied, a chore or responsibility left to someone who had to face what to do with all that stuff. Once all that is dear (or coveted) is parceled out, what do we do with the rest?

Whatever else we might imagine, someone in the family from which the *Junk Drawer* objects came had to sort through the accretions of generations. They had to work their way through things held on to for what must have been over a century, given the vintage of the child's photograph. Who would, after all, want these things? What damage does it do finally to shed them? Even with all we know about our families' pasts via sources like Ancestry.com, what do we have the right to shed, or shred? How might one transform what is left from the past into something new, held if only for a time in someone else's care? Isn't this what Von Eckardt has done?

Laura and I have looked hard at the photo of the child and the shoes. We want them to add up to something, those empty well-cared-for shoes belonging to a different baby, canted against that uncomfortable baby solemnly dressed up for what? Some ritual? Those little feet, a blur of movement in contrast to the sepia solidity of the rest of the photo, raise another question for me: why was this photograph saved in the first place? In all of my looking at old photos where the subject had to hold still, before candid photographs were ubiquitous, I don't remember seeing any like this. Why wasn't it thrown away by the photographer? Was it impossible to make that baby be still? I am making up a story: the family had to be upset with the sloppiness of this photo shoot. The baby is boxed in by the camera, a box camera, and the shoes taunt from the future, with the diagonal lines of the arrangement energizing and challenging the stillness.

Finally, who would want Von Eckardt's photos? What if she put them on eBay? Who would bid, take them home, and do something new with them? That speculation, of course, is what this collection of essays invites.

(LAURA)

I keep thinking about the things I have of my father's. There is a small box that I took from my mother's dresser years ago. Inside that box are locks of hair—my father's baby hair, golden curled strands. There is nothing to identify them as such. Wrapped in a small white handkerchief, they stand as silent testimony to the tiny person my father once was. Even with pictures of him, a traditional Eastern European Jewish boy in America who would wait for his hair to be shorn until he was at least two or three years old, there they are.

I think about this hair having written about other hair, the horrible bales of hair shrouded in dark shadows in a huge room-sized case at Auschwitz that I saw for the first time in May of 2022 in Poland. Though my small sample does not carry the weight of history, it speaks in the language of intimacy. It mattered enough to my father to give it to my mother for safekeeping—a gift she held close until the day she died. And now it is mine. What happens to it after I die, I do not know. Perhaps it too might show up in a collection of discarded objects like those on sale on eBay, but this hair brings me back to those shoes and perhaps the baby in that photograph to whom they may or may not have once belonged. We cannot hold on to everything. We need to know how to let go, and so some once-precious objects may fall out of grace and become junk to be thrown away or put up for auction. But the tenderness I feel for those delicate shoes, the fact of their abiding persistence, the care it took to keep them in such pristine condition does make me think that they belonged to someone who cared not only for them but also for some baby who once wore them, not unlike my mother tending to my father's locks of hair.

RUTH'S CODA: A RETURN TO THRIFT SHOPS

When my mother Astrid retired—Trid was our nickname for her—she volunteered at the church thrift, The Frippery, her way of serving Communion. Though she wouldn't have put it this way, she liked how thrift shops shelve the past and sell it with the promise of the future.

If linens worth saving were dropped off at the Frippery, Trid would take them home; they would come back washed, ironed, and ready. (Trid knew her way around an ironing board. Her mother, widowed with six small children, took in laundry to make a living.) She had a lot to say about people who dropped off real junk.

Cornell, Saar, and Schapiro would surely find something in the Frippery they could use for their art; Barnes, too, but he would be looking hard at the ensembles, taking in how the stuff is arranged, examining whether different relationships among the objects would make them more interesting. When I show up from time to time at the Frippery even now, I always find something. On tap in this place: affection, tenderness, and connection wrap the gifts that come in and go out the door.

In honor of this piece, I owe Laura a trip to the Frip some Tuesday or Thursday when she isn't teaching or perhaps over winter break, weather permitting.

1. For Trid and Irv.
2. Maggie Nelson, *The Red Parts: Autobiography of a Trial* (Greywolf Press, 2016), 120.
3. I draw here on the three years of courses I took in the Barnes Method at the original Barnes Foundation, from 1989 to 1992. My teachers included Richard Segal, Barton Church, and Richard Wattenmaker. The Barnes Foundation continues to offer classes in the Barnes Method of how to look at art. The Foundation from its beginning was about education. It was never intended to be a museum. Barnes's method contradicted the museum tropes of labels and chronology.
4. Ruth notes that her postcards share an affinity with those of Ellsworth Kelly. Kelly's postcards were recently on exhibit in two exhibitions, *Ellsworth Kelly: Blue*

Green Black Red and *Ellsworth Kelly: Postcards*, at the Matthew Marks Gallery in New York, June 2022.

5. Lewis Hyde, *The Gift: How the Creative Spirit Transforms the World* (Vintage, 2019), 4.

6. Lewis Hyde, *The Gift*, 4.

7. Charles Simic, *Dime-Store Alchemy: The Art of Joseph Cornell* (1992; New York Review of Books Classics, 2011), 14.

8. Maria Stepanova, *In Memory of Memory*, trans. Sasha Dugdale (New Directions Paperback, 2021), 292.

9. Robin Pogrebin, "Barnes Museum Chooses Architects," *The New York Times*, Sept. 10, 2007, https://www.nytimes.com/2007/09/10/arts/design/10barn.html.

10. Nico Saieh, "Venice Biennale 2012: Wunderkammer/ Tod Williams Billie Tsien Architects," *ArchDaily*, November 22, 2012, https://www.archdaily.com/272440/venice-biennale-2012-wunderkammer-tod-williams-billie-tsien-architects.

11. James Christian Steward, et al., *Betye Saar: Extending the Frozen Moment* (University of California Press, 2005), 64.

12. Sara Cochran, "Interview with Betye Saar," in *Betye Saar, Still Tickin'*, ed. Sara Cochran (Scottsdale Museum of Contemporary Art, 2017), 13–14.

13. Thalia Gouma-Peterson, *Miriam Schapiro: Shaping the Fragment of Art and Life* (Harry N. Abrams, 1999), 80.

14. Helène Aylon, *Whatever Is Contained Must be Released: My Orthodox Girlhood, My Life as a Feminist Artist* (Feminist Press, 2012).

15. Many years ago, Ruth stitched something for Laura out of this robe as well. It is in her office at Temple University.

16. Hyde, *The Gift*, 189.

17. Ziyah Gafić, "Everyday Objects, Tragic Histories," TED Talk, filmed March 2014, https://www.ted.com/talks/ziyah_gafic_everyday_objects_tragic_histories?subtitle=en.

18. For more on Gafić's work, see M. Scott Brauer, "Ziyah Gafic's Quest for Identity: Building a Visual Record of the Items Left Behind by Those Killed in the Bosnian War," *Witness*, July 17, 2019, https://witness.worldpressphoto.org/ziyah_gafics-quest-for-identity-d6a928abbf46.

19. "The Ian Parry Scholarship: Benefit Auction 2021," *Artsy*, accessed October 1, 2022, https://www.artsy.net/artwork/ziyah-gafic-quest-for-identity-items-recovered-from-mass-graves-in-bosnia-and-herzegovina. The Ian Parry Scholarship Benefit Auction to support young and emerging photojournalists took place in 2021.

20. Brauer, "Ziyah Gafic's Quest for Identity."

21. Brauer, "Ziyah Gafic's Quest for Identity."

22. Rachel M. Lindsey, "Borderlands of the Sacred," *The Imminent Frame: Secularism, Religion, and the Public Sphere*, October 30, 2018, https://tif.ssrc.org/2018/10/30/borderlands-of-the-sacred/.

23. Lindsey offers a powerful account of this work in "Borderlands of the Sacred."

24. Lindsey, "Borderlands of the Sacred."

25. Laura Levitt, *The Objects that Remain* (Penn State University Press, 2020).

26. Nelson, *The Red Parts*, 120. *The Red Parts* was republished in 2016 with a new subtitle, *The Red Parts: Autobiography of a Trial* by Graywolf Press. I have been working primarily from the original edition and continue this practice here.

27. Nelson, *The Red Parts*, 120.

28. Roland Barthes, *Camera Lucida: Reflections on Photography* (Hill and Wang, 1981).

29. Svetlana Boym, *The Future of Nostalgia* (Basic Books, 2001), 212.

30. Boym, *Future of Nostalgia*, 210.

31. Boym, *Future of Nostalgia*, 210–11.

32. Ruth reached out to Ron Padgett, inquiring about his poem and received this response:

From: Ron Padgett
Sent: Thursday, August 11, 2022, 3:48 PM
To: Ruth Z Ost
Subject: [External] Re: Nothing in that city? Plymouth Salem High School, Plymouth, MI

Dear Ruth Ost,

Thanks for your nice message. FYI I wrote that poem ca. 1964, published it in an "underground" little magazine ca. 1965, and then put it in a book that came out in 1969, about ten months after I started helping kids write poetry (in the schools). I don't recall being in Plymouth, but who knows?

Honestly, when I wrote it I thought of it as a passing fancy of very little heft, but over the years it has taken on a life of its own, not only for me but for a number of readers. Go figure.

Good luck with the junk drawers.

Best wishes,
Ron Padgett

Ruth wrote back to Ron and asked if she could share this email and he said yes.

CHAPTER 7

ARTIFACTS AND ACCESS

RHODA ROSEN AND AMANDA LEIGH DAVIS

Behind Barbara Von Eckardt's *Junk Drawer* project lies the premise that objects are "at least in part, testamentary" (see page 6). Hers is a practice that explores what she calls the "readability" of the artifact. She hopes, imagines, and even claims that an object, even a photograph of an object, can provide access (albeit partial) to the person to whom it belonged. To be sure, the composition of her photographs—isolated, carefully arranged objects on a dark, flat background out of which silvers, sepias, and whites emerge for our viewing; the use of mostly black and white; the washed-out color when color is evidenced; and the silver filter—all produce a beautiful, evocative feel. Arguably, it is the photographs' crafted aesthetic that provides the illusion of conjuring the person to whom the objects belonged, more so than the objects pictured do. In that conjuring, the photographs presume to reference a past in which person and object might have been in relationship, producing meanings together. For the photographer, these meanings may still be glimpsed in the present. While Von Eckardt posits the irretrievable separation of person from beloved object, the aesthetic hopes to conjure the meaning of those objects to their past owner.

Von Eckardt thus performs the work that Sander Gilman, in this volume, compares to that of his grandfather, who salvaged other people's trash to sell for his living, a work that Gilman claims has the power to transform the affects of disgust at garbage into curiosity about its potential value. Like a trick of transforming mere water into valuable wine, Von Eckardt sets scenes of salvation—artwork, it seems, can give new value to the junk that has been decontextualized of exchange relations or production conditions. But how, specifically, is this work wrought? In Gilman's account, it is through his written interpretation of his grandfather's peripatetic labor; in Von Eckardt's case, this salvation has been digitized: she scrolled and searched through eBay's massive archives for objects to rescue. In both stories, bits and fragments are salvaged from archives of possible materials, a few selected in provenance events that are nigh untraceable.[1] Previous ownership and how those objects came into or left human lives is here absent. So stripped of historical and human contexts, the objects that were once junk enter the art world as valuable art, "aura" now created not by history but by the application of a nostalgic atmosphere and a pronunciation declaring this atmosphere "art." "Readymades" become aestheticized, which Marcel Duchamp claims never to have been his aim. For Duchamp, the "readymade" was an incomplete challenge to art; the full challenge would have been to return everyday use value to that which had already been designated as art, his example being that a Rembrandt canvas should become an ironing board.[2] In Von Eckardt's archive, readymades are aestheticized not as a challenge to the assignment of artistic value—as in the Duchampian example—but precisely to give them exchange and display value, while precluding any possible use value.[3]

The process through which past objects are selected for present value salvation might be understood through the concept of the archive, or the larger body of materials from which these individual objects were selected and isolated. Michel Foucault wrote that "the archive is first the law of what can be said, the system that governs the appearance of statements as unique events."[4] The archive, in other words, is a work and an institution of power, the "rules of a practice that enables statements to both survive and to undergo regular modification."[5] For the archive is not the totality of everything possible, but rather, as Jacques Derrida put it, "a house, a domicile, an address, the residence of superior magistrates, the archons, those who command."[6] The archive, then, is not even a set of materials or objects, but rather a specific place where authority does its discriminating work: "On account of their publicly recognized authority, it is at their home, in that place which is their house (private house, family house, or employee's house) that official documents are filed. The archons are first of all the documents' guardians ... They have the power to interpret the archives."[7] It is Von Eckardt's interpretive act as a sort of archon that gives the junk in her project value within the archival house of art history. And this particular act mystifies the provenance of these objects, makes them the hazy reverie of speculations on the present of an unknowable past—creating, not excavating, aura. In a time when provenance research must be a priority for art institutions to be ethical actors in the global world, art historians must also emphasize and prioritize human use and access.

There are certainly Herculean efforts in contemporary art to claim space in the archive while acknowledging the historical exclusion of these efforts. In doing both, these extraordinary projects expose the power at work in the medium and technology of photography and point to the heartrending limits of belonging or not belonging—or belonging in a partial or inauthentic way—in and to the archive. An example of such a necessarily ambitious contemporary art project is the work of L.A.-based artist Adam Davis, who is traveling across the country to historically Black cities to photograph twenty thousand Black people, producing forty thousand tintype photographs (one for the sitter; one for the archive). His aim is to create the largest Black photographic archive to date. The tintype is a particularly important technology for him, not least because from the 1850s it was accessible to white people only, yet used to produce, among other things, images of the enslaved to create a scientific archive of alleged, eugenically informed, inferiority. On one hand, this project claims a medium as well as a space in the archive for self-definition of Black identity against the images shaped by white human traffickers and scientists that so many have explored (see, for example, Molly Rogers's *Delia's Tears*).[8] On the other hand, it asks how many Black portraits it would take to make up for the absence of historical self-representation. So far, that answer is not less than forty thousand. But tintypes are important for another reason too: the images do not sit on a support, but float within the emulsion in a liminal space that, Davis suggests, mirrors Black life in the United States.[9]

As opposed to Von Eckardt's photographs, which mystify the provenance of her selections, the form of Davis's work conceptualizes the devastating history of medium, technology, and image and knowledge production that is at the core of the very exclusionary nature of the archive. Although Davis claims a space within the archive, pointing to its already always porous character, the sheer scale of his project also suggests an ambition to architect an unprecedented alternative archive with a decentralized distribution of interpretive power. He does not interpret the meaning of the objects produced by his work, but rather emphasizes the means of their production, which is social engagement. His negotiation with potential sites, development of networks, travel to sites, and meeting and speaking with twenty thousand community members and all those who come as witnesses to his portrait sessions in churches and coffee shops and other communal spaces all point to the fact that his project is about social engagement with Black people in Black spaces. The distribution of copies of the portraits to their human counterparts precludes any rarified aura in the archive that Davis engineers to create clear pathways of human access. This work is about life, interaction, engagement, collaboration, participation, joy, and celebration, honoring all contemporary Black creators and innovators and all the ancestors who were creators and innovators who sustained life in ways the scientific archive has chosen to ignore and erase.

It is through understanding archival work as a space where power can be either reinforced or decentralized and redistributed, a space where objects become housed or unhoused, that our essay argues four points with regard to Von Eckardt's *Junk Drawer* series. First, that the junk drawer objects do not themselves retain the aura of their prior owners, but the photographic representation itself, here Von Eckardt's photographs of objects, produces aura. Second, that objects do not—in fact, cannot—provide access to human interiority; rather, simply put, only connection and interconnectedness with another human provides such access. Third, that rather than becoming locked into an argument for or against photographic representation and the problem of whether it offers access to human interiority (clearly there are nuanced conditions discussed in this book in which it legitimately does so), we want to focus on a medium that has come to be known as social practice. That we do so is our fourth point, because it answers the question of how to live in an immanent present, not an archived historical past or utopian future.

Von Eckardt writes in her artist statement that "Interestingly, this broader reconception led to a revision of my purpose in creating and photographing the junk drawer collection: from restoring the meaningfulness of the junk drawer objects from their devaluation via commoditization by photographing them, to also giving them new meaning by creating the opportunity for related scholarly exploration" (see page 13). What Von Eckardt is doing is creating beautifully composed photographic commodities, distancing objects from their presumed original owners, and integrating them into the archive of art history. She claims to mediate human interiority through the detritus of consumer culture or ask scholars to do so, yet we have no context for any value connection for the original owners of the objects. Indeed, it seems more like the intimacy between object and owner is through her attachment to these objects as their current owner. Whether they had display, use, or exchange value to presumed previous owners seems less palpable than the intimate attachment with which the current owner has imbued them, ironically, through the typical distancing techniques that have come to signify care (and to conceal plunder) in the traditional archive.[10] These techniques include organizational methods such as grouping, classifying, and arranging; formal techniques such as highlighting objects, sharply contrasting objects with abstract or blank backgrounds, or emphasizing object contours; and conceptual techniques, such as constructing objects for study ("creating the opportunity for related scholarly exploration") and the very idea of rescue itself ("restoring the meaningfulness of the junk drawer objects"). All Von Eckardt's techniques reduplicate the techniques of care for objects in the Western archive.

The archive (whether institutional or personal) is itself a strategy of taking ownership, and the current owner here takes ownership of this fascinating group of objects through a medium, photography, described by the term "capture" because of its association with acquisition. Von Eckardt's alluring photographs remind us that the archive is active: it is an active doing, a doing that takes possession. The objects in the photographs, however evocative they may be, are silent about people. For the doing to create meaningful intimacy with interiority, art must be done in connection with others, for which there is no substitution or mediation.

Because Von Eckardt seeks human connection through mediation, what she ends up salvaging is aura itself, a quality Walter Benjamin proclaimed had been killed by mechanical reproduction.[11] Crucially, Benjamin's original understanding of aura was not reducible to human individuals but was rather a unique accumulation of specific history; aura was the quality of an object's historical embeddedness, its retention and accumulation of time and place, and hence its utterly unique, unreproducible, and indeed priceless (in the sense of very expensive exchange value) qualities. While it may initially appear that Von Eckardt is conceptually responding to Benjamin by returning to the junk of the mechanical age, what her work formally achieves actually overturns what Benjamin found so exciting about mechanical reproduction. She reintegrates the mechanically reproduced object back into the feudal archive, where hallowed objects were foci of exclusive ritual and magic, such as the "related scholarly explorations" in which privileged insiders are granted power from on high to worship through study and interpretation. She effectively conserves institutional power by acting as archon, rather than revolutionizing art in this moment of global crisis when art must be based in social relations if it is to be ethically oriented to contemporary power dynamics. In Benjamin's well-known essay, mass producibility destroyed aura by making once-cloistered objects available to the masses: once desacralized, objects were ready to be integrated into the rhythms of everyday life. Mechanical reproducibility held the promise of revolting against subservience to the objects deemed sacred by archons, but Von Eckardt reverses that process, reordaining objects with sacred access to a fetishized past. The next section of this chapter resists her claim that the *Junk Drawer* objects point us to human interiority, and we argue that she instead reifies interiority by unproblematically aligning it with the ideological promises of property ownership.

DOING INTERIORITY

In her artist's statement, Von Eckardt claims that viewers of material objects or their photographic representations have access to the interiority of the objects' owners. The *Junk Drawer* series hence reproduces capitalist, colonialist, and middle-class ideologies surrounding human interiority. This section outlines the content of that hegemonic ideology before this chapter concludes by proposing alternatives to challenge and iterate on the restrictive and exclusive model of democratic home ownership.

The assumption that objects might grant access to interiority is housed within an ideology summarized by Diana Fuss when she writes that "modernity is simply another name for the reign of interiority, that moment in history where exteriority is driven indoors by the domesticating passions of the bourgeoisie."[12] These "domesticating passions" include home ownership—or the possession of drawers in which to store junk—as foundational to the very possession of subjectivity. The specifically American iteration of this Western ideology includes a retreat from the street, with its consequent emphasis on size as providing protection from others, and possession as the precondition for subjectivity itself.[13] This "reign of interiority" holds that surfaces and objects contain and hence are the access point for the "insides" of human doing and being, which has made privacy an increasingly unattainably expensive commodity and the Commons an increasingly surveilled arena.[14] Lauren Berlant wrote that the Commons is where humans can go "not to possess but to be possessed, to submit to being dispossessed of property in the self by the immediacy of a nature that dissolves the attachment to sovereignty and instrumentality."[15]

The ideology of democratic homeownership became hegemonic over the latter half of the twentieth century (a period the importance of which is outlined below). Under this social system, state institutions supposedly ensured that home ownership would be distributed equally and fairly, cultural factors forged conditions under which interiority became spatialized, and material surfaces (like a house, artifacts, or a face) came to signify access to that interiority. When an ordinary person not only can but ought to own a house, Foucault's archival place of power becomes itself mass reproduced, making anyone an archon with the power to decide what (or whom) is selected for preservation. It is not coincidental, therefore, that Von Eckardt's objects come from the post–World War II era, in which home ownership was democratized, hearkening back to the mid-century exiled German philosophers Benjamin, Hannah Arendt, Theodor Adorno, and Martin Heidegger, for example, who explored houselessness as both a social problem and transcendental concept against the backdrop of the massive refugee crisis and enormous political displacement during and after World War II.[16]

While democratization of homeownership may strike some as a utopian ideal, it is crucial to recognize that this mass production of places of power is precisely what creates the social problem of houselessness, the *raison d'être* of the next section of this essay. Capital may house some, but it is insufficient to comprehensive human or cultural belonging. Within the regime of democratic homeownership, houselessness robs humans not only of privacy, but of their very humanity. Meanwhile, the privileged with the power of discernment over what matters in the present are housed, living materially together with belongings but literally separated from common belonging with others. For artists to aspire to build "a world worth attaching to that's something other than an old hope's bitter echo," they must eschew the role of archon and adopt instead the role of architect.[17]

DOING SOCIAL PRACTICE

Social practice is a contemporary genre that manifests in many ways, but that we here argue can be understood as acts of architecting infrastructures for social Commons. Capital reifies subject positions, limiting them to the singular—consumer, producer, authority (such as art historian, critic)—but architecting the Commons requires that we demolish rigid cultural structures, which are as much structures as ones of brick and mortar. Social practice requires that we honor fluidity and interconnectedness, and allow literally any interiority to occupy the Commons. For the purposes of this essay, we will concentrate on two aspects of social practice that are typical of the genre and that are important for our own practice. First, social practice often leaves the studio and enters real life, and as such it blurs the distinction between creative labor (demarcated by studio space and posited as an individual pursuit) and the activity of living. When social practice is located in the real world of the Commons, it isn't displayed in typical art spaces, like galleries or museums, it isn't hung on a wall, but frames reality itself. Second, that social practice can be antirepresentational in form, foregoing description for common experience. In many instances, social practice brings into the frame connectivity with individuals—people in community together, often across class or identity formations. It sometimes views this connectivity as having aesthetic value, or it moves beyond the concept of the aesthetic altogether. For social practice that is relational, the labor can be long-term, enduring, and isn't necessarily expressed as a marketable object, but is, rather, endlessly renewed in the deepening of community bonds, of belonging to one another.

In terms of its antirepresentational aspects, social practice challenges the art world to shift focus away from objects and toward what has come to be termed "world building." "World building" is a term long recognized within art history, literary studies, and affect studies as naming the range of daily sensory activities that both produce and apprehend a sense of the historical present, and Berlant has described the need for aesthetic modes that "make demands on the sensorium for adjudication, adaptation, improvisation, and new visceral imaginaries for what the present could be."[18] Centering world building, in other words, as opposed to market value or social saturation, means not only sensing and describing human worlds, but also enacting change within them.

When social practice takes empowering community as the subject of its world building, what constitutes artistic labor shifts from the individual artist producing capitalist commodities to collaborative work and work that includes expertise across disciplines not narrowly defined by studio practice. For example, creative labor may include research, administrative labor, fundraising, community facilitation, marketing, and event and project management, to name but a few of the functions comprising the entire field of art that can now also be claimed as social art practices. Our social practice is called Red Line Service (RLS), after one of the twenty-four-hour elevated ("El") commuter train lines in Chicago, which serves as shelter for many houseless Chicagoans. Our practice moves away from an object-based critical gaze toward a relationality between historically marginalized people (here, unhoused artists), academically credentialed cultural workers, and traditional art audiences—all connected by ongoing collective aesthetic work that reimagines and iterates on the very grounds for our interactions.

This kind of social practice is careful not to fix identities through representation—a methodological answer to what Catherine Grant and Dorothy Price call a recent need to "decolonize art history."[19] The community rejects reduplicating the strategy of making people or the objects of which they have been dispossessed vulnerable to any static or aesthetic gaze: among a myriad of other ways, unhoused artists are frequently separated from their possessions when the latter are left on the pavement after hurried evictions or looted by the sanitation trucks that regularly purge tent communities in their so-called off-street cleaning initiatives; or these artists are stripped of property rights through the sales of their objects at auction—including on eBay—that they had kept in unpaid-for storage lockers.

Rather than reduplicating the static aesthetic of rescued objects such as in Von Eckardt's photographs, in this kind of social practice neither objects nor unhoused people seek rescue. The unhoused artists are at the center of a self-designed community in which they build sovereignty through decentralized, distributed power-sharing. When invited to do so (and where possible), their art world-credentialed community members secure resources and open channels so that the ongoing world building of people—which takes place against all odds throughout the violent process of losing a home and the ongoing traumatic experiences of being unhoused—can continue.

This creative world building by unhoused artists is neither a form of repair (always anyway illusory), nor is it a counter-archive (always anyway a strategy of power), but rather it is an ongoing assertion of making and claiming a common home in the mainstream art world, from which they (and for that matter, even credentialed yet precarious cultural workers) have been rendered excluded.[20] The work is centered on a number of principles:

> 1) Cocreation—all projects, from design to implementation are created in consultation with houseless artists who are paid for their labor;
>
> 2) Safe(r) space—everyone must feel equally empowered to participate, to bring their full selves, be supported in their healing from trauma as much as in their art-making, and be encouraged to take intellectual and artistic risks;
>
> 3) Positive perceptions—instead of seeing houselessness as a deficit, art is used to destigmatize houselessness;
>
> 4) Accessibility—it must be easy for people to make, use, or attend to art; and
>
> 5) Regularity—houseless artists are able to count on supportive networks from one another and from Chicago's cultural community.

Because the world building work of social practice takes place in and through time, and because the raw materials are humans, it is necessarily messy and can't aspire to the enduring, fixed (both chemically and through careful arrangement of forms) quality Von Eckardt produces in her photographs. This messiness does, however, aspire to a shared interest in intimacy, or scenes of attachment formations. Where Von Eckardt's interest is in lost attachments to objects, our interest is in scenes with no preconceived notions of the forms or ends of the attachments that may or may not take or shift shape: even aesthetic objects are not presumed to dictate such engagement, though they do play a role in igniting interests, sparking discussions, and even combusting disagreements. The ever-shifting nature of this work makes formal analysis tricky, but attempting it sheds light on "the glances, gestures, encounters, collaborations, or fantasies that have no canon," which Berlant has identified as the unrecorded and impermanent forms that intimacy can take in the present.[21]

The formal elements of this particular art practice include: hosting lectures by art historians, curators, and museum directors; holding workshops with artists; removing barriers to authorizing, enjoying, producing, and consuming art through sharing meals with the professionals at each event; providing train fare and stipends as compensation for making and presenting art; allowing artists to retain intellectual copyright of their work; and insisting that the work be community-led.[22] At workshops and on art field trips, participants think critically aloud, work on translating their thoughts into critical writing, share and debate ideas, and listen to one another's concerns and growing pains. To protect the sovereignty of the community of unhoused artists, we mandate that unhoused Chicagoans make up 50 percent or more of our board and that those leadership positions are paid. In addition, the community is organized around a committee structure that is also stewarded by unhoused artists who are financially compensated for their labor. These elements are indicators of the way that participatory art practice encourages us to forego the powerful visual regime of distancing subject from object, and art from life, and keeps us from mistaking the transactional for the relational as often happens in the art market.

The meaning of the art project is multilayered and is also made concrete in the world as an active part of creating new lifeways. The ways these layers of meaning are made concrete include: destigmatizing houselessness (in this sense it is pedagogy as art); decreasing social isolation; increasing social belonging; mainstreaming the art of unhoused artists; transferring the considerable resources and power of the institutional art world to unhoused artists; creating a full ecology of care by and for unhoused artists, and the artists and museum institutions enlisted to support them when they are so invited; and insisting that art is embedded in social relations and can, therefore, enact solutions, perhaps quietly, in the everyday sphere. Our social practice posits art as neither doomed to be an asset class (such as stocks or real estate) nor a commodity nor an individual expression;[23] rather, art is a social practice that re-enters the stream of life, in which the conditions of cultural production, shared in community, are themselves a resistance to being warehoused or forgotten, and a choice, renewed daily, about how to live together in the present.

BEING PRESENT

The community built within RLS practices ongoing, ordinary acts of care. RLS unhoused artists know and look after one another, visit each other in the hospital, and encourage each other in creative work as much as in self-care. This community is the medium of the work. In discussions of local politics over dinner at a museum or gallery, RLS artists enact a "historicity of epistemologies immanent to living at a particular moment, where feeling it out becomes identical to the activity of being in history and in the aesthetic."[24] In other words, we resist the "eventification" of history—the collapsing of a vast collection of ordinary realities into exceptional, singular occurrences that shape the way a present is later understood—through creating art that enacts "the presented present by being in it, touching, tasting, over hearing, and tracking how we are responding to it."[25] By sharing meals and experiences, and keeping records and data, RLS creates art that connects with human interiorities through multisensorial engagements of and in the present.

The value of the historical present is relatively new to critical studies. Institutions from the realms of education and politics to churches have overwhelmingly looked to past traditions for value—an impulse reflected in the nostalgic sepia tones of Von Eckardt's photographs of twentieth-century American mass consumer culture. Von Eckardt asserts that the pictured objects express choice and personal meaning, yet a view of their actual historical present would include the marketing forces and supply chains shaping the objects available for purchase and the contexts of their availability to the people who eventually bought them, perhaps without thought, picking up just another commodity screaming for attention out of many similar options, presented in ways driven by market research into manipulating consumers into making impulse buys. We insist on resisting aestheticizing the detritus of a culture that values the production, sale, and consumption of commodities above the safety and wellness of the humans operating the machines (or replaced by the machines) that produce them. At stake is how, or indeed even whether, we imagine the role of art in everyday human life. RLS refuses to cede art to capital storage or growth; our art is community, which we create by staging the present activities of connection and embedding participants in a sense of belonging, a sense that is fundamental to human survival and wellness.

It may seem odd to include in the present collection an essay proposing an alternative art to that which organizes it. Yet one argument for this anomaly could go that, only now, after Von Eckardt's photographs have engaged an audience tied together by the ordinary and interdependent activities that go into producing a critical text, will her work become art. Until now, the objects and photographs at the center of the discussion have been what they always had been: commodities and images of commodities elevated only through the present human exchanges that create, rather than excavate, meaning. The conversation around the objects and photographs—the writers, thought partners, editors, assistants, publishers, and communities supporting the survival of all of the above—is the art that points our attention to our own present vantage point, looking back on the remnants of twentieth-century consumer culture.

From this bird's-eye perspective, Von Eckardt's work has value in displaying the disconnect of contemporary art practices from the present and can serve as a call to all those participating in cultural fields to bridge that divide. In a world in which art and junk are interchangeable, perhaps we can finally turn to critical and robust engagement with our ordinary historical present. As Harvard University's Joint Center for Housing Studies emphasizes, ours is a reality in which housing is officially unaffordable for a majority of Americans, and renters particularly bear the burden of rising living costs—a reality in which the possession of drawers, let alone junk to put in them, is increasingly at risk. After years of being told their patriotic and moral duty was to stay home, Americans are facing record eviction levels, and "in 2019, some 7.8 million unassisted households with very low incomes faced severe cost burdens, lived in severely inadequate housing, or both." Lest anyone think that surely somebody must be doing something about this, "just one out of every four income-eligible renter households actually receives assistance. There were 737,000 households on waiting lists at just 44 housing agencies in 2021." Housing stock has also been under threat by climate change, affecting "14.5 million residential properties in 2021, at a cost of $56.92 billion."[26]

While this ordinary historical present may seem dauntingly cataclysmic, art can and must belong to it and promote belonging within it. Elevating junk to art status will not rehome it; only embedding art in community gives it the aura that comes from belonging to a historical present. Elevating junk to art at this time is not only spectacularly disconnected from the ordinary present reality in which most struggle to keep stable rooms of their own, but it is also first and foremost a work of directing the flow of capital, from the initial exchanges of consumers with distributors (and the supply chain that brings the object to the distributor) to the artist's exchanges with eBay (and that particular platform making those objects available) to the artist's exchanges with the cultural institutions that will inevitably imbue their work with monetary value. That such institutions will name this value "Art" will not change that the primary value driving this work is capital. We cannot reach people's interiorities through supply chain junk, but we can connect with people here and now, and sometimes we can even do so through what we call junk—or what we classify as art. The materials and objects around which community gathers are interchangeable; it is the community of humans, being present together, that matters.

1. It is worth noting that these artistic acts making provenance unavailable are being published at a time when museums worldwide are coming under scrutiny for inadequate provenance research, which has resulted in stolen objects making it into their permanent collections. Objects that were often meant for daily use in communities are now held under lock and key and kept in carefully controlled basements hidden from human view. For recent research into this phenomenon in the Swiss museum context, see Astrid Tomczak-Plewka, "Uncertain Provenance Is the Norm," *Horizons: The Swiss Research Magazine*, Jan. 9, 2022, https://www.horizons-mag.ch/2022/09/01/uncertain-provenance-is-the-norm/.

2. Duchamp gave this example at his 1961 presentation to the Museum of Modern Art's Art of Assemblage Symposium.
3. The primary distinction Marx makes in *Capital: A Critique of Political Economy*, vol. 1, trans. Ben Fowkes (1867; Penguin, 1990) between types of value is use-value versus exchange value (126). Use-value includes the material realities of the objects and the human needs they fill. Exchange value, by contrast, flattens objects into interchangeable commodities.
4. Michel Foucault, "The Historical a priori and the Archive," in *The Archeology of Knowledge*, trans. A. M. Sheridan Smith (Pantheon Books, 1972), 126–33 (129).
5. Foucault, "Historical a priori," 130.
6. Jacques Derrida, *Archive Fever: A Freudian Impression*, trans. Eric Prenowitz (University of Chicago Press, 1998), 1.
7. Derrida, *Archive Fever*, 2.
8. Molly Rogers, *Delia's Tears: Race, Science, and Photography in Nineteenth-Century America* (Yale University Press, 2010).
9. For more on the project, see Evangeline Barrosse, "LA Artist Building One of the Largest Troves of Contemporary Black American Portraits," *Los Angeles Times*, March 20, 2022, https://www.latimes.com/entertainment-arts/story/2022-03-30/la-artist-adam-davis-tintype-portraits-black-americans.
10. Ariella Azoulay, *Potential History: Unlearning Imperialism* (Verso, 2019), 15–20.
11. Walter Benjamin, "The Work of Art in the Age of Mechanical Reproduction," in *Illuminations: Essays and Reflections*, ed. Hannah Arendt, trans. Harry Zohn (1935; Schocken, 1969), 217–65.
12. Diana Fuss, *The Sense of an Interior: Four Writers and the Rooms That Shaped Them* (Routledge, 2004), 12.
13. Nancy Kwak has charted how this ideology was packaged into a massive American export in the post–World War II era in her *A World of Homeowners: American Power and the Politics of Housing Aid* (University of Chicago Press, 2015).
14. Deborah Nelson in her *Pursuing Privacy in Cold War America* (Columbia University Press, 2002) traced this phenomenon in a book on Cold War influences on privacy as a concept. The theory of the Commons arose in the nineteenth century with a Marxist reinterpretation of the common law notion of a finite good, such as a public space, being managed, for good or for ill, by a collective. This theory was expanded notably in the twenty-first century by scholars like Silvia Federici and Lauren Berlant as way of historicizing resistance and the reorganization of society in times of social injustice. See Silvia Federici, *Caliban and the Witch: Women, the Body and Primitive Accumulation* (Autonomedia, 2004).
15. Lauren Berlant, "The Commons: Infrastructures for Troubling Times," *Environment and Planning D: Society and Space* 34, no. 3 (2016): 393–419 (400), https://doi.org/10.1177/0263775816645989.
16. See Theodor Adorno, *Minima Moralia: Reflections on a Damaged Life*, trans. E.F.N. Jephcott (1951; Verso, 2005); Martin Heidegger, "Building, Dwelling, Thinking," in *Poetry, Language, Thought*, trans. Albert Hofstadter (Harper Colophon Books, 1971); Hannah Arendt, "We Refugees," in *The Jewish Writings*, ed. Jerome Kohn and Ron H. Feldman (Schocken Books, 2007), 267–74; Walter Benjamin, *The Arcades Project*, trans. Howard Eiland and Kevin McLaughlin (Harvard University Press, 1999).
17. Berlant, "Commons," 414.
18. Lauren Berlant, "Intuitionists: History and the Affective Event," *American Literary History* 20, no. 4 (Winter 2008): 845–60 (847), https://doi.org/10.1093/alh/ajn039.
19. Catherine Grant and Dorothy Price, "Decolonizing Art History," *Art History* 43, no. 1 (2020): 8–66 (10).
20. "Culturally unhoused" is the term used by John A. McClure in *Partial Faiths: Postsecular Fiction in the Age of Pynchon and Morrison* (University of Georgia Press,

2007) to describe Native American characters in novels who undergo a painful return to a culture they had been displaced from. Although culture is not technically a sheltering structure, it is a deeply ontological form of belonging, which is necessary to human survival.

21. Lauren Berlant, "Intimacy," *Critical Inquiry* 24, no. 2 (Winter 1998): 281–88 (288), https://www.journals.uchicago.edu/doi/abs/10.1086/448875.

22. We do not pay all RLS artists the obscenely low Chicago minimum wage, but rather the current actual Chicago housing wage. This is the amount that a person working a forty-hour work week for fifty-two weeks per year must earn to afford a one-bedroom apartment at fair market value in the city. In other words, we are mindful of two things: first, the potential trap in which not-for-profit organizations often turn people into passive recipients of aid—by contrast, we are building a community of active artists producing and creating worlds by appropriately compensating artists, who retain copyright for their work; and, second, the assumption on the part of the social service charitable model, in which if an art group or class is created, cultural labor is not compensated, yet the copyright remains with the organization who uses the cultural labor of participants to raise funds through auctions, or through brochures in which the artists' work is used to show organizational efficacy. RLS sets a model for community arts in Chicago.

23. For more on art as an asset class, see Georgina Adams, *Big Bucks: The Explosion of the Art Market in the 21st Century* (Penguin, 2014) and her *The Dark Side of the Boom: The Excesses of the Art Market in the 21st Century* (Lund Humphries, 2018)

24. Berlant, "Intuitionists," 849.

25. Berlant, "Intuitionists," 849.

26. Harvard Joint Center for Housing Studies, "The State of the Nation's Housing 2022," 43, last modified 2024, https://www.jchs.harvard.edu/state-nations-housing-2022.

CONTRIBUTORS

MARY BERGSTEIN is Professor Emerita at Rhode Island School of Design in Providence. She won the American Psychoanalytic Association prize for *Mirrors of Memory: Freud, Photography, and the History of Art* (2010). Among her other books are *In Looking Back One Learns to See: Marcel Proust and Photography* (2014) and *The Sculpture of Nanni di Banco* (2000). Her essay "Faux Nudes and Body Art 1900" about body stockings and women's tattoos appeared in *History of Photography* (2022). Her most recent book is *Visual Culture in Freud's Vienna: Science, Eros, and the Psychoanalytic Imagination* (2024).

DANIEL CAVICCHI is Professor of History, Philosophy, and the Social Sciences at Rhode Island School of Design in Providence, where he also has served as dean, vice provost, and provost. His books include *Listening and Longing: Music Lovers in the Age of Barnum* (2011); *Tramps Like Us: Music and Meaning Among Springsteen Fans* (1998); and *My Music: Explorations of Music in Daily Life* (1993; co-editor). He established the *Pop Conference* with Eric Weisbard in 2001 and was the inaugural editor of Wesleyan University Press's *Music/Interview* series. His public work has included the exhibit *Songs of Conscience, Sounds of Freedom* at the Grammy Museum, Los Angeles, and the *Witness Tree Project*, a history and design curriculum with the National Park Service. His latest book is an anthology, edited with Stephan Michael Schröder, titled *Admirers, Fanciers, and Devotees: The History of Early Fandom* (2026).

AMANDA LEIGH DAVIS is an independent scholar who has taught courses at institutions as diverse as Brigham Young University, the University of Chicago, and the School of the Art Institute of Chicago. They are also a performance artist who uses fire as their medium. They serve on the Board of Red Line Service and earned their PhD in English Language and Literature at the University of Chicago.

SANDER L. GILMAN is a distinguished professor emeritus of the Liberal Arts and Sciences as well as emeritus professor of psychiatry at Emory University in Atlanta, GA. A cultural and literary historian, he is the author or editor of over one hundred books. His most recent books are *Doc or Quack: Science and Anti-Science in Modern Medicine* (2025) and his coedited volume *Readers for Life: How Reading and Listening in Childhood*

Shape Us (2024). For twenty-five years, he was a member of the humanities and medical faculties at Cornell University, where he held the Goldwin Smith Professorship of Humane Studies. For six years, he held the Henry R. Luce Distinguished Service Professorship of the Liberal Arts in Human Biology at the University of Chicago. For four years, he was a distinguished professor of the Liberal Arts and Medicine at the University of Illinois at Chicago, where he created the Humanities Laboratory. He has been a visiting professor at universities in North America, South Africa, the United Kingdom, Germany, Israel, and New Zealand.

JOHN P. JACOB is the McEvoy Family Curator for Photography at the Smithsonian American Art Museum in Washington, DC. He was co-curator of "Carrie Mae Weems: Looking Forward, Looking Back" and "J. P. Ball and Robert S. Duncanson: An African American Artistic Collaboration," both exhibited in 2023. He was also curator of "Diane Arbus: A box of ten photographs" and "Trevor Paglen: Sites Unseen," both exhibited in 2018, and "Harlem Heroes: Photographs by Carl Van Vechten," exhibited in 2016. Previously, Jacob was director of the Inge Morath Foundation. He also was program director at the Magnum Foundation for its Legacy Program. Jacob began his career as an artist, working with reproductive media including photography, rubber stamps, mail art, and artist's books.

LAURA LEVITT is Professor of Religion, Jewish Studies, and Gender at Temple University in Philadelphia, PA, where she has chaired the Religion Department and directed both the Jewish Studies and the Gender, Sexuality and Women's Studies programs. Levitt is the author of *The Objects that Remain* (2020), *American Jewish Loss after the Holocaust* (2007), and *Jews and Feminism: The Ambivalent Search for Home* (1997), and a coeditor of *Impossible Images: Contemporary Art After the Holocaust* (2003) and *Judaism Since Gender* (1997).

MARGARET OLIN, Senior Lecturer Emerita, Department of Religious Studies, Yale University, in New Haven, CT, is a scholar and photographer. Her fields of study include art historiography, critical theory, visual culture, Jewish art, spatial practices, and photography. Among her recent publications are *Touching Photographs* (2012), *Photography and Imagination*, edited with Amos Morris-Reich (2020), and *The Bitter Landscapes of Palestine*, with David Shulman (2024). She coedits, with Katrin Kogman-Appel, Steven Fine, and David Sperber, the journal *Images: A Journal of Jewish Art and Visual Culture*. As a photographer and curator, her work has been shown in in the United States as well as in Germany, Israel, and the United Kingdom.

RUTH OST was the director of Temple University Honors Program for over two decades. She has a PhD in Religion and completed the original Barnes Foundation Art Education Program. Her scholarship and teaching are located at the intersection of art, ritual, and gender, with a focus on the role of art in everyday life. She has written on Jewish feminist artists, notably Helène Aylon; currently, she is working on an essay about Miss Gladys, who lived in a car and curated her "Garden of Imagination" in an empty lot in North Philadelphia, now plowed under. Ost curates small constructions made from found objects, torn/scissored paper, fabric, glue stick, and thread. She is one of the "100 People Listening," as part of "100 People Listening: A Shared Decade," a project commissioned by the arts organization Philadelphia Contemporary.

RHODA ROSEN is executive director of Red Line Service, a socially engaged artistic community led by and for people with the lived experience of being unhoused. Since 2009, she has also served as adjunct associate professor at the School of the Art Institute, Chicago, where she teaches courses on modern and contemporary art. She earned her PhD from the University of Illinois in Chicago, and her MA and BA from the University of the Witwatersrand, in Johannesburg, South Africa.

BARBARA VON ECKARDT is Professor Emerita at Rhode Island School of Design in Providence, where she was a full professor and Dean of Liberal Arts. She is both an analytic philosopher with past appointments at Yale University and the University of Nebraska, and an artist, with certificates in photography and painting from RISD. As a philosopher, she specializes in the philosophy of cognitive science, publishing the book *What Is Cognitive Science* in 1993. Her photography has been exhibited in numerous group shows. She is currently indulging her artistic interests as a student in the MFA Painting Program at the Savannah College of Art and Design.

INDEX